from the

KITCHEN

of

THE
NEWLYWED
COOKBOOK

The Newlywed Cookbook

FRESH IDEAS & MODERN RECIPES
FOR COOKING WITH & FOR EACH OTHER

by Sarah Copeland

Photographs by Sara Remington

CHRONICLE BOOKS
SAN FRANCISCO

For András, my dream guy

Text copyright © 2012 by Sarah Copeland.
Photographs copyright © 2012 by Sara Remington.
Illustrations copyright © 2012 by Jessica Hische.

Library of Congress Cataloging-in-Publication Data available.
ISBN 978-0-8118-7683-4

Manufactured in China

Designed by Anne Donnard and Alice Chau
Prop styling by Dara Donovan
Food styling by Sarah Copeland and Lillian Kang
Camera assistance by Kassandra Medeiros
Typesetting by Helen Lee and Hallie Overman

10 9

Chronicle Books LLC
680 Second Street
San Francisco, California 94107
www.chroniclebooks.com

CONTENTS

INTRODUCTION

There's a moment in a marriage, whether two days or two hundred and twenty-two days into it, where you're standing side by side in the morning barefoot on the cool kitchen floor. Everything is quiet but the hum of him making you coffee just the way you like it, with all that frothy milk and sugar. You're stirring together his favorite pancakes, sprinkling a few blueberries in the batter, and then it hits you: these simple moments are somehow the best in life.

This could happen over a fork fight for the last peach in the jar, or playing rock-paper-scissors for whose turn it is to do dishes. It can happen, and will happen over and over again if you let it. That is the essence of this book.

Fresh food, prepared with love, is a key ingredient to happy, healthful, and playful relationships. It's much easier to laugh through a disagreement when your bellies are full of delicious, nurturing food {believe me, I've softened an argument more than once with a bowl of something sweet} and it's easier to continue loving a person through their faults when that's the same person you get down-and-dirty with in the garden and at the kitchen sink, wiping up the pots and pans of a feast you'll remember. It's hard not to love the person who just spent their evening making chocolate pudding from scratch or who missed an hour of extra sleep to have a fat stack of pancakes waiting for you on Saturday morning when you wake up.

This book is all about how sweet life can be when the kitchen is your playground. It's a book as much about good living as it is about good eating. It's a book about the story of your life together.

The part of my story that became the inspiration for this book began in Hungary, with András, my best friend and playmate in life. It was my second trip to Hungary with him, and I had already fallen in love with his family, his culture, and the foods that grew all over the backyard of the house where he grew up—parsnips and carrots, wild strawberries, plump plums, and sour cherries that his mother turned into mouth-puckering soup. Food became the only form of communication I had with his family. I learned about the devotion of his mother while standing grating home-grown potatoes at her side for rösti. I learned about the passion and peace of his father, walking with him among the fruit trees, learning the words of our favorite foods.

On the third day of that trip, András took me on a hike up into the Bakony hills behind the farmhouse where he'd spent his summers as a kid. We hiked to the top of the peak where all you could see for miles was forest, fields, and his little village. On the hike back down, as the forest swallowed us in a sea of ferns, András stopped, got down on his knees, and asked me to be his wife.

It wasn't all romance. I had been a grump the whole way, hungry and fidgety, wishing I'd worn something cuter every time he snapped a photo. But András, steadfast, was smiling the whole way, confident in his plan. And, true to form, just minutes after he pulled the ring out of his pocket, he held out a handful of fruit and asked, "Do you want a fig?" as if he was thinking "Phew, she said yes, now we eat." I wanted time to stop, to make a screen grab of this moment, to hold his gaze. And he wanted to eat. I had to laugh—we really are different creatures, and that is why life is so good together.

And so goes our story. He makes me laugh, and then we eat. And eat we did. We celebrated over many meals that week. Before we left, his grandmother spent a whole day teaching me how to roll her homemade strudel, as if it were now in my hands to provide his favorite foods, to nurture and restore him through the loving act of cooking.

At the airport when we left Hungary, knowing they wouldn't see us again until the wedding, his family looked at him first, then me, and spoke a few simple words. András translated: "Take good care of each other," they said. "It's the most important thing."

On the plane home, as I got used to the glimmer on my finger and thought about what it meant, I played those words over and over again in my head. Suddenly I heard my granddad and saw him reaching over to grab my dad's arm as he said goodbye to my own parents on their visits back home, "Take good care of each other now." I had heard him say it a dozen times. Sitting next to the man who would become my husband, I suddenly realized that those simple words were at the heart of every marriage we admired. It seemed that the secret to a rich life together was to make it our pride and joy to take good care of each other.

Cooking together and for each other is a loving act, one of the most enduring ways to nurture each other, and your first opportunity to invest in each other's health and happiness. Food is a love language, one most of us speak. This book is here to add a few more words to your vocabulary. It is a place to turn to for new ideas and inspiration to put down the take-out menu and cook up something all your own.

THE TABLE COMES FIRST

I can never understand how young couples starting off buy a television, or a sofa, or a bed. Don't they know the table comes first? —Fergus Henderson

Long before we ever ate those figs together in a forest, or took our first toast as husband and wife, András sat at my table in my apartment in New York City eating baba ghanoush and homemade crackers. How he got there is another story for another day, but you could say that in our life, the table always came first. Our first meal together set the tone for everything that was to come. How much he must have trusted me, to eat whatever I put in front of him without giving it a second thought, and how much I trusted him to have him sit with me there at my own table while I shared the most personal of gifts with him—my cooking.

Between that first meal and the grand meal that eventually followed {the wedding supper}, I fed and nurtured his body with food, while he nurtured my dreams, my decisions, and my hopes. And despite the state of his buckwheat pancakes {got to love the guy for trying}, I realized I utterly loved him.

When we got married, and made our home together, the table became an even bigger part of our lives. In our case, the table is the kitchen counter that sits smack in the middle of our apartment. It is our bar, our desk, my potting shed, and his workshop—the epicenter of our life together. We start our days there over breakfast and end them there too {usually with something sweet}. We host brunches and pizza parties and pasta-making feasts, plan our budgets, and dream up our plans for the future over simple meals that all start right there. The table is our foundation, the magnetic core of our life together.

As a newlywed, you too are building your life with the one you love. With this book, I hope to help you build it around a table strong enough to hold a lifetime of tradition, good humor, and good meals with the people you love the most. Don't worry if that first table you share is physically tiny; I know firsthand that the size of the table doesn't matter. One day your table will grow to fit more friends and family, but it all starts with just the two of you across from each other in those first amazing years after you say "I do."

IT'S YOUR LIFE: *This book is full of the kinds of stories, recipes, and adventures that have made my marriage my greatest haven, the place I'm the happiest, the most at home and alive. But this is your book now, and your marriage. Make these recipes your own, write your own stories, and make every day an occasion for a delicious, satisfying life together.*

STRATEGIES

There are dozens of rules to good cooking. I've probably broken most of them. I snip chives with kitchen shears when I'm in a hurry and rarely chop anything in perfect dice. Forget the rules—cooking is supposed to be fun! Here are ten strategies to make your kitchen the spirited and well-seasoned center of your nest.

1. GET SMART, GET FRESH Learn as much as you can about ingredients, and, when you can, start with the freshest ones you can find. Use the Stocked {page 11} and To Market {page 31} chapters of this book to become an educated cook and you'll get a lot more flavor and satisfaction out of the time you spend in the kitchen.

2. GLAM UP EVERYDAY INGREDIENTS One of the secrets of savvy cooks is knowing how to make the most of frugal ingredients. Never is this more important than when you begin life together. You can throw a great party and eat like a king and still save for that dream house.

3. USE FLAVOR TO THE FULLEST Many of the things our mothers were taught were unhealthy, like butter and egg yolks, are full of flavor. We now know that whole, natural foods {even those high in fat} like butter, are always better for us than processed foods, like margarine. Use these ingredients with intent and enjoy every delicious bite.

4. LEARN THE ART OF READING RECIPES Read a recipe all the way through before you begin cooking. Watch for clues—they are there to help you—but understand these are just guidelines. Times and temps may vary slightly depending on the quality of your cookware, your style of range, or how often you open your oven door {use your oven light please, darlings!}. Use suggested cooking times as a guide, but let the visual clues {like cook until golden brown} be your touchstone as to how and when things are cooked properly.

5. GET IN THE GAME Whether you're cooking for two or ten, have everything you might need to pull off a recipe handy in advance. Having all your tools at the ready will greatly ease any pressures that could boil up if you hit a part that's new for you.

6. BE FLEXIBLE Some of the best meals come from improvisation. If you're dead set on making a recipe but forgot one ingredient, you probably don't need to go out on a last-minute mission that turns your evening into a tailspin. Improvise. That said, baking is a science that commands precision. Don't take chances with your chocolate cake!

7. MAKE EXTRA Now that you're a great cook, make extra. Stockpile your supper successes in the freezer for lunches, lazy days, and the first night home after a week away. And while you're at it, keep plenty of all kinds of foods in the house—big bowls of fruit, a jar of mixed nuts, an extra gallon of milk, and bread in the freezer. Guys can eat a lot more than you think.

8. DON'T PANIC The food in this book is not built on perfection, but on pleasure. Whether you've been cooking for one day or one decade, somewhere deep inside you is a very competent cook, a masterful cook even, completely capable of making simple and sublime deliciousness happen at your very own table. Trust your instincts.

9. BREAK THE RULES It's your life and your dinner. One of the very best things about being a grown-up is you can make your own rules, or break the ones you know. There is life beyond meat and potatoes. Fix breakfast for dinner or eat your dessert first. And make things the way they sound good to you. If you don't like olives, leave them out. Do whatever feels right to the two of you and enjoy every bite.

10. FLIRT WITH THE SOUS CHEF Make cooking a source of joy and fun in your lives. Make a meal, make a mess, and make any excuse to make yours a happy, healthy kitchen full of constant delights.

CHAPTER 1

STOCKED

PANTRY

Can you imagine anything more exciting than thick slices of ripe summer tomatoes, drizzled generously with golden, glistening olive oil and a sprinkling of salt? When you bite into one, you get a crystalline burst of salt that tastes of the sea, little moments of pleasant heat where the freshly ground black pepper hits your tongue, and finally a wash of buttery, acidic sauce created when the tomatoes juices melt into the olive oil.

What if I told you the secret of every brilliant chef or home cook lies in their bottle of extra-virgin olive oil? A carefully selected olive oil can elevate the simplest meal from good to great in an instant. Why do you think you can't resist dipping your bread in the little plate of oil over and over again at the best restaurants in town, or diving back into the butter dish? Most likely the chef had put a lot of thought into which olive oil or butter to buy for his tables, which baker to buy his bread from so that even this simplest taste experience of bread and oil or bread and butter could be superb.

The most exceptional meals have a common crux—very thoughtfully selected components that when put all together require only a loving, guiding hand from the cook. As newlyweds, this is your first chance to show each other you want the very best for each other. That doesn't always mean expensive ingredients {though occasionally it does}. Fifty or one hundred years ago, probably in your very own family, it was second nature for both a husband and wife to know how to choose the very best. Often they were the most simple ingredients—salted meats and cured sausages with a perfect balance of fat and flavor, fresh hand-made breads, sweet creamy milk, and eggs that were hours old and laid nearby—but the standard for them was very high.

Much has changed about the way we get these foods onto our plate, but the basic principle remains the same: quality ingredients in, equal quality meals out. And with quality ingredients within your reach, the rest becomes quite easy.

Now, imagine your dream pantry, with all your shelves arranged neatly by when and how you might use each ingredient, with a tidy list that suggests recipes that correspond with what's in stock. There might even be a digital alert that tells you when your hubby's eaten up all the chocolate chips you needed for making cookies this weekend. Well you don't need to be that savvy to have superb meals every day. But it does make it a little easier to stock and navigate your pantry if you think of it in three different categories—your everyday pantry, which supplies your daily meals; a healthy pantry, which boosts nutrient quality of your diet; and an entertaining pantry, full of goodies that are good to have on hand for special occasions. Get to know them all and keep an eye on what you go through quickly, which will help you keep ahead of the daily pleasure of filling your plates.

A well-stocked pantry {which includes some basics that are kept in the fridge} is instant gratification for flavor fanatics and makes the journey to satisfying meals fast and easy, day after day. Some of these flavors are much more potent or exotic than extra-virgin olive oil, but the premise is the same. Wherever you live, your local farmers' market, grocery store, and gourmet markets offer a wealth of adventure to explore together. This list is full of starting points from which you and your beloved can launch out toward the most pleasing plate of food you can imagine. Don't be intimidated by new ingredients. They are there to expand and excite your dinner plate.

A Pantry for Two

ARBORIO RICE

This is risotto rice and consists of plump grains that are full of starch, which make the creamiest risotto.

BUTTER

Most of the recipes in this book call for unsalted butter, which makes it easier to control the amount of salt added to a recipe. Keep plenty of everyday unsalted butter on hand to cook both sweet and savory dishes without a special trip to the store. It freezes well, so if you find a better deal in bulk, go for it. Bigger commercial brands are consistent from season to season, and some are much better than others {I like Land O'Lakes}. When baking something where the flavor of the butter is crucial, splurge on the best.

Good salted butter is a must for the table, and there are several premium brands available, most notably French, Irish, or Belgian butters. But a pot of golden, freshly churned butter from a local dairy or cheese maker is a treat like no other. Like cheese, butter is a living thing, so flavors can vary depending on how it's processed and what the cows eat. Since locally churned butter from pasture-raised herds is higher in omega-3s and wonderfully nuanced, it's a worth-while splurge for special guests at your table {you and your love count too!}.

BREAD

With a good loaf of bread in your breadbox, you can create a most delicious meal. Starting with fresh, artisan breads really does make a difference. While you can't keep a world-class baker locked up in your cabinet, consider your local bakery an extension of your pantry. If it's convenient, make a habit of stopping by on your way to or from work once a week. Since fresh, artisan breads don't have preservatives, they last about three days at best {baguettes, specifically, should be eaten the day they come out of the oven}. I find that hearty, nutty, and whole-grain breads last longer than white breads, and are tastier and more healthful too. To get the most out of each loaf, slice it in half; wrap one half tightly in plastic and freeze for later in the week. Eat the other half fresh. Avoid storing bread in the fridge, which rapidly declines the exquisite texture of fresh artisan breads. Always save the ends or scraps of bread, even if slightly stale. They'll come in handy to make croutons and bread crumbs for Green Beans with Tomatoes & Bread Crumbs {page 199}.

CHICKEN BROTH

Sometimes water is a perfectly acceptable broth for cooking soups, particularly if there's a vegetarian in your duo. Other times, broth or stock adds a richness, warmth, and flavor that can't be beat. There are several organic and free-range broths on supermarket shelves that, like the free-range and organic chickens themselves, yield better-flavored broth. Whether you buy organic or conventional broth, taste before you cook with it. If you decide the flavor is too strong, dilute it with water.

{ BETTER BROTH }

The best broth is the one you make yourself at home. If you don't make chicken enough to keep a constant batch of broth bubbling on the stove {I don't!}, stock store-bought quarts in your pantry. But don't waste opportunity to turn bones of your Double-Dip Roast Chicken {page 143} into broth. Here's how: Put your roasted chicken bones in a pot and cover with water. Bring to a boil and skim off any foam that rises to the surface. Add two each peeled and chopped onion, celery, and carrot; a few sprigs of thyme and parsley; 2 bay leaves; and 1 teaspoon black peppercorns. Simmer and cook for 2 hours. Strain and cool. Store in the fridge for 4 days and in the freezer for up to 1 month. For a deeper chicken flavor, add one boneless skinless chicken breast to the bones {the meat can later be shredded for chicken salad}.

CHEESE

HARD CHEESE Hard cheeses like Parmigiano-Reggiano or pecorino are excellent for grating over soups, stews, and pastas and add depth and a touch of salt. Parmigiano Reggiano can be bought in large wedges and kept for a few months wrapped well in a cheese drawer. Cheese is living, and likes to breathe, so wrap it in butcher or wax paper, not plastic wrap/cling film. Label and date it, and refresh the wrapper every so often. When recipes in this book call for freshly grated Parmigiano-Reggiano, use a microplane {see Tools, page 24} to grate it fresh from the block.

SEMIHARD CHEESE Gruyère, Comté, Fontina, Manchego, and Cheddar. These are five of the most versatile cheeses that also keep well for several weeks. While not completely interchangeable, with two of these on hand at any time, your repertoire could include omelets, quesadillas, enchiladas, sandwiches, soufflés, cheeseburgers, mac'n'cheese, and more.

CHOCOLATE-HAZELNUT PASTE

Tucked away in the back of a top shelf and out of plain view {where it can't tempt you}, chocolate-hazelnut paste {such as Nutella or CocoaHaze, made without hydrogenated oils} is not a bad thing to have on hand when you need something sweet fast. It always makes for easy entertaining when served with soft cheese or spread over warm Golden Zucchini Bread {page 75}.

COCOA

If you like hot cocoa and cookies in your house, you won't want to run out of this. The recipes in this book use Dutch-processed and natural cocoa powder interchangeably, but not all recipes do {since they react differently with leavening}. Use Dutch process for deep, dark cocoa color and flavor, and natural cocoa if you prefer the old-fashioned chocolate experience.

EGGS

Never be caught without a dozen eggs in the fridge. In fact, when I find only six left in a carton, that's my signal to head to the store. There is no faster, cheaper go-to ingredient to have on hand. Cage-free, organic, or natural eggs may seem like a splurge, but not when you consider the meals that can be made from this one humble ingredient. Plus the flavor is far superior to those raised in a pen. To taste the difference, hard-boil a half dozen organic, free-range eggs and another half dozen standard eggs until they are just set. Taste them side by side. May the richest, creamiest egg win.

FISH SAUCE

Sounds kind of icky, but it's the secret ingredient to all things Asian. Look for it in the international or Asian section of your supermarket, or in an Asian market. A little goes a long way, so a small bottle will probably suffice for a long time.

FLOUR

ALL-PURPOSE FLOUR All-purpose/plain, white whole-wheat/wholemeal flour, and whole-wheat/wholemeal flour are all pantry staples in our house. In some recipes, they can be used interchangeably. Whole-wheat/wholemeal flour surpasses milled white flour in nutritional benefits, but white flour produces the lightest baked goods. Blend them, or meet halfway with white whole-wheat/wholemeal flour, which is milled from white whole-wheat berries {rather than red whole-wheat berries} for a milder flavor but with the benefits of whole grains.

BREAD/STRONG FLOUR Though you may not make fresh bread from scratch often, two outstanding taste experiences in this book—Dowry Dinner Rolls {page 132}, and homemade pizza dough {page 158}—require it for the most success. It keeps well in an airtight storage bin or in a self-sealing plastic bag in the freezer.

FRESH HERBS

Fresh herbs are one of the fastest routes from zero to delicious. Though it's valuable to have a good starter set of dried herbs and spices, fresh herbs not only deliver more on flavor, they actually pack a surprising nutrient punch as well. Sure, you can't keep fresh herbs in your actual pantry, but you can keep them on your windowsill. Look for Green Thumb clues throughout the book on how to grow your own. An inexpensive potted plant of fresh thyme can last you all year round, which is comparable to the price of one bunch of cut thyme in the store. When you do use dried herbs instead of fresh, use less. They can have a more intense flavor and texture than fresh herbs. Replace them if they smell musky or old.

REAL MAPLE SYRUP

This is a must in any house where pancake lovers reside. The "syrup" you get in restaurants and in almost any bottle with a face are often made with corn syrup and colorings. Look for pure maple syrup, grade B if possible, which is tapped straight from trees and has trace minerals. In moderation, it's a perfectly healthful, natural sweetener enjoyed drizzled over your Sunday stack, Greek yogurt, oatmeal, or even in your morning coffee.

ONLY THE BEST Organic eggs, milk, cream, and butter have a richer flavor, taste fresher, and really are better for you. They also cost more. Splurge. And if kids are anywhere in your future as a couple, you'll be doing your body, and theirs, an extra favor by starting this habit now. Save a little by buying in-store brands of organic whenever you can find them and in bulk when it's something you use often.

MILK

BUTTERMILK Long live buttermilk, which makes for wonderful biscuits and pancakes, is delish drizzled over oatmeal and summer berries, and makes the best pre-soak for fried chicken. Buttermilk can be faked on the fly with 1 tsp of lemon juice dropped into a cup of whole milk. Set it aside for 15 minutes until it looks curdled, then stir and use in place of buttermilk in equal parts.

WHOLE OR 2-PERCENT MILK No matter what style of milk you drink, always keep a bit of whole or 2-percent milk on hand for cooking and baking. Used in moderation, they will not wreak havoc on your hard-earned waistlines, but they give wonderful texture to pancakes, muffins, cakes, and scones. Cooking with 1-percent or skim milk can work, but I don't advise it for baking or for anything that deserves a rich texture like Overnight Egg & Cheese Strata {page 81}, Grown-Up Mac 'n' Cheese {page 135}, Chocolate Pudding {page 234}, or any other custards or cakes. I prefer organic milk both for drinking and baking, which usually has the most wholesome, clean milky flavor.

NUTS

Walnuts, pistachios, pine nuts, hazelnuts, pecans, peanuts, and cashews all make superb and heart-healthy, high-protein snacks and add texture and substance to salads and baked goods. Sprinkle them over oatmeal or yogurt, blend them into Green-on-Green Pesto {page 209} or pulse them in the food processor and turn them into nut flours {see A Pantry for Health, page 20}. You'll find dozens of recipes for fresh or toasted nuts in this book. Because of their healthy fats, they can go rancid if not used quickly. Store big bags of raw or toasted nuts in plastic containers in the freezer.

{ TOASTING NUTS & SEEDS }

Toasting improves the texture and flavor of many nuts and seeds. To toast large nuts {walnuts, hazelnuts, or pecans}, spread them in a single layer on a baking sheet/tray and bake in a 350°F/180°C/gas 4 oven until just golden brown and fragrant, about 15 minutes, shaking the pan halfway through. For smaller nuts like pine nuts and some seeds like sesame seeds, toast them in a skillet over low heat in a thin sheen of oil. Turn them frequently until they are evenly golden brown. Always set a timer and watch carefully with your eyes and your nose; nuts burn easily.

OATMEAL

Oats are known for their heart-healthy qualities. They are also a whole grain that is full of fiber and really sticks with you. I'm a fan of their soothing and familiar flavor. As a breakfast cereal or a baking grain, keep plenty of these on stock. You'll need them for Oatmeal-Yogurt Pancakes with Blackberry Crush {page 62} and Oatmeal Scones with Brown Butter Glaze {page 69}.

OILS

A solid pantry has a variety of oils in it. The four basics are vegetable oil for cooking and baking, extra-virgin olive oil for cooking, a premium extra-virgin olive oil, {sometimes called finishing oil} for dressing, and peanut oil for frying and flavoring.

{ THE MAGIC DUO: OIL & BUTTER }

Many cooks use either oil or butter, but the secret of the best cooks is to cook with both. Oils like olive oil have a healthier profile and a higher smoking point than butter, which means it's great for cooking on higher heat. But butter delivers on flavor that certain dishes would be amiss without. Sometimes one or the other does the trick or is the right profile, but together they are the perfect cooking fat—flavorful, rich, and healthful.

VEGETABLE OIL An all-purpose/plain, flavorless oil that's cheap and useful for cooking, frying, and baking. Buy it in bulk and keep small portions handy in a squeeze bottle near the stove as a go-to cooking oil. I often mix canola and extra-virgin olive oil for a cheaper but slightly more flavorful cooking oil.

EXTRA-VIRGIN OLIVE OIL Olive oil is one of the healthiest fats on the planet. "Extra virgin" just means that it's a first pressing of the olives, usually cold press. At one time, olive oil was considered too fancy for daily use, but there are now several brands of quality extra-virgin olive oil, affordably available in bulk, for everyday cooking. Use this in most savory recipes {meats, vegetables, and pastas all love a little of its luscious flavor} unless the flavor of olive compromises or conflicts with the other flavors of a dish, in fried rice for example.

Stock a bottle of a very high-quality {or premium} extra-virgin olive oil, often called finishing oil, for dressing, drizzling, and finishing, a technique you'll see called for often in this book. This is one of the principal ingredients in the Little Meals chapter {page 83}, and affords you an easy night in the kitchen since it does wonders to create a "wow" out of the simplest raw ingredients.

{ EXTRA SPECIAL EXTRA VIRGIN }

A good extra-virgin olive oil {or finishing oil} is generous, adding beautiful, luscious flavor to cooked and raw foods. The most flavorful finishing oils can be pricy, so if you can, buy from a store that offers tasting before you buy. There's nothing worse than getting home with an eighteen dollar bottle of fine oil that tastes bitter to your palate. One great way to find one you like is to ask the maitre d' at a restaurant where you enjoy their dipping oil which brand they use, or steal a peek at the brand at your best friend's house where you had that amazing salad.

When you taste, look for one of these five basic flavor profiles, and find the one that's the most pleasing to you.

- Full-bodied and peppery
- Mostly fruity with a little bite
- Smooth and buttery
- Fruity and herbal or grassy
- Mildly nuanced and delicate

Don't get too bogged down in the details. What's important, as with anything where flavor is concerned, is to buy the one that tastes the best to you.

PEANUT OIL For certain things, like fried rice or fried chicken, the flavor of peanut oil can be magnificent. It's awfully cheap, and it turns out that it's also considered a healthy fat. For a splurge, try toasted peanut oil for stir-fries.

PEPPERCORNS

If you don't already have a good peppermill, buy one and keep it filled with black peppercorns. It's one of the best investments you can make toward your mealtime. Freshly ground black pepper is a flavor experience wholly unlike that of the crackled flecks that come from a pepper shaker. Since it's very hard to measure black pepper as it's being cracked fresh from your grinder over your food, most recipes in this book call for black pepper to taste, except when a specific amount is imperative to the success of the dish. Learn your tastes and tolerance for the heat of black pepper, and play around with fine or coarse settings on your mill until you find just the right balance for you.

SAN MARZANO TOMATOES {WHOLE AND PEELED}

The best canned tomatoes on the market are this variety of plum tomatoes from Italy. If you have the space, save by buying them in bulk to have on hand at all times, especially in the winter. In thirty minutes you can turn them into homemade sauce for dressing pastas and Make-Ahead Lasagna {page 137}, and quick soup for your Grilled Cheese & Tomato Sliders {page 98}.

SALT

In a good restaurant kitchen there might be as many as six or seven kinds of salt, each with its own unique purpose. While you don't need quite that many at home, they aren't all interchangeable and it helps to know a little about where they are best used. I keep the following four salts on hand. The first three are cooking salts, the fourth is finishing salt.

IODIZED SALT In this book, iodized can be used interchangeably with fine sea salt. We all need a little iodine in our diet, so if this is your choice house salt or table salt, carry on.

KOSHER SALT This is your all-purpose roasting, brining, boiling, and seasoning salt. Its coarse texture makes it easy to control when seasoning meat and large vegetables. I don't recommend kosher salt in baking since the coarse grains don't blend as easily as finer salts.

FINE SEA SALT This is my first line of defense in house salts. Natural sea salt is flavorful, cheap, and can be used in baking and cooking alike. It works like iodized salt, but with trace minerals that are essential to our body's physiology.

FINISHING SALTS As a general rule, you get the most from your food when you salt gently throughout cooking, and add small amounts of high-quality finishing salt at the end for distinctive texture and flavor you won't want to miss. My favorite finishing salts are Maldon sea salt, fleur de sel, smoked sea salt, and gray salt. There are dozens of other finishing salts worth a try, like volcanic salt or Himalayan pink salt. Those belong in your entertaining pantry, but with this warning: you may develop the habit of making them an everyday luxury.

SPICES, DRIED

Ground spices add instant flavor to numerous dishes and some, like curry powder, deliver on satisfaction in a way that makes it possible to replace excess fat with flavor. Not all spices are created equal. Smell them if you can before you buy. They should smell fresh and potent, not musky. Technically, ground spices should be used or replaced within a year. If you only dip into them once in a while, buy the

smallest portion available, or buy them whole and grind them yourself with a mortar and pestle or in a coffee grinder reserved for this purpose.

SUGAR, UNPROCESSED, ORGANIC

Fair trade organic sugar, also labeled evaporated cane juice is now easy to find at regular supermarkets. The small grains give the same tender texture to baked goods as white sugar, but without chemicals and bleach, and can be used in all the recipes in this book.

SUNFLOWER SEEDS

This is my go-to power seed. They provide you with extra vitamin E {our body's favorite fat-soluble antioxidant}, vitamin B_1, minerals, and texture when added to granola, hot cereal, and quick breads like Rise & Shine Muffins {page 68} or Golden Zucchini Bread {page 75}.

SOY SAUCE

Try to buy soy sauce from the international aisle of the super-market or at an Asian market that carries the better brands. Low-sodium is good, too, if you're watching your salt intake.

VINEGARS

There are as many types of vinegar as oils, and you will quickly learn which ones you and your sous chef prefer. The most adaptable for cooking, pickling, and dressing are white wine, red wine, apple cider, or champagne vinegar. Many organic brands of apple cider vinegar have a superior flavor. You can fancy up your pantry with champagne and sherry vinegars if those flavors appeal to you.

WHOLE GRAINS

Whole grains, full of fiber and protein, are also rich in flavor. There is a nuttiness in them that you just don't get from refined grains and flours. Though these are in your Pantry for Health, don't reserve them for once in a while. They are a key part of your everyday diet. One of the best ways to keep them a constant in your daily diet is to cook them in advance in big batches, since they don't lose flavor or texture in reheating. Add them to soups, use them for stuffing, stir together and sweeten for breakfast porridge, or stir into green salads. Try some of these favorites.

BARLEY You may find barley, or pearl barley, the polished version of this grain that is more tender and slightly quicker for cooking. Both are pleasingly chewy and are delicious.

BROWN RICE If you think white rice is good, get ready for its heartier, healthier sibling. Discover the nurturing simplicity of brown rice served warm with butter and sea salt. Or give it a sweet finish with pure maple syrup and warm milk as breakfast porridge.

FARRO This nutty, almost buttery grain is delicious hot or cold. Usually imported from Italy and partially hulled, it cooks in 20 to 30 minutes and can then be stirred into chicken soup, tossed in cold salads, or cooked like risotto. You may also find spelt, a heartier wheat kernel full of protein that is left whole, and therefore takes much longer {50 to 60 minutes} to cook. Once cooked, it can be used much like farro.

QUINOA The Incas called quinoa the "mother grain" and considered it sacred. And, for good reason. Slightly crunchy and mild mannered, this grain delivers a huge dose of protein and is also one of the simplest grains to cook ahead. Keep extras on hand to stuff into burritos or enchiladas, stir into hot cereal, and serve as a healthy side with fish, chicken, and vegetables.

Buy whole grains, rice, and flours in bulk whenever you can. Organic grains are wonderful, but costly.

YEAST

Baking bread from scratch may be on the horizon for this week, or something you hope to grow into. Give it a try when you're ready. You'll need a packet or two of yeast. Look for granulated active-dry yeast {not rapid rise}, for the recipes in this book. Store in the fridge.

GREEK {STRAINED} YOGURT

Greek yogurt is a thick, strained yogurt used all over the Mediterranean and in Middle Eastern cuisines. It's just as welcome and useful in American and Mexican foods and makes a healthful substitution for both mayo and sour cream. It's getting easier and easier to find, and it comes in 0-percent fat, 2-percent fat, and whole-milk versions. The 0-percent is so rich and luscious you'll never miss the fat. It can become breakfast or dessert in an instant {check out Greek Yogurt with Fresh Figs, page 236}, makes superb spreads for sandwiches {Herb Mayo, page 207, and Spicy Mayo, page 207} and is so darn versatile you won't ever want to be without it.

A Pantry for Health

Many things in your everyday Pantry for Two are inherently healthful. In fact, if you're cooking with whole foods from scratch most days of the week, you are very well on your way to a lifestyle that is built for longevity. But if you and the hubs have made a pact to pay particular attention to increasing whole grains, healthy fats, and fiber in your diet, get good and cozy with some of the additional ingredients in this section.

AGAVE NECTAR

Perfect for sweetening sauces to coffee to sweet tea and drinks, agave nectar has a low glycemic content {which means your body processes it in a healthier way than sugar} and it takes far less of it than other sweeteners to make strong, bitter flavors like cocoa palatable. All sugars are packed with calories, and agave is no different, but used in moderation it can help get a handle on a sweet tooth. Nothing quite replaces the way granulated sugar works to tenderize baked goods like cakes and cookies, but this is just the thing to stir into creamy frostings instead of pounds of excess confectioners'/icing sugar.

FLAX SEEDS & FLAX-SEED MEAL

Whole flax seeds can be stirred into bread batter or oatmeal for added fiber and omega-3s. Whole flax seeds provide excellent fiber, but pass through your system virtually undetected by your cells. Try crushing or cracking them in a coffee grinder, or buying flax-seed meal to gain the maximum benefits. Sprinkle either over yogurt, add to your Monday Morning Muesli {page 66}, and stir into batters like Golden Zucchini Bread {page 75}. Store in the fridge for longer shelf life.

FLOUR

GLUTEN-FREE FLOURS There are numerous gluten-free flour options available on the market today including amaranth, barley, millet, quinoa, brown rice, buckwheat, and chickpea flours, as well as cornmeal. Though these flours were not tested for this purpose in the recipes for this book, I encourage gluten-free bakers and eaters to read more on the subject and give these flours a whirl. It's important to note that there is no exact replacement for wheat flours, so foods baked with gluten-free flours respond differently.

NUT FLOURS Like nut oils, nut flours can boost the flavor of baked goods, and depending on how finely they are ground, can add texture and nutrients as well. Almond, hazelnut, and walnut flours are readily available in gourmet and health food stores, and are sometimes labeled almond meal or hazelnut meal. You can make them at home as well {like oat flour} by grinding finely in a food processor. Since nuts have higher fat content, they can quickly turn into nut paste like peanut or cashew butter, so use the pulse feature to pulse the nuts gently into a meal. Stop before it starts sticking together, and scrape the sides and corners of the bowl frequently to keep it loose and light.

WHOLE-GRAIN FLOUR Whole-grain flours, like the whole grains themselves, have been milled in a way that preserves both the wheat and the germ of the grain for maximum protein and fiber. Use whole-wheat/wholemeal flour for standard baking and whole-wheat/wholemeal bread/strong flour for yeasted dough. White whole-wheat/wholemeal flour is a good starting point or middle ground if you're new to whole-grain flours.

Other whole-grain flours with lovable, versatile flavor profiles are millet, oat, and barley flour. Quinoa flour is also delicious but slightly stronger and more grassy, and buckwheat has a furtively whole-grain flavor and should be used in moderation or blended with other flours. If you can't find any of these, make your own by grinding whole oats to a fine powder in your food processor. Use in the same amounts as oat flour. Since these flours have more going on in the

{ WORKING WITH WHOLE-GRAIN FLOURS }

Fiber-rich whole-grain flours soak up liquid more quickly in batters. So watch for this when baking and note that you may occasionally need to add a touch more water, milk, or buttermilk if you substitute whole-grain flours for white flour in a recipe. This is especially true for buckwheat flour. Add extra liquid slowly, a teaspoon at a time.

nutrient department, unless you use up a bag in about 2 weeks, preserve them by storing them in big plastic bags or bins in the fridge or freezer.

FROZEN FRUIT

Keep frozen {organic, when possible} berries, cherries, or peaches on hand for quick smoothies, sauces for ice cream, and to stir into pancakes and quick breads. Frozen berries are more economical, and tastier {since they are flash frozen in peak ripeness} than buying off-season fresh fruit.

GRAPESEED OIL

Flavorless and versatile like vegetable oil, grapeseed oil has a high smoking point like peanut oil, and is healthful like olive oil, so it's a superstar winner in every category. I frequently use this oil for both cooking and baking.

HOT PEPPER SAUCES & PASTES

Hot pepper pastes from around the world give heat, aroma, and well-rounded flavor to many savory foods. Since flavor is a great satiety substitute for fat, keep one or all four of the following sauces on hand and you might find yourself reaching for an unhealthy snack a little less often.

HARISSA A North African hot pepper paste, harissa is made from piri piri peppers. Spicy hot, it is incredible stirred into mayo cut with Greek yogurt for a delectable spread for sandwiches.

HUNGARIAN HOT PEPPER PASTE If you can't find harissa, Hungarian red pepper paste is a wonderful alternative. When I first started making vegetarian soups, I missed the deep, satisfying flavors of chicken stock. I quickly learned that onions cooked in oil, plus red pepper paste and water makes a fragrant, filling broth with all of the same satisfaction of the best chicken broths I'd ever had.

SAMBAL OELEK If you like spicy, even a little, you will have so much fun with sambal oelek sauce in the house. Primarily used in Asian cooking or as a condiment throughout Indonesia, Singapore, Malaysia, and the Philippines, sambal is primarily made of a variety of chiles, and a little goes a very, very long way.

SRIRACHA SAUCE This smooth and spicy sauce is actually made in America but has become the ketchup of Thai cooking. It's made with chiles, garlic, vinegar, sugar, and salt and comes off as a blend of spicy and sweet. You can mix it into mayo for dipping fried zucchini/courgette or spreading on sandwiches, and stir it into your soup or fried rice. I even use

it to add kick to the sauce for Succulent Barbecued Chicken {page 139}. I keep both sambal oelek and Sriracha in the refrigerator, but one or the other usually does the trick.

NUT BUTTERS

Natural nut butters like those made from peanuts, cashews, almonds, and hazelnuts are pure joy. Creamy, filling, flavorful and just a touch sweet, they are great for a breakfast or mid-morning fix.

NUT & SEED OILS

Oils pressed purely from nuts and seeds can wow with their flavor and their fabulous health benefits.

WALNUT, ALMOND, OR HAZELNUT OIL All nut oils are better used for flavoring than for cooking, since they break down quickly under high heat. Buy amber-colored oils made from roasted nuts {rather than raw nuts}, which have deeper flavors. How you use these or which one you choose depends entirely on how much you like the nut itself. Replace part of the olive oil in the Olive Oil Cake {page 251} with almond oil and you'll get the same moist cake with a completely different flavor profile. Mix walnut oil with olive oil for your Classic Vinaigrette {Window Box Green Salad for Two, page 86} to deepen the flavor without overpowering. Store these oils in the fridge for a longer shelf life, and keep away from light and heat.

SESAME OIL AND TOASTED SESAME OIL Most commonly used in Asian cooking, these give a potent flavor and aroma to Kitchen Sink Fried Rice {page 113} and can give an Asian flair to simple salads. Use these oils sparingly, particularly the deeply flavored toasted variety, which I prefer.

RAISINS & GOLDEN RAISINS/SULTANAS

Raisins add iron to sweet and savory dishes, and give a soft, round flavor when you need a touch of sweetness. Golden raisins, sometimes called sultanas, are slightly milder in flavor. Both are great to keep on hand and can be quickly turned into an impromptu trail mix for mid-meal munchies.

{ GOOD OLD RAISINS & PEANUTS }

Where would the world be without GORP? This simple trail mix, made of handfuls of raisins and peanuts, is perfect for staving off the grumps between meals. Add in sesame seeds, pistachios, walnuts, and a few chocolate chips for extra fiber and flavor.

A Pantry for Parties

Back in the day, folks used to just drop by when they saw the light on. Today, that could send the hosts of the house into a tailspin. Planning for friends in your married life is in invitation for growth and excitement. With a well-stocked specialty pantry, you can open your doors and your heart to impromptu parties with just a few things in the fridge, most of which keep very well and turn your table for two into the most popular table in town with very little effort. You'll earn your reputation as accomplished hosts with just a few of the following things in stock.

BREAD

ARTISAN BREAD {IN THE FREEZER} Find a local baker you love and buy their loaves—olive, whole grain, walnut-raisin, or cranberry—two at a time, one to eat now, one to freeze. Wrap one well in plastic wrap/cling film, then aluminum foil, and stick it in the freezer for rainy day guests. They refresh like new in a hot oven, particularly one with a pizza stone, and make an instant party served with wine and a wheel of cheese.

PAR-BAKED FRENCH BAGUETTE Big brands and bakeries at gourmet groceries now stock par-baked goodies for you to keep on hand. Pick up a few loaves or rolls on your next grocery trip, and bake them off, hot and crackly, just before dinner is served. If you've baked on a pizza stone, your guests {or your spouse} will never guess that your freezer is the baker's best friend.

CHEESE

FRESH RICOTTA CHEESE Having a pint of fresh ricotta in the fridge makes an awfully good excuse to invite a few friends over. Dollop it on flatbread or pizza or dress it up as a side or sweet. For more on how to choose and serve it, see A Beautiful Bowl of Ricotta {page 213}.

SOFT CHEESE Soft cheese is by nature not a pantry staple, since it doesn't keep long and needs to be picked for ripening based on when you plan to eat it. If you have an extra hour before company arrives, swing by the cheese market or gourmet grocer on your way home and pick up a well-ripened cheese {ask your cheesemonger for a recommendation}. Many farmers' markets now feature at least one local cheese maker. Get to know them and their cheeses. Taste and try until you find a go-to favorite you're proud to slice and serve.

CHOCOLATE, BITTERSWEET

If you like chocolate, it won't take much convincing to encourage you to taste and find your favorite brands. You can now buy premier brands like Valrhona and Callebaut in blocks or *pistols*, the way chefs buy them, at many supermarkets and gourmet grocery stores. For big baking projects without a big budget, I like the Pound Plus Belgian bittersweet chocolate baking bar from Trader Joe's.

CRÈME FRAÎCHE

Très special for little bites, crème fraîche is also a good choice for the occasional sour finish on a sweet dessert like Bittersweet Chocolate Tart with Smoked Sea Salt {page 247}. It always makes Don't-You-Dare Mashed Potatoes {page 187} extra memorable.

GHERKIN, CORNICHON, OR ARTISAN PICKLES

Pickling is back—if you're lucky enough to have a pickling habit, a friend who pickles, or an expert pickler at your weekly farmers' market, stock up. A fast plate of pickles and charcuterie can be made from pickled beets/beetroots, green beans, or okra and gives spunky contrast to a plate of fat-marbled charcuterie. Cornichons do the job too, especially if you suddenly come into a thick slab of country pâté or a pot of pork rillettes.

HEAVY CREAM

Sometimes nothing in the world but fresh whipped cream will do. Real cream is expensive, but it keeps for quite some time. And leftovers make a quick treat out of fresh fruit or even pre-made pudding pots someone slipped into your cart on the last trip to the store.

OLIVES

Olives with their pits are generally of a higher quality and more flavorful than pitted olives and make a better presentation, too. Anything from kalamata to niçoise black olives can be found cured or flavored in jars, at deli counters, and more and more, in specialty olive bars in supermarkets. My personal favorites are picholine, green olives from France with an elegant shape and mild flavor.

PIE DOUGH, HOMEMADE

Once you become the ace pie maker you'd always dreamed you'd be, get in the habit of making extra pie dough and keeping it in the freezer as a pantry staple. There it will keep for up to 3 months. With 1 hour on the countertop or a night in the fridge to thaw, it'll be ready to roll and use for sweet and savory pies, the perfect one-dish wonder for any style of entertaining.

PIZZA DOUGH, FROZEN

Making pizza dough {see Gardener's Pizza, page 158} is too fun to miss out on. Don't deny yourself the pleasure, but do keep an extra pound of good frozen dough {either your own or from the grocery store} in the freezer for emergencies, like when you need a lovely Grilled Flatbread {page 280} to put out with your party spread.

SAUSAGE, DRIED, CURED

Saucisson sec or any good cured meat—Spanish, French, Italian, Hungarian—is a welcome partner to any cheese at a party. It keeps for weeks in the fridge. Slice it up on the spot for an instant charcuterie platter.

VANILLA BEAN & VANILLA BEAN PASTE

Fresh whole vanilla beans/pods are filled with the most sumptuous pulp. A plump Madagascar vanilla bean/pod warrants its price tag. If you only find thin, dried-looking beans in the market at eight dollars for two, chances are the pulp is dried out and difficult to use. For the price, you're better off getting vanilla bean paste made of scraped pulp and syrup, which offers more beans for your buck. {Check Sources, page 293}.

VANILLA: A WORLD OF AROMA AWAITS

Keep fresh vanilla beans/pods in a small jar filled with bourbon or vodka, which will keep the beans plump and make the precious pulp much easier to remove. It will also turn the liquor into your own vanilla extract, one that is likely to be of better quality than what you find at most stores. After you use the beans, dry them out on a plate or paper towels/absorbent papers on your counter and then add to a jar of sugar to create vanilla sugar for baking or sprinkling into sweets.

TOOLS

The most essential tool in any kitchen is your sense of adventure, followed very closely by your eyes, nose, ears, and hands. Keep those hands washed and be prepared to use them because there's no faster way to get to know food and learn how to cook.

Once you're comfortable working with your hands, you need little more than a good sharp chef's knife, a set of nesting stainless-steel bowls, a whisk, and a wooden spoon. But, since the advent of electricity and the brilliance of gadget-makers across the globe, cooking has become faster, easier, and neater. There is no better time than when you first set up house together to invest in some essentials. Friends and family will want to know what you need and want. All the better if it's something that helps you invest in time together in the kitchen and at the table {trust me, grandmas, aunts, and moms will love to hear that you can't wait to cook together!}. Consider this your kitchen wish list.

Cook's Essentials

BAKING SHEETS/TRAYS

For cooking or baking, get at least two. You'll use them to bake cookies/biscuits, roast vegetables, and hold lots of little things that bake at once like French Onion Soup {page 134}.

BOX GRATER

Use this to grate your own cheese from larger pieces of cheese, a cheaper and better option than using purchased pre-grated cheese. This tool is also useful for grating zucchini/courgettes for Golden Zucchini Bread {page 75}, carrots for Rise & Shine Muffins {page 68}, and cucumbers for Tsatsiki {page 210}.

CAST-IRON GRIDDLE-GRILL PAN

This is the item I'd most like to have with me on a deserted island. The griddle side makes pancakes {see pages 60, 61, and 62} and is easier to control the heat than a single skillet {cast iron holds heat well}. Flip it over for a grated grill {not as hot as an outdoor grill} that's wonderful for pressing panini or grilling veggies and smaller cuts of meat or fish. Like all cast iron, season it before use. Wipe down with a cloth and rinse big messes with warm water. Dry it completely before putting it away. Never wash in the dishwasher, or with soap.

COLANDER

An essential tool for draining pasta and rinsing fruit.

CUTTING BOARD

Every kitchen needs at least one sturdy wooden or bamboo cutting board for food prep. It will also serve as a cheese or charcuterie board in a pinch. It's great to also have a few lightweight, dishwasher-safe cutting boards dedicated to meat and fish prep, with another for fresh fruits and vegetables. If you have space, keep one small board just for garlic and onions, which have strong flavors that stick to wood. It can be scrubbed out but better safe than stuck with garlic watermelon cubes in your fruit salad.

FINE-MESH STRAINER

You'll love the texture that a quick strain gives sauces. It's also great for rinsing smaller fruits like berries.

HONING STEEL

Keep knives aligned and in shape with a honing steel, which comes with most knife sets. Learn how to use it and you'll only have to sharpen your knives once or twice a year.

KNIVES

CHEF'S KNIFE Find one that feels very comfortable in your hand. German or Japanese steel is worth the investment. It should rock easily back and forth against a wooden cutting board and make big cuts fast and easy.

PARING KNIFE Cut the tips off strawberries, core apples and pears, or trim and tidy fruits and vegetables, all with this versatile thin, short-bladed knife.

SERRATED KNIFE Perfect for slicing bread and tomatoes without crushing either. Wash well after slicing tomatoes; their acidity can dull knives.

MEASURING SPOONS

Accurate teaspoon and tablespoon measurements are the cornerstones of successful baking.

MICROPLANE

I travel with this portable, rasp-style grater in my suitcase, and leave one for every friend I visit. Grate cheese, chocolate, and lemon zest with this slim little tool that will earn its place in your tool kit.

OVENPROOF STAINLESS-STEEL FRYING PAN

8-IN/20-CM The all-purpose/plain pan for two, you can use it to fry two eggs, cook two chicken breasts, one T-bone, or an omelet for two.

10- OR 12-IN/25- OR 30.5-CM It's just right for bigger portions, stir fries, and pan-searing larger cuts of meat.

PARCHMENT/BAKING PAPER

For baking, line just about anything from baking sheets/trays to cake pans/tins, and your baked goods will be so much easier to turn out and clean up, too.

PEPPER GRINDER

Pretty please, don't buy cracked black pepper in a jar. Like all spices, pepper is best ground fresh, right into the pot or over your salad or pasta. Buy whole black peppercorns and a peppermill and watch every meal come alive. You'll taste the difference; I promise.

REAMER

Use this small wooden, plastic, or stainless-steel device for getting the most juice out of citrus fruits. A fork will do, but this will do it faster. Electric citrus juicers are also nice if lemonade or mojitos are a regular in your house.

SAUCEPAN, 2-QT/2-L

Suitable for simmering soups, oatmeal, hard-boiled eggs, and hot cocoa.

SLOTTED SPOON

Choose one with a long handle for lifting cooked vegetables or Fried Zucchini {page 191} from a pot. This tool will save your arms from splashes of hot water or oil.

SOUP PAN/PASTA POT, 8-QT/7.5-L

Necessary for large batches of soup or long pastas.

THERMOMETER, LEAVE-IN OR INSTANT-READ

A leave-in thermometer lets you check the doneness of meat by monitoring its internal temperature. It stays in the meat throughout cooking. With an instant-read type, you insert the probe briefly into meat to get a temperature reading and remove it. You can also use either type to test the temperature of oil for frying and liquids for proofing yeast.

WHISK

So useful—anytime you need to whisk or whip, reach for this tool.

{ WASTE NOT; WANT NOT }

Keep your kitchen a little greener by keeping a compost pail on the countertop. Turn kitchen scraps like eggshells and apple peels into plant food for your garden. In our house, this makes the essentials list. Get a pail that's small and easy to keep on the counter. A good one has filters that keep the whole process smelling clean. If you don't have a garden, the local farmers' market or community garden will likely take scraps off your hands to turn them into organic fertilizers for their soil.

A Baker's Tool Box

BAKING RACKS

Big baking projects or even a couple layers of cake will benefit from a set of cooling racks. Transfer hot baked goods or casseroles to baking racks to cool quicker and save your kitchen counters.

CAKE PANS/TINS, ROUND 9-BY-2-IN/23-BY-5-CM

Look for high-quality {professional standard} pans with straight sides. You'll need two for layer cakes. Use often for all-occasion cakes like Better-Than-Boxed Chocolate Cake {page 257}. It is also the right size for Skillet Corn Bread {page 130} if you're without a cast-iron frying pan.

COOKIE/BISCUIT CUTTERS

You can use a thin rimmed glass to cut biscuits or cookies into perfect rounds, but sharp-edged biscuit cutters or round cookie cutters win my vote for best repeat performers in this category. Have at least two, 1½ in/4 cm and 2½ in/6 cm diameter. Serious bakers will want a set of graduated round cutters that start with tiny ½-in/12-mm rounds and go up to 3 in/7.5 cm or 4 in/10 cm in diameter.

ELECTRIC HAND MIXER

Whipping cream and egg whites is a breeze with a mixer, and it really outdoes a wooden spoon in many instances.

KITCHEN SCALE

It's a small investment and won't take up much space. If you plan to bake at all and use chocolate regularly, a scale will prove very helpful for this book and others.

LOAF PANS/TINS, 9-BY-5-IN/23-BY-12-CM

For quick breads—the fastest way to say "I love you; I baked." They are great for gifting, brunches, and basic morning foods. It helps to have two loaf pans for the Golden Zucchini Bread {page 75} and for making double batches of all your favorites.

MEASURING CUPS

DRY MEASURING CUPS Key for dry measures like flour and sugar. If you bake frequently it won't hurt to have an extra set.

LIQUID MEASURING CUPS A 1-cup/240-ml size is a must, but 2-cup/480-ml and 4-cup/960-ml sizes will also come in very handy for measuring larger amounts of liquids.

{ HOW TO MEASURE }

When baking, a successful outcome depends on the accuracy of the baker. Here's how dry and wet ingredients are measured for the recipes in this book.

To measure flour {of any type}, cocoa, and other dry ingredients for the recipes in this book, spoon flour lightly into a graduated dry measuring cup until it is full. Level off by sweeping across the cup with the edge of a spatula or knife without packing down the flour.

To measure wet ingredients, pour into a liquid measuring cup. Set on a level surface and view the measuring line at eye level to ensure the liquid is at the desired mark.

PIE PANS OR PIE PLATES

Have a 9-by-1½-in/23-by-4-cm standard glass or metal pie plate for sweet and savory pies, plus a deep-dish version for bigger baking enthusiasts.

ROLLING PIN

Sure, empty wine bottles will do, but if you get a good rolling pin, you'll be passing it along to your grandchild one day. I like French wooden tapered pins.

SILICONE BAKING MAT

Cookie lovers will want a set of silicone baking mats {in sizes to match your baking sheets/trays}, which are ovenproof and dishwasher safe and make baking sheets/trays nonstick. Designed to use and reuse over and over, these will keep your cookie jar full and your baking sheets/trays clean.

SPRINGFORM PAN, 9-IN/23-CM

Cheesecakes, as well as Olive Oil Cake with Tangerine Marmalade {page 251} and Lazy Chef's Fruit Torte {page 244} all require a springform pan, as does any cake that you want to come out easily. The sides open with a hinge and lift off from the base for clean serving and cutting—genius!

Tools for the Gourmand

Now that you've got the basics, you may want to consider adding a few more toys if space or budgets permit. Here are my favorites that make it that much easier to open your kitchen doors to bigger challenges and crowds.

BLENDER

FULL SIZE Smoothies, daiquiris, dressings, and more are quick to come together in a sturdy blender. The opportunity one affords for the occasional homemade milkshake is a very good justification to acquire a blender.

IMMERSION BLENDER For the smoothest smoothies, soups, and sauces and ease of use, an immersion will be your constant companion in the kitchen. It purees right in the cooking pot, so you don't have to transfer food to a blender.

CAST-IRON FRYING PAN, 8- OR 10-IN/20- OR 25-CM

Certain foods shine when cooked on cast iron. Steak, corn bread, fried eggs, and griddle cakes all benefit from its built-in flavor {which builds up over time}. Buy a pre-seasoned cast-iron pan and never, ever use soap. Read the care instructions carefully, and you'll have this for life! Vegetarians, this is an excellent way to get more iron in your diet.

FOOD PROCESSOR

FULL SIZE Consider this your first priority on your upgrade list. Mix pie dough, scones, sauces, or soups, and turn grains and nuts into flours. I'll teach you how to do these things by hand, but a food processor saves time and mess and makes big batches a no-brainer.

MINIFOOD PROCESSOR One takes up little space and turns making dips and spreads like Herb Mayo {page 207} into an ultrafast, everyday proposition.

FRENCH PRESS

Makes the perfect cup of coffee in small amounts when needed. And it's sleek and so much fun to bring to the table.

KNIFE SET

Go ahead and register for the full knife set. Tomato knife, boning knife, carving knife, santoku. You can do just fine with good chef and pairing knives, but you'll find a way to use them all if you get them. Be sure the set includes kitchen shears.

NONSTICK STAINLESS STEEL FRYING PAN

6-IN/15-CM To complete the stainless cookware listed in Cook's Essentials.

12-IN/30.5-CM If weekend guests or holiday entertaining is in your future, add this to your cookware set.

SPICE GRINDER

Freshly ground spices smell and taste the very best. You can buy whole spices in bulk, which last longer and cuts down on costs in the grocery store. This electric device is interchangeable with but faster than a mortar and pestle.

STAND MIXER

True to its name, this electric workhorse appliance stands up and does half the work for you while you're free to set the table or sip wine. Many things you can do with a stand mixer you can also do with a hand mixer, but both your hands and attention are required. If you own one, make sure you get all three attachments: paddle, whisk, and dough hook.

The paddle works for most dough and batters and is used when a recipe says to cream or beat ingredients, as in butter. Use the whisk for dry and wet ingredients and for whipping or beating, as in eggs. The dough hook is immeasurably helpful for yeast breads—like Gardener's Pizza {page 158}, or Dowry Dinner Rolls {page 132} in this book.

PIZZA STONE

For pizzas, flatbreads, or simply reheating breads, a stone makes crusts crispy and holds heat evenly. I vote this the best gift to give or get as a newlywed, especially if you have a hankering to make pizza {Gardener's Pizza, page 158} a regular for date night at home.

TOASTER OR TOASTER OVEN

You can toast bread in a hot oven, but a toaster uses far less energy to do the same job quick. Toaster ovens are great for hearty eaters who love leftovers. Heat and re-crisp things as you would in a regular oven, but without turning your whole kitchen toasty.

For a Good Time

Of course you don't actually need a crêpe pan, but it sure does make date night a lot more fun. Here are a few more goodies to accessorize your kitchen and get the less eager cook in the house to pull up a whisk next to you at the kitchen counter.

CERAMIC RAMEKINS, 4-OZ/120-ML OR 8-OZ/240-ML

Think of all the pretty little single-serve foods you can make when you have a set of these! You'll need them for Little Beauty Baked Eggs {page 78}.

CAST IRON PANINI IRON

Made of heavy cast-iron, this is a great companion for your grill pan and gets my vote as the most useful tool for DIY Dinner for your Dude. It makes amazing grilled cheese and turns simple sandwiches into a hot dinner. Dare I suggest, Nutella panini?

CRÊPE PAN

One cannot live on crêpes alone, but almost. Sure you can make crêpes in a 6-in/15-cm nonstick, but nothing will inspire you to get in the kitchen and serve them up for your sweetheart and friends like a little French crêpe pan.

CAST-IRON FRYING PANS

Splurge on four 4-in/10-cm or 6-in/15-cm sizes to cook little things to order for the two of you or friends. Individual omelets, Dutch Babies with Poached Rhubarb {page 58}, or your favorite cookie dough baked as a frying pan cookie {topped with ice cream, of course} are good advertisements for investing in these little pans.

JUICER

What is better than fresh carrot, apple, and ginger juice? Okay, maybe hot cocoa. But there's truly no other way to juice certain fruits and veggies than an expeller juicer. A worthwhile investment for gardeners, fresh-food fanatics, and athletes.

SALT GRINDER

Use a salt grinder to grind large-crystal sea salt into tiny flakes as a finishing touch.

TORTILLA PRESS

This is a small investment with a big return. Handmade tortillas are delicious, simple, and addictive.

WAFFLE IRON

Go Belgian or go home. The deep grid of professional-style Belgian waffle irons make for crispy, delicious waffles. I also vote this appliance "most likely to get hubby in the kitchen with you!"

WOK

You can stir-fry and make Kitchen Sink Fried Rice {page 113} in a 10- or 12-in/25- or 30.5-cm frying pan just fine, but woks are fun. Go for cast iron, preseasoned.

CHAPTER 2

TO MARKET

The Seasonal Kitchen

EAT FRESH

If you are at the market and you ask the fruit man if you can taste one of his beautiful grapes, he will immediately recognize you as someone who cares and will give you respect. —Jamie Oliver

Let's get back to that plate of juicy summer tomatoes you two were sharing. In a perfect world, those tomatoes would still be warm from the sun, a flawless blend of sweetness and acid. But it's not only the flavor that has captured you. You can practically smell the earth, and you can't help but wonder at all the beautiful colors, so vibrant, so refined that only nature could have made them possible. Every one of your senses is enraptured with the experience, and suddenly you're sure it's the best thing you've ever eaten. Even with the best olive oil on the planet, it doesn't quite work the same way if the tomatoes were overpriced, watery winter slices, beaten and bruised from a cold week in a shipping truck.

The same intoxicating experience could happen just as easily with a ripe summer peach, a plate of roasted beets, or pasta all swirled up with mushroom, fresh sweet corn, and cream. Welcome to the heart and soul of good cooking—fresh seasonal ingredients. They are the defining detail between merely just good or truly delicious food. With a little time and attention paid to the details of your plate, vibrant, fast, and imaginative meals like these can become an easy, everyday occurrence with very little work from you. The fresher and more alive your ingredients are when you start, the easier it is to cultivate healthful, daily abundance in your kitchen. And paying attention to the ingredients makes shopping for those foods together fun and engaging, rather than just a humdrum routine.

When it comes to most produce and protein, there are three easy ways to make sure you're getting the best quality ingredients: Buy fresh, buy seasonal, and buy local. These standards build on and complement one another. Here's how:

BUY FRESH

Consider freshness an insurance policy for delicious daily meals. The fresher your food, the more it is already bursting with life and flavor—which means it requires less skill, time, or money from you to make your meal shine.

BUY SEASONAL

Buying in season is not only the best deal, you'll also be buying food when it is at its very ripest, which means supreme flavor, luscious juices, and nutrient values that are through the roof. It also makes it even easier to buy fresh, since in-season products haven't been shipped from another climate. There's absolutely nothing wrong with wanting and needing a little fruit in the winter time {that's when frozen berries gain celebrity status}, but imagine how much better that first May strawberry will taste when you've waited for it all winter long. So how do you know what's in season?

BUY LOCAL

Buying local is a safety net for both freshness and seasonality. When you buy from your local farmers you are almost always buying in season and most likely buying something that's been off the vine, tree, or stalk for less than 48 hours—an advantage you can taste. Everyone has a different version of what "local" means, anything from food grown within 50 to 400 miles from home base. Start somewhere you feel comfortable and enjoy the pleasure of getting to know the people who provide you with your daily grub. You may even find your favorite food source is in your own backyard!

Supporting your local economy and reducing your carbon footprint are excellent reasons to shop locally and vote with your fork. And if your primary purpose is simply getting the most flavor and nutrients on your plate tonight, you'll be far ahead of the game by starting with these three principles. Choosing to eat locally grown, seasonal food is a goal, not a religion. I love a Maui Gold pineapple and Calimyrna figs, neither of which is grown anywhere near our home in New York. Even a table where locally grown ingredients predominate has room for a steady fling with the far-off and exotic {like cocoa and coffee}, especially when they are chosen and enjoyed with great care. Some days we run out of fresh fruit or vegetables before the weekly farmers' market rolls around again, which means we occasionally eat a tomato grown in a greenhouse somewhere. But most days I'm looking for something that looks and feels the most like it came from my garden, like zucchini and peaches with fuzz on them or tight green bundles of lettuce — all indicators that our produce hasn't been overly handled, or rubbed the wrong way over a long journey to get to us. This is key if either flavor or nutrients are your goal, since almost every fruit or vegetable begins a slow decline the minute it's picked, losing moisture and nutrients every mile along the way to your table.

And of course, the added benefit of shopping local is the personal care and service that comes to you by the bushel. Frequent the same farmer or butcher and they'll begin to learn your preferences, save special items for you, and maybe even throw in an extra one of their prized peaches once in a while.

{ FAIR TRADE }

The Fair Trade label, seen on certain brands of ingredients like bananas, tea, sugar, coffee, rice, and chocolate, was created to ensure that fair prices are paid for products grown in developing countries. It also certifies that the farmer had no exposure to toxic pesticides, isn't involved in child labor, and uses environmentally sound farming methods. It's often a good bet for a better tasting product too.

Shopping this way is so much easier and more fun once you get to know the resources you have in your neighborhood. Spend some time sussing out your local farmers' market, a good butcher and fishmonger, and the best artisan baker in town. Check out a local food co-op, Community Supported Agriculture {CSA} groups, small locally owned supermarkets, and health food stores that may buy direct from farmers.

{ CSAS: CHIC. SMART. ACCESSIBLE. }

Community Supported Agriculture, also called a CSA, is like a club for fresh fruit and veggie fans. When you join a local CSA, you pay a local farmer in advance for the promise of abundant boxes of vegetables and fruits from their fields week after week, all season long. It's the best way to support the farmers and keep your crisper drawer stocked. Check Sources {page 293} for resources that will help you find a CSA near you.

And by the way, this isn't something that only one of you needs to know and understand. If you're the chief shopper in the house, and your better half is slow on the uptake giving up a favorite prepackaged food they may have grown up with, make quick trips to the market together a part of your weekend routine. Make a subtle point of showing off all the colors and flavors you've discovered there, and let them pick out a few things that piques their interest as well {you'll learn a lot about what they like this way!}. Just don't leave your honey hanging there too long if it was your idea {trust me on this one}, and by all means, don't preach! Your carefully shopped, lovingly cooked meals will be a much more delicious form of evangelism.

{ ABOUT ORGANICS }

There are a number of sound arguments as to why buying organic is often the very best thing for the health of you, your spouse, and the earth. In certified organic food, there are no synthetic growth hormones, no persistent pesticides {which after all are designed to kill living organisms}, no antibiotics, and no genetically engineered crops. The animals that live on organic farms are likely to be healthier, as are the farmers themselves since they're not exposed to frequent chemicals. It's also likely that since organic farmers feed their soil a rich array of organic compost to nourish your food, the nutrient density of that food is higher as well. These are all very good reasons to take that label seriously.

A savvy shopper should also know that the nuances of the word organic can be tricky. Organics doesn't always signify a small family farm where the growing and picking happens almost as if it would in your own backyard. Sometimes that is true. When you find those farms and farmers, get to know them; they are gems. But organics can just as often be about big business.

Farmers who use organic practices deserve our respect, but they are not the only farmers to trust. Sometimes locally grown is an equally good option. Since our agricultural system is based primarily on dollars and cents, farmers have to make all sorts of difficult choices to stay in business. On some small family farms, this could mean forgoing the expensive organic certification and working instead in good conscience to bring you their best. Some may label their foods "natural" or "sustainable," which are likely to mean good things, but since they are not certified, ask for details about what sort of practices that farm uses.

These gray areas are more good reasons to shop where you can ask your own questions. When you do, you might find, delightfully, that those rosy locally grown strawberries aren't sprayed with pesticides. In a good season, some nonorganic farmers avoid chemical pesticides by employing some of the same methods as organic farmers {introducing birds to their fields to eat bugs, planting cover crops}. But since they aren't certified organic, they do reserve the right to spray when a crop is about to go downhill fast, so ask.

When you do buy organic, be prepared to get over sticker shock. Farmers who commit to growing only organic crops also commit to losing a portion of their crops every year to bugs and blights that can't be recovered. But consider this: the hidden costs on the other side of some of the cheaper options can catch up with us quickly, affecting the health of humanity and our generous planet.

When it can be found, both local and organic is ideal. I buy organic meat, poultry, milk, dairy, eggs, and produce when I can, particularly when I know I plan to eat the whole fruit with the peel {apples, peaches, grapes, and berries}. And when local produce is a better bet in terms of freshness and flavor than an organic option grown all the way across the country, I feel good about that choice too.

Either way, I use a homemade fruit-and-veggie wash made with equal parts apple cider vinegar and water. Keep this sink-side in a spray bottle. Spray your fruits and veggies well, wipe with a paper towel and then rinse in cold water. It's a cheap and easy solution for making all fruits and veggies a little cleaner.

GROW YOUR OWN GARDEN

Now that you're salivating, dreaming about that perfect sungold tomato, take a peek out your back window and consider making your own fertile ground the most rewarding marketplace of all. It doesn't get more local than that, plus you don't need a fancy sticker or costly certification to grow organically in your own garden. All you need is some good soil and a little practice to watch your harvest grow ever richer and more rewarding each year.

Having a backyard or even a patio is not a prerequisite for becoming a gardener. A local community garden or even a fire escape is a very good starting spot to dig in a little dirt and plant a patch of something green. I even know urban farmers who got started with a pot of herbs on their windowsill and never looked back.

Someday, you and your beloved might raise a dog, or a baby—why not start with a plant? And besides, you'll have so much muddy fun digging in the dirt together. There's nothing like a splash of cold water from a garden hose to end a heated debate and bring a little laughter back into the picture.

With more than two thousand varieties of fruits, vegetables, herbs, and greens in existence, and dozens of heirloom and organic seed companies popping up each year, it's hard to know where to begin. Your best bet is to start small and easy. Add and experiment each year as your knowledge and space increases. Here's a good group of things to get started with to fit the space you have.

COMMUNITY GARDENS: THE SOIL THAT BINDS

Whether or not you have a backyard, community gardens are perhaps the very best way to get growing. In most parts of the country, you can pay nominal dues {as little as twenty dollars a year} for a little plot of dirt within a bigger community space. The benefits of a shared space are numerous including seed swapping, community composts bins, better deals on soil and compost, and usually a shed full of tools that are yours to use without making an investment.

I earned my green thumb in a community garden in New York City, where we still grow most of our summertime greens. I've learned more from those around me than from any garden guide, and the swapping {our tomatoes for our neighbor's squash blossoms} keep us coming back year after year. And there is always someone to ask to do the watering when we are away on our next adventure.

{ A COOK'S GARDEN }

HERBS

WINDOWSILL: parsley, thyme, dill, basil, rosemary
BACKYARD: sage, lemon verbena, sorrel, lavender

GREENS

WINDOWSILL: cut-and-come-again lettuce, mesclun mix, arugula/rocket
BACKYARD: mustard greens, spinach, kale, romaine, red leaf, watercress

VEGETABLES

WINDOWSILL: cherry tomatoes, pole beans, hot peppers
BACKYARD: beefsteak tomatoes, bell peppers, bush beans, okra, pumpkin, squash, summer squash, cucumbers

FRUITS

WINDOWSILL: strawberries
POTTED OR BACKYARD: blueberries, raspberries, blackberries; currants, dwarf peach tree

COMPOST

I've found the most exciting things growing from our compost pile—heirloom melon plants, volunteer tomatoes, and purple carrots. I'm an admittedly lazy composter, preferring to dig our kitchen scraps into unplanted patches of dirt between healthy rows of our garden, and cover them with soil to let nature take its course. Of course, there is a science to composting. If you're composting in a bin above ground, mix equal parts wet kitchen scraps to dry {leaves, unbleached used paper towels, bark, mulch, or shredded newspaper}. Or, leave science to scientists and drop off your compost at the farmers' market, local nursery, or community garden.

BIODIVERSITY

Nature thrives when a huge variety of plants and animals coexist. Genetic varieties support both the flavor of our foods and the health and safety of our food supply. When you garden, you have a huge opportunity to plant heirloom fruits and veggies, and nurture a food supply that is exciting, diverse, and endlessly flavorful.

THE SEASONS

No matter where your goodies grow, it's helpful to know what's in season when, since foods that are in their prime tend to go very well together {nature's clue for encouraging harmony on your plate}. While it's much more fun to taste your way through the seasons than to talk about them, it does help to have a grasp on what to look for when, and how to buy and store some of the fruits and vegetables you'll be using in the recipes that follow. Here's a guide.

Spring

Spring is a seasonal food junkie's delight. After hibernating with your honey bun all winter long, even the most primitive of greens can taste enlightened. Lighten your dinner load with all the fresh, perky pea shoots you can handle, and feel your moods elevate.

ASPARAGUS A little asparagus goes a long way toward dressing up a humble dish. See this for yourself in the Overnight Egg & Cheese Strata {page 81} Starting in early spring, you can find both fat, meaty asparagus and its slender, snappy counterpart, which also have thinner skins. It's your preference, but with either type, look for firm stalks with pert, smooth skin and fresh tips. Asparagus is full of water and wilts quickly, so if you can't cook the stalks immediately, store them upright in a glass with a little water, like flowers, and cover the tips with a damp paper towel in the fridge. To clean them, snap off the woody stems where they break naturally and peel any fat stalks about half way up from the bottom.

BEANS Green beans, sugar snaps, favas, limas, mayflowers. The list of fresh beans is endless, especially now that heirloom beans have come back on the scene. Beans grow vigorously and should be picked young, and are usually a great deal at the farmers' market. Many varieties, like green snap beans and irresistible sugar snaps can be eaten raw off the vine. Cook them quickly in boiling water and refresh them in ice-cold water for crudités or turn them into tangy pickles. Beans that spend longer time on the vine and develop heartier pods, like favas or cranberry beans, are called shell beans, and should be shelled and split and their inner beans boiled fresh or dried and put up for fall and winter soups. Both types should be firm and plump, and if you get the chance to taste for flavor before buying, do so. Later in the season, look for haricots verts, tiny and thin French green beans that should be picked while young and just barely cooked.

LETTUCES AND LEAFY GREENS Many lettuces, and leafy greens like spinach, Swiss chard, mustard greens, and kale, are cold weather–loving plants. You'll find them in farmers' markets and supermarkets year-round, but they may look especially inviting in the crisp, cool spring and fall months. Lettuce comes in all colors and textures from pale green and striated with deep purples, to curly and sweet to spiky and bitter, and can be expensive at the green market. Grow them, they're easy. Here is another chance for big savings. Leafy greens are cheap, superbly nutritious, and very filling. They are also easy to grow in almost any soil. And they last much longer when picked fresh from your garden or purchased at the farmers' market, since they are mostly cells filled with water. When I can't grow it, iron-rich spinach is one leafy green I make a point to buy organic, since it's often sprayed heavily to fight off greedy bugs. All greens should be washed very well with several dunks in a bowl of clean water. Lift the greens out, drain the water, and wash them a second and sometimes a third time before eating or cooking.

MUSHROOMS Morels are the choice mushroom in spring. Their earthy aroma has turned mushroom lovers into committed devotees who will splurge for the price and glory of a good batch. Cook them soon after getting them home if possible, or store them in the fridge in a paper lunch bag so that they can breathe {never keep them in plastic}. To clean, halve large morels lengthwise and only rinse them in water if they seem especially dirty or sandy. Morels quick-cooked with shallots and butter can't be beat. They also make an extra-special topping for a plain cheese omelet, or as the topping for Wild Mushroom Toasts {page 216}.

PEAS & PEA SHOOTS Fresh peas are a very special treat and should be eaten the minute they come home. Full of life and sweetness, they need little more than a quick dip in boiling water, followed by a sprinkling of sea salt and a bit of butter to be appreciated at their best. They complement countless flavors and textures, but truly shine with radishes and fresh ricotta as in Fresh & Pretty Peas with Radishes {page 200}. Their shoots are sold at markets just before actual peas appear, and their tendrils are sweet whisper of what's to come. They make a gorgeous garnish for Chef's Scramble Crostini {page 96}.

RADISHES Oh the humble radish, a punchy little creature with so many colors, textures, and flavors. They're incredibly easy to grow and cheap to buy by the bunch week after week at the market through early summer. Whether served sliced, quartered, raw, or blanched, radishes love a good soak in ice-cold water when they get home from a hot day at the market.

RHUBARB A vegetable that masquerades as a fruit, rhubarb tends to be polarizing, though few people I know can resist Sticky-Sweet Rhubarb Upside-Down Cake {page 255} or Dutch Babies with Poached Rhubarb {58}. Thin, bright ruby-pink stalks are full of tart flavor {leaves are discarded, since they can be toxic}. Add only enough sugar to give it balance, and cook it low and slow just until it softens but keeps its pretty color. You'll find rhubarb again for just a bit in the winter in some states, too.

SPRING GARLIC Also called green garlic, this is the baby version of bulbous garlic you get later in the year. Mild, herbal, and slightly tender, it's much like a scallion or small leek but smells distinctively of garlic. Get it while it lasts to slice for a garnish or stir into vegetables that get a quick cook.

SPRING ONIONS Either purple or pale white, spring onions are pretty things with as much to offer in the flavor category as they do in their good looks. Buy them with light bulbs and perky green tops, both of which can be used. These are delicious raw {now is the time to stack them on your Better Beef Burgers, page 120} and cooked on the grill/barbecue as a star in The Man Sandwich {page 103}. Later in the year the same onions, left in the ground, need longer cooking to bring out their sweetness.

STRAWBERRIES Spring sings its arrival with glorious straw-berries. If you've waited all winter long you may not mind paying the dear price that good market berries sometimes command. These are worth every penny. Tiny, tender, and sweet as a summer day, you won't need much reminding to eat them fast. They go downhill quickly after they are picked {why the sturdier, less flavorful varieties are more widely sold in supermarkets}. Keep them in a cool place, and don't give them a rinse until just before you plan to eat them.

Summer

Of all the seasons, summer is a love affair with fruits and vegetables. There are endless opportunities to let them steal the show on your plate, and many of them need little in the way of cooking or garnish. What a beautiful pardon to indulge in lazy afternoons sipping rosé and splashing in a swimming hole while you dream away the day.

APRICOTS Depending on where you live, you might find apricots from late May through June. Their season is fleeting and a good apricot can be hard to come by. Look for ripe ones with a little blush on their skin {they don't ripen off the tree}. Bake, poach, or eat them fresh.

AVOCADOS Though you'll find them year round in the grocery store, it is in summer that the black-skinned Hass, the most commonly found variety, is the creamiest. Avocado is such an astoundingly healthy fruit, with over twenty essential nutrients from Vitamin E to the B vitamins, folic acid, and potassium, that I'd like to argue the case for completely ignoring any concerns you may have about its fat content. It's healthful fat, and fat that gives tremendous flavor and texture to both hot and cold dishes. Avocados can be pricy, because unless you live in California or Florida, most of them are shipped from warmer climates. Buy them in bulk and if you're looking to save, skip organic since you'll peel them before eating. Keep two on the counter to ripen quickly, and store the others in the fridge to soften more slowly. Pull them out a day before eating.

BERRIES Raspberries, blackberries, mulberries, blueberries—pick a berry, any berry, and bring it home. Eat them by the handful for their marvelous healthfulness {antioxidants galore} and bursting good flavor. Stir them into Steel-Cut Oats {page 65}, sprinkle them on Multigrain Pancakes {page 61}, and cook them until they burst into Blackberry Crush {page 62} to top pancakes or ice cream sundaes. Buy them all when plump and full of juice. At the farmers' market, you can ask for a taste before you buy, which is important because taste trumps good looks in this case. Most berries are a touch delicate. Handle them gingerly. Store them in the fridge in single layers if possible, eat them quickly and wash them only when you are ready to eat them. White or purple mulberries are harder to find but grow wild on trees all over the United States and reward the faithful forager. When possible, buy organic berries, since pesticides can remain on berries even after washing.

CHERRIES The dark, deep-staining juices of fresh cherries signal two very important things—these are supremely delicious and absurdly nutritious. The season for both sweet {red, white, or Queen Anne} and sour cherries is fleeting. Grab hold of the season with every dime you've got. Fill little bowls with cherries, pit them and stir them into Lazy Chef's Fruit Torte {page 244} with peaches and plums, and stew them with a little sugar as a sweet topping for ice cream {Warm Cherries with Pistachio Ice Cream, page 239}. Taste before you buy them, since good looks can be misleading. And by all means, wear an apron when you pit them!

CORN Fresh corn kernels begin to turn from sugar to starch as soon as they're picked, so try to buy them from the farmers' market, still in the husk {which locks in moisture} within a day or two of eating them. Look for bright green, tightly fitting husks that surround plump, milky kernels.

CUCUMBER Persian, Blonde, and Kirby are just a few of the sprightly varieties of cukes available to buy or grow that might inspire you to rethink just how fun these veggies are to have on hand. Grow or buy them by the bunch {they're cheap}. You'll find yourself stacking them on sandwiches {Pan-Fried Striped Bass Sandwiches, page 104}, serving them up as relish {Mint & Chile Marinated Cukes, page 189}, shredding them into Tsatsiki {page 210}, and slipping them into your water for a refreshing summer elixir.

EGGPLANT/AUBERGINE Many varieties of eggplant can be found in markets and supermarkets alike. Whatever color or shape you buy {they can be big and deeply purple, fat and white, long and lavender}, look for ones that are evenly plump with shiny skin, void of blemishes. Eggplant has a bitterness that can send wary vegetable explorers crawling back to home base. A fresh eggplant's flavor will be milder. Sliced, grilled, and salted just enough, eggplant is great stacked in veggie sandwiches. Charred and smashed with olive oil and garlic and you've got luxurious eggplant caviar, known in this book as Babaghanewlyweds {page 211}.

FIGS What would a newlywed diet be without the fig, considered both to be an aphrodisiac and a sign of fertility? In late summer and early fall, the sun's summer magic comes to life in the sweetness of a properly tree-ripened fig. They are mostly grown in California and in Mediterranean countries, and can be harder to find fresh across the United States. If you find them, green or purple skinned, consider the ease and ecstasy of Greek Yogurt with Fresh Figs {page 236} to finish your meal.

MELONS From mid-summer to early fall, melons arrive with myriad names and labels in markets and farm stands. There are dozens of varieties with colors from pale green to peach to bright pink, and textures and flavors to match. Melons can be vegetal and taste of cucumber, or dripping sweet with flesh that yields in an instant to eager teeth. They need nothing but a napkin to be enjoyed at their sublime peak. To choose most melons {except watermelon}, smell the stem end. Orange and green-fleshed melons should smell sweet and floral. Watermelon should sound hollow when tapped, and as for all melons, should be very heavy for its size.

PEACHES & NECTARINES The perfect peach should be unbruised and tender to the touch but not soft. Most important, it should smell intensely and intoxicatingly like the peach of your dreams, a good indicator that the sugars have ripened properly and it's ready to eat. Tree-ripened peaches are fragile and should be eaten soon after you bring them home since they won't last more than a day or so when they are at their juicy best. Store them on the counter for that fresh-from-the-tree sunny texture, or in the fridge to stop ripening. Buy organic peaches when you can if you plan to eat the skins.

PLUMS There are a great many varieties of plums grown around the world, especially in Central Europe and along the coasts of the United States. Elephant Heart, Shiro, mirabelle, and cross-hybrids like pluots {a plum-apricot mix} are exciting detours from the classic and more familiar pink and purple European plums. Most have tart skin and juicy flesh that varies from pucker-worthy to sweet and juicy enough to make a good mess of your chin. They are excellent eaten out of hand, sliced into fruit salads, and added to tarts and tortes, like Lazy Chef's Fruit Torte {page 244}. The best ones should yield a little to light pressure. Though they will soften slightly on the counter, they don't actually ripen off the tree.

POTATOES In many ways, potatoes are actually year-round foods, and the bigger varieties keep well in a cool place for a long time. But come late spring and throughout summer, little, nugget-size potatoes of all shapes, sizes, and colors start to appear at farmers' market. I buy them by the greedy handful for their buttery texture and smooth skins that love to be boiled, broiled, smashed, or sliced and served up simply with butter or olive oil and fresh herbs {Boiled Baby Potatoes with Garden Chives, page 184}. Since they are grown in the soil, they absorb both the chemicals and nutrients found there, so thank organic farmers by buying potatoes from them when you can.

TOMATOES Is there any fruit more beloved than a summer tomato? They might be nature's perfect food. My best piece of advice is to grow them in every hefty pot or patch of soil you can come by. They are increasingly more expensive at supermarkets and farmers' market {due to their susceptibility to blights, fungus, and rot}, while seeds and starters for any number of heirloom varieties are getting easier to find every year. You need good soil and lots of uninterrupted sunlight to grow them successfully, but it's not hard. Tomatoes are a bit like wine, but far less intimidating. There are hundreds of varieties, and you really have to taste to know what you like best. But even a basic homegrown tomato will taste superb next to a standard supermarket version. When you buy them at the market, look for firm fruits that are heavy for their size {which means they are juicy, but since you pay by the pound, also expensive}. And like most of the world's best vine- or tree-ripened fruits and vegetables, the ugly Betty of the batch might be the best find. Keep these on the countertop. Tomatoes lose their flavor, texture, and sun-ripened succulence when stored in the fridge

ZUCCHINI/COURGETTE, SUMMER SQUASH & SQUASH BLOSSOMS Zucchini is easy to cook. Sadly though, most people have only tasted slick, rubbery zucchini and summer squash cooked over low heat in a crowded pan. Zucchini and summer squash, which come in dozens of varieties, should be bought when firm and still fuzzy without nicks and scrapes all over the skin. Bring them home and try them shredded in Golden Zucchini Bread {page 75}, grilled in The Man Sandwich, {page 103}, served raw in Shaved Zucchini with Ricotta & Walnuts {page 192}, and breaded. When you cook them plain, cook them over high heat with oil, salt, and pepper, either on the grill or in a pan large enough to make sure they don't touch. You want to eat them crispy on the outside and still slightly firm throughout. I have a particular devotion to squash blossoms. They are crispy and lightly vegetal. They are an elegant raw topping for Gardener's Pizza {page 158}. The flower is the forebearer to the fruit that's to come, so if you grow your own, grow an extra plant just for their flowers.

Fall

This is the season of soups and sweaters, football games and gatherings. After a sunny summer to plump up, pumpkins and squash arrive for roasting, sweet potatoes soften into smooth purees, and apples await, graciously, amply ready to fill your belly between hayrides and hikes.

APPLES Affable, amiable apples are praised for their long-storing qualities, exactly why you'll see them all year round. But never was there a better time than autumn to head to the country to pick them straight from the tree. Seek out some of the hundreds of varieties that have come back in vogue. Many cooks prefer firm, crisp, and tart varieties like honeycrisp, Mutsu {Crispin}, Gala, or Macoun for eating, and crisp, sweet to tart varieties that hold their shape, like Jonathan, Jonagold, or Golden Delicious for baking. Often the best flavor for pies and sauces comes from mixing a variety of apples, so I buy a couple of varieties of what's in season locally for most recipes. Store them in a cold spot {fridge, basement, or cool garage} where they'll stay crisp. Buy organic or wash well if you plan to eat the skin.

GRAPES Fresh Concord or Muscat grapes are one of Earth's greatest jewels. They are harder to find in certain states, though the rise in winemaking enthusiasts from Illinois to Idaho is changing that. Some of the best Concord grapes I ever had were from a farm stand in mid-Missouri. Buy local for the best flavor, and organic when you can. Because you generally eat the skin, it's worth the splurge to buy organic since grapes are toward the top of the list of foods found to have heavy pesticide residue.

PEARS It's not always easy to find a ripe pear, but pears will soften slightly on the countertop or in a brown bag until they are juicy and yield to the touch. When ripe, they don't need much to be enjoyed. Slice and serve with fresh whipped cream, alongside cheese, or in salads. Local markets and orchards offer the best textures and heirloom varieties. Buy organic when you can, since we tend to eat them skin-on.

PUMPKIN & SQUASH Pumpkin and squash come in as many shapes and sizes as you could possibly dream up, from fat and squatty to long and lean, with skin that is smooth or warty, orange or sage green. Try them all, they are wonderfully varied and their meaty, mild-to-deeply-flavored flesh can soothe and satisfy in many forms. Roast them {Roasted Winter Vegetables, page 193} to top Baked Risotto {page 115} or toss into cool-season salads.

SWEET POTATOES I could live a good long while on a diet of baked sweet potatoes, which turns into a buttery mash in minutes on your plate. Usually, the sweet potatoes we think of first in this country are actually Garnet or Jewel yams, deeply orange-hued and sweet as can be. Steam, roast, or bake {even quickly in the microwave}, top with a little pat of butter or drizzle of fruity olive oil and coarse sea salt for finishing. Store them in a moderately cool place {think root cellar, not fridge} like potatoes.

TURNIPS Try not to turn up your nose at the innocent little turnip. They can be cooked horribly, but I assure you, when braised in butter and salt, they are like earth's candy. {Ditto for rutabaga/swede.} You can grab a bunch of baby turnips in the spring, but wait till fall for bigger bulbs. In any size, they blend beautifully with most aromatics, like onions, carrots, and celery, and add much to fall and winter braises like Plenty of Pot Roast {page 148} and Big-Flavor Braised Short Ribs {page 178}. Their tops are mighty tasty too. Cook them like mustard greens.

WILD MUSHROOMS Wild mushrooms are the prime rib of produce. There's a time in the year where I could get carried away wandering the forest floor after a week's rain, hoping to find it flush with chanterelles, black trumpets, and porcini. This rarely happens, because it takes a true expert to safely forage in the wild, and therefore worth the price they command for discerning the heady, delicate, edible versions from imposters. Mushrooms do very well in high-heat, low-moisture cooking techniques. Cook them stovetop in butter and oil or roast in a hot oven. Herbs and sea salt are their astute companions. Look for mushrooms that are relatively clean {by nature's standards, not greenhouse standards}, fragrant, and earthy smelling. Avoid anything musty or damp, or those that have turned spongy or slippery. They are most likely past their prime.

Winter

It's time to get cozy. Winter foods like squash and larger cuts of meat require longer cooking times, and fill the house with warming aromas that ward off winter blues. Everything slows down, and suddenly you have even more time for each other. Now is a choice time to open that bottle of red wine you've been saving and to savor all its promised flavors.

BROCCOLI & CAULIFLOWER In terms of greens, there's not an awful lot to shout about this time of year. You might find new appreciation for broccoli, cauliflower, cabbage, kale, all of which will stick with you when more lightweight vegetables have had their day. Broccoli, simply steamed, is truly something. Cauliflower can be stunning too, more so when roasted or cooked quickly at high heat and topped with lemon, capers, raisins, and breadcrumbs.

CITRUS {GRAPEFRUIT, ORANGES, LEMONS, LIMES, AND TANGERINES} You will never find my fruit drawer without lemons or limes, any time of the year. They brighten almost anything, even a glass of water. But now is the time to explore all the other citrus like pink grapefruits, Seville and blood oranges, kumquats, and hybrids like Tangelos. One orange bursting with bright flavor brings a warm winter salad to life and does the same for the Brown Rice Bowl with Watercress, Walnuts & Winter Citrus {page 112}. Grapefruit makes a splendid start to the day, and it complements the snap of shaved fennel in Arugula, Grapefruit & Fennel Salad {page 88} as a fresh first course alongside charcuterie.

Tangerines and lemons make luxurious marmalade to top Olive Oil Cake with Tangerine Marmalade {page 251}, and all kinds of citrus sit pretty in the fruit bowl to keep you in vitamin C through the weariest winter months.

POMEGRANATES For a fleeting few months in early winter, these clever fruits hide their ruby jewels beneath their skins. One of the fruits eaten for their seeds rather than pulp, the pop and crunch of pomegranate is matched only by its anti-oxidant profile. Slip the seeds in salads or winter sangria, or quarter the fruit and use it on your holiday table to add color to a platter of turkey or prime rib.

PERSIMMONS Hachiya and Fuyu persimmons, grown in southern states, require some devotion. They deserve it, for they are a special treat, unlike any other fruit. They can be hard to find, and even harder to find ripe. Buy Hachiyas very soft, and don't eat them until they feel like custard inside. Then they are heavenly. Fuyus should be rounder and firm with deep orange skin. They taste great cold and sliced in salads. Neither appears in recipes in this book, for I enjoy both most of all on their own.

Year-Round

There are a number of loyal, evergreen fruits and vegetables that keep the world going round when half of it is buried in snow. You can find most of these in the supermarket any time of the year.

BEETS Long live the numerous restaurant chefs who have brought the beet back into fashion. Fresh beets, thinly shaved, slowly simmered or roasted in rich olive oil and sea salt, are a far cry from the canned version so many of us know. These are a vegetable to get excited about! They still deserve any bad press received for the way they stain your hands or your aprons, but you won't mind when you taste them in A Real Good Salad {page 87}. Though these are a true summer crop, you can find them year round and you are more likely to turn on your stove to cook them in cooler months. Before you bring them home, feel to make sure they are rock hard. If you buy them with the tops on, look for vibrant green and pink-veined tops that can be lopped off and cooked like Swiss chard.

CARROTS Pulled fresh from the soil, with dirt still clinging, carrots are an exciting bunch worth giving a little thought and care. No offense to the little preshaved nubs we've become accustomed to snacking on, but the baby carrots of the farmers' market in summer are an altogether different sort. Sweet, sometimes brightly colored purple, deep orange, red, or pale yellow, they make a stunning surprise served on a platter with fish or braised meats. If you can find them with their curly tops attached, bring them home and trim the tops low to keep the moisture and energy concentrated in the roots that will become your dinner.

FENNEL The bulb, fronds, and seeds of fennel, a regular in restaurant kitchens, are too often overlooked at home. They are mildly sweet and smell of anise, or licorice, and give tremendous flavor whether used raw or cooked. If used raw, I like to shave fennel very thin as in the greens that garnish the Pan-Fried Striped Bass Sandwiches {page 104}. Look for fennel with the feathery fronds still attached, which can spruce up simple salads and garnish fish. Remove the stalks and core before shaving with a sharp knife or mandoline, but the core can be left in if you plan to quarter and roast in bigger pieces.

FRESH HERBS Fresh herbs add color, flavor, and flourish to even the simplest supper, and there are many that you can grow or buy year round. Including fresh herbs on the daily menu shouldn't require you to break the bank {or throw away half a bundle every week}. They are one of the most expensive things to buy in the grocery, and also the easiest to grow. Start with hearty rosemary, oregano, and thyme, and then move into chives, parsley, and chervil. Look for Green Thumb hints for how to grow specific herbs.

GARLIC We have garlic to thank for the depth, aroma, and success of so many treasured dishes. It can sting in its raw state, so use moderately, but when cooked long and slow on low heat, it softens to an almost-sweet, resonant roundness. Look for tight bulbs without any green shoots. If you find a little green germ inside, halve your clove and cut around it.

ONIONS Try to never get caught without onions. A good number of recipes depend on them. For basic cooking, buying in bulk is a good idea if you use them weekly. Look for firm, unsprouted onions and avoid storing them with potatoes or other root veggies, which can cause them both to sprout.

POTATOES Varieties with a creamy yellow flesh are rich and flavorful, and delicious tossed in butter, smashed with sour cream or crème fraîche, or roasted on high heat and added to salads. Drier, fluffy Idaho, baking, or russet potatoes are best for baking, for making Don't-You-Dare Mashed Potatoes {page 187} and Easier-than-Pie Oven Fries {baked, not fried} {page 219}, and as the starting point for Dowry Dinner Rolls {page 132} and Homemade Gnocchi with Summer Beans {page 162}.

SHALLOTS If I had to choose, I might pick a shallot over onion. It's milder and less abrasive than onion both cooked and raw, and even a novice can coax the same sweetness out by braising it in butter.

Sliced or minced and soaked in warm salty water for 10 minutes, shallots add delicate crunch and savory notes to salads and complement classic vinaigrettes very well.

WATERCRESS Peppery watercress adds gumption to just about everything, especially salads and sandwiches. Thank goodness it's easy to find year round. Add it to meals in the winter when you need a bit of spunk. Choose watercress with fresh, upright, deep green leaves. Avoid anything that is yellowing or looks wilted. Wash it well and store it in very slightly damp paper towels/absorbent paper for up to 2 days. Pull the leaves and smaller stems from the woody stems before serving.

THE MEAT & FISH MARKETS

Fruit and vegetables are hardly our only opportunity to be choosy. There are just as many if not more thoughtful choices involved in choosing meat, poultry, dairy, and eggs, and confusing labels to go with them. Choice or Prime? Grass-fed or Pasture-raised? Hormone-and-antibiotic free? With meat, poultry, dairy, and eggs, a good start is foods labeled "natural" and "hormone-and-antibiotic free." "Organic" is also a good benchmark. Distinctions like "pasture-raised" or "grass-fed" on beef, and "cage-free" or "free-range" for poultry and eggs, can all put you one step closer to eating animals raised the way nature intended, but even these labels are not cut and dry. There are numerous books and articles from which to learn more. The health of you and your spouse are your most precious assets, and it's worth your time to learn about your food and make the best choice for you both. In the meantime, look for Eat Green call-outs on recipes in this book that call for specific meat or fish. And as always, seeking out sources where you can ask questions is the best way to get the highest quality proteins on your plate.

THE MEAT MARKET

Even after years of cooking professionally and a keen interest in the anatomy of most mammals, I've found it's still no easy task to make sense of my grocer's meat section. Since most grocery stores no longer employ their own butchers, it can be hard to find an expert to ask. If you do find a grocery with an on-site butcher, you're in luck! Don't be afraid to request one {they might be in the back cutting up your dinner} and ask plenty of questions.

Luckily, butchery is an art that's experienced a renaissance, making it far easier to find a good brick-and-mortar butcher shop now than it's been since before World War II. Take advantage. Their cuts may cost a bit more, but it's likely the meat will be of high quality, and it comes with a free and very reliable resource—the butcher!

Wherever you buy your meat, here are some basic rules of thumb to bring home the best.

- Only shop in clean, well-kept butcher shops. High standards show in clean countertops and floors.

- Look for meats that are well displayed and clearly marked, which allows the butcher and you to both make better sense of when the meat came in and when it should go.

- Ask questions about where your meat came from, if it's organic, pasture-raised or grass-fed {for beef}, or free-range, cage-free, or vegetarian-fed or both {for chicken}. If the butcher doesn't know the answers or seems unwilling

to make an effort to find out, chances are your meat is a long way from home, and there's no telling what's happened between the farm and your plate.

- Meat should smell clean, look matte or dry to the touch {not bloody or wet}, and be wrapped in butcher paper for you to take home. Be wary of meat that's sitting in its own blood or wrapped in plastic film.

- Beef or lamb should be rich, dark red with creamy fat around the edges and throughout, which keeps it moist while cooking.

- Pork and chicken should look and smell clean.

A NOTE ON GAME MEATS

If you're up for something new, give game meats like duck, venison, bison, or rabbit a try. Venison and bison are leaner, and by the nature of wild game, often more natural red meat choices. Ground, they can substitute quite nicely for any recipes that include beef including Fresh Pappardelle with Pork Ragu {page 168} and Make-Ahead Lasagna {page 137}.

THE FISH MARKET

There's an eternity to be explored under water. Fish and seafood are in many ways the world's greatest protein. They taste brilliantly of the sea and are full of the vital fatty acids our brains and bodies thrive on. In almost every couple, there's usually one who wrinkles their nose at the very mention of seafood. If a plate of fish in childhood consisted of frozen orange roughy or farmed tilapia, get ready to have your world rocked by fresh, locally line-caught fish.

It can be tricky to navigate the waters, so to speak, of fresh fish. If you grew up in the land-locked Midwest, as I did, learning what to look for is an acquired, not innate, skill. Mix in the iffy and always-changing reports on the quality of our planet's waters, and warnings for things like mercury, and it can be a daunting area to dive into.

Don't let that scare you off. There are still plenty of fresh, sustainable fish in the sea. Start by looking for a local fish-monger. If you don't have one, don't give up yet! Though many grocery stores don't have well-stocked fish sections, there are some that pride themselves on information, freshness, and quality. Find the fishmonger or manager and ask plenty of questions: Is the fish wild or farmed? Line- or net-caught? Is it sustainable? And most important, what day did it arrive at the store? If they don't know the answers or are unwilling to find out, run for the hills. Don't worry about seeming picky. They probably respect their pickiest customers the most and will remember to give you the very best next time you come around.

LIVING WATERS

The nature of the earth's waters is such that it is affected by the habits of every creature that interacts with them, so conditions are constantly changing. Check for the latest standards on the Monterey Bay Aquarium's Seafood Watch to help you learn about the most sustainable choices for you and the planet. Arranged well by Best Choice, Good Alternative, and Avoid, the site will help you quickly learn the greenest choices available in any given month or time zone.

With fish and seafood, as with all ingredients, your own eyes and nose should always be your first line of defense against a rotten deal. You'll give even the most trustworthy fishmonger reason to raise his or her standards when they see you, their savvy customer, choosing only the best based on these basic guidelines:

- Fish should smell clean, of the ocean {if it's a saltwater fish}, and without any strong or unpleasing odors.

- Fish should be packed on shaved ice, not on cubed ice, which can bruise the fish's flesh.

- Eyes should be clear, bright, and shiny. If they are cloudy or glazed over, give it a pass.

- The gills {lift to check just below the fin behind the head} should be deep red, never brown, sticky, or murky looking.

- The skin and scales should glisten and be neat and intact. If patches of skin seem to be missing, the fish has likely been mishandled.

- If the type of fish you want is mangled or badly cut, ask if they have fresh cut in the back.

MEATLESS MONDAYS: Big hunks of meat weren't meant to find their way to the dinner plate every night. It's time to get jazzed about all of the meatless recipes and "Make it Meatless" options throughout the book that can help you go meatless a few times a week. When you do have meat, enjoy it, and look for meat that was well cared for and raised on a natural diet.

- It's easiest to tell the freshness and quality of whole fish, so even if you want to take home fillets, consider choosing one whole and asking to have it filleted. You may pay a little bit extra for the luxury, but it will be easier to judge its value with the head on.

- Whole fish or fillets should be stiff and spring back quickly when touched. If it holds your fingerprint it's most likely old or hasn't been stored correctly.

- Don't be afraid to ask for center-cut fillets and pieces that somewhat match in size, which cook more evenly, especially if you're new to cooking fish.

THE FISH IN YOUR FREEZER

Some fish, shrimp/prawns, and seafood {like scallops} are always frozen, especially if you live in land-locked states. Fish that have been flash-frozen or frozen at sea are sometimes in better shape than fresh fish that are days old. Check these fish the same way you check for fresh fish. If still frozen, it should be rock hard and sold from a clean, very cold freezer section with high turnover. Check to make sure scallops have been dry stored. Those stored in brine will be plump but pumped with liquid, which raises their cost per pound and makes them harder to cook.

Once you've found the good stuff, buy fish and seafood on the same day you plan to cook it if you can, or not more than 24 hours ahead. Store it in the coldest part of your fridge, in a plastic bag set on crushed ice or an ice pack if possible.

If you're planning a menu for a special meal or guests, call ahead. A good fishmonger should know what's coming in that day, and you'll likely get the freshest fish on the market. And finally, before you buy, ask if they will scale or portion fillets for you, and pull the pin bones from your fillets. Neither is hard to do at home, but it's messy. It's a time saver you can feel good about since you've already gone the extra mile to get the best fish available.

CHAPTER 3

BRUNCH

Brunch is the beloved meal of newlyweds, a celebration of long, lazy Saturdays where one meal turns into the next and time stands still for the two of you. Those are the days for Oatmeal-Yogurt Pancakes with Blackberry Crush {page 62} and Cheddar-Cornmeal Biscuits {page 70}. Days for breakfast in bed or for passing on the paper and dreaming up your next big plan together over a plate of Whole-Grain Croque Monsieur {page 77}.

Making time to start your day at the table together is not only a good habit for your health, but a good habit for a healthy relationship too. It's the most hopeful time of the day, side by side in your pj's before you let the rest of the world in. When we first got married, we sometimes found that we were quite content to stay nose to nose on our pillows. But evenings are unpredictable. Between workouts and dinner dates with friends, it turned out breakfast is our very best time to count on being together every day. Sometimes you have to throw caution to the wind and make the morning wait for you. This chapter is made up of meals to send you off into your day with the feeling that you've already gotten more out of life {and your marriage} than most people dream of all day.

Brunch is the perfect and not-too-expensive first chance to extend your table for two and invite friends. There are no finicky wine pairings to worry about {everyone loves a mimosa}, no tables to be set, just glorious Rise & Shine Muffins {page 68} and Golden Zucchini Bread {page 75} that can be made in big batches the night before and laid on a cake stand with bowls of fresh fruit and hard boiled eggs.

Not every day is a brunch day. There are days for Monday Morning Muesli {page 66} and Two Breakfast Sandwiches {page 76}, fast morning meals for busy workdays that sustain you until lunchtime without putting a cramp in your morning schedule. Those are the days you're grateful you tucked the extra weekend muffins into the freezer to make your midweek morning that much more exciting.

When you just can't wake up, shake it up a bit and serve breakfast for dinner. What could feel more liberating than Sunday Buttermilk Biscuits & Gravy {page 72} on a Tuesday night?

Eat breakfast like a king, lunch as a citizen, and dinner like a beggar.
—Hungarian Proverb

DUTCH BABIES
· · · · WITH · · · ·
POACHED RHUBARB

serves 2 to 4

{share} Dutch babies, or German puffed pancakes, are such a memorable treat. Although they're incredibly simple to make, they invoke the same delightful gasp as a soufflé, making you feel like a star. With all the butter and half-and-half, these aren't for every day, but are truly too special to miss when you need to start your day with something sweet.

POACHED RHUBARB	DUTCH BABIES
1 plump vanilla bean/pod	6 tbsp/85 g unsalted butter
2 small stalks rhubarb, sliced {about 3 cups}	4 large eggs
¾ cup/150 g sugar	½ cup/120 ml half-and-half/half cream
2 tbsp water	½ cup/60 g all-purpose/plain flour
2 tbsp/30 g unsalted butter	2 tsp sugar
1 lemon wedge	Confectioners'/icing sugar

Preheat the oven to 425°F/220°C/gas 7.

TO PREPARE THE RHUBARB: Split the vanilla bean/pod lengthwise and lightly scrape the little black flecks of vanilla seeds out of the bean with the back of a knife. Add the seeds to a medium saucepan along with the pod, the rhubarb, sugar, and the water. Cook over low heat until the rhubarb just begins to soften and all the sugar has dissolved, about 20 minutes. Remove from the heat and stir in the butter. Squeeze a little lemon juice over the top and stir in. Set aside to cool slightly.

MEANWHILE, MAKE THE PANCAKES: Divide the butter between two 6-in/15-cm cast-iron frying pans or small, shallow, ovenproof baking dishes. Melt the butter over low heat and swirl to coat the pans. Set the frying pans on a baking sheet/tray.

Combine the eggs, half-and-half/half cream, flour, and sugar in a blender and puree until smooth, about the consistency of eggnog, about 1 minute. Pour the batter directly into the pool of butter in the frying pans and transfer the baking sheet/tray to the oven. Bake until the pancakes are puffed about 3 in/7.5 cm above the pans and are golden brown on top, with a little pool of butter in the center, about 20 minutes.

Spoon over warm poached rhubarb and lightly dust with confectioners'/icing sugar. Serve the Dutch Babies straight from the oven {on a tray in bed, if you're feeling so inclined}.

P.S. *These pancakes also make a dramatic dessert and are excellent served with lemon juice and confectioners'/icing sugar, or your favorite preserves.*

RICOTTA SILVER DOLLARS
····· WITH ·····
NECTARINE SYRUP

serves 4

{from summer's finest fruit} Ricotta cheese gives pancakes a sweet, tender texture that is heavenly when warm. Summer nectarines create their own seductive syrup when tossed with sugar and lemon juice. These little lovelies literally melt in your mouth, so stack them high, served fresh from the griddle, and watch them disappear.

NECTARINE SYRUP

4 large firm-ripe nectarines

Juice of 1 lemon

½ cup/100 g sugar

PANCAKES

1⅓ cups/155 g all-purpose/plain flour

½ cup/70 g medium or finely ground cornmeal or polenta

½ tsp fine sea salt or iodized salt

½ tsp baking powder

½ tsp baking soda/bicarbonate of soda

Scant 2 cups/480 ml buttermilk {see page 16}

½ cup/120 ml fresh whole-milk ricotta cheese

2 large eggs, separated

Pinch of freshly ground nutmeg

Pinch of finely grated lemon zest

1 tbsp sugar

Melted unsalted butter, for the pan

TO MAKE THE SYRUP: Halve and pit the nectarines. Cut halves crosswise into thin slices. Toss with lemon juice and sugar in a bowl and set aside for 30 minutes. Stir occasionally to encourage the fruit to release its juices and create a syrup.

TO MAKE THE PANCAKES: Whisk together flour, cornmeal, salt, baking powder, and baking soda/bicarbonate of soda in a large bowl. In a separate bowl, whisk together the buttermilk, ricotta, egg yolks, nutmeg, and lemon zest. Make a well in the center of the dry ingredients, and whisk in the wet ingredients until just incorporated.

Beat the egg whites and sugar with an electric mixer or a whisk in a clean bowl until they just hold stiff peaks. Gently fold the egg whites into the batter with a spatula or whisk until evenly incorporated, but don't overmix, which can deflate the egg whites.

Heat a cast-iron or nonstick griddle or heavy frying pan over medium-high heat until a drop of water sizzles when splashed on the pan. Brush the griddle lightly with melted butter. Pour a scant ¼ cup/60 ml of batter per pancake onto the griddle, leaving about 2 in/5 cm between pancakes. When little bubbles form all over the surface of the batter, after 1 to 2 minutes, gently lift and flip the pancakes with a flexible spatula. Cook on the other side until the pancakes are golden brown around the edges, about 2 minutes. Repeat, adding more butter to the pan as needed.

Serve immediately with sliced nectarines and their syrup.

MULTIGRAIN PANCAKES
· · · · WITH · · · ·
CHOCOLATE SHAVINGS

serves 4

{sensibly decadent} Who says there's no place for chocolate at breakfast? Subtle flecks of dark chocolate mixed with whole grains make this the most sensibly indulgent breakfast. Pancakes made with a blend of whole-grain flours are the best in flavor and texture, so if you have a few of these flours on hand, mix them together. If not, you can use all white whole-wheat flour or a blend of all-purpose white and whole-wheat flours totaling 2 cups. Whole grains need a touch of sugar for tenderness, as well as melted butter, which keep these soft and fluffy.

If a bit of morning chocolate is not your style, serve these sprinkled with fresh, frozen, or wild blueberries as your go-to blueberry pancakes. For my taste, both versions love a little butter and pure maple syrup on top too.

1¼ cups/175 g whole-wheat/
wholemeal flour or
white whole-wheat/wholemeal flour

½ cup/40 g oat flour, barley flour, or millet flour

¼ cup/35 g buckwheat flour

3 tbsp sugar

2 tsp baking powder

1 tsp baking soda/bicarbonate of soda

1 tsp fine sea salt

2½ cups/600 ml buttermilk

8 tbsp/115 g butter, melted, plus more for the pan

2 eggs {at room temperature}, beaten

⅔ cup/75 g shaved or finely chopped bittersweet or semisweet chocolate

Confectioners'/icing sugar or maple syrup

Whisk together the flours, sugar, baking powder, baking soda/bicarbonate of soda, and salt in a large bowl. In a separate bowl, whisk together the buttermilk, the melted butter, and eggs. Make a well in the center of the dry ingredients, and whisk in the wet ingredients until just combined and evenly wet with some small lumps remaining.

Heat a nonstick griddle or heavy frying pan over medium-high heat until a drop of water sizzles when splashed on the pan. Brush the griddle with melted butter. Pour a scant ¼ cup/60 ml of batter onto the griddle per pancake, leaving about 3 in/7.5 cm between pancakes.

When little bubbles form all over the surface of the pancakes, sprinkle over about 1 tbsp of the chopped chocolate on each. Top the chocolate with just one or two spoonfuls more batter per pancake {so the chocolate doesn't scorch on the griddle} and let them set another 30 seconds. Gently lift and flip the pancakes with a flexible spatula. Cook on the other side until the pancakes are golden brown around the edges, about 3 minutes. Repeat, adding more butter to the griddle as needed.

Serve warm with butter and confectioners' sugar or maple syrup.

OATMEAL-YOGURT PANCAKES
· · · · WITH · · · ·
BLACKBERRY CRUSH

serves 4

Oats add great flavor, texture, and a little nutritional boost to almost any baked good. I love their flavor, but in this dish, the oats fade into the background behind the ethereal texture of perfectly plump, tender pancakes. The Greek yogurt works like buttermilk or sour cream, giving these pancakes a dependable rise that makes them our classic weekend pancakes.

Deep, dark purple blackberries, crushed over heat, polish off your meal with a decadent finish that's antioxidant rich and delicious. When blackberries are out of season, replace them with any juicy berry, like blueberries or black raspberries.

BLACKBERRY CRUSH

2 cups/480 ml fresh blackberries

¼ cup/50 g raw or turbinado sugar

¼ cup/60 ml pure maple syrup, plus more if needed

PANCAKES

1⅔ cups/190 g all-purpose/plain flour

⅔ cup/55 g old-fashioned rolled oats

2 tbsp granulated sugar

1¼ tsp baking powder

¼ heaping tsp baking soda/bicarbonate of soda

¼ tsp fine sea salt or iodized salt

1 cup/240 ml Greek yogurt, plus more for garnish

1 cup/240 ml whole milk

4 tbsp/55 g unsalted butter, melted, plus more for the pan

2 large eggs

TO MAKE THE BLACKBERRY CRUSH: Combine the blackberries and sugar in a medium bowl and mash slightly with a fork. Strain the juice into a small pot and reserve the berries. Heat the juice over medium heat and simmer until it is thick, syrupy, and easily coats the back of the spoon, about 8 minutes. Remove from the heat and stir in the maple syrup. Cool slightly, and pour over the berries. Adjust the sweetness with additional maple syrup if needed. Set the syrup aside.

TO MAKE THE PANCAKES: Whisk together the flour, oats, sugar, baking powder, baking soda/bicarbonate of soda, and salt in a large bowl. In a separate bowl, whisk together the yogurt, milk, the melted butter, and eggs. Make a well in the center of the dry ingredients, and whisk in the wet ingredients until well incorporated. The batter should be thick, with little bubbles on the surface.

CONTINUED

Heat a cast-iron or nonstick griddle or heavy frying pan over medium heat until a drop of water sizzles when splashed on the pan. Brush the griddle lightly with melted butter. Drop about ⅓ cup/75 ml of batter per pancake onto the hot griddle, leaving about 1 in/2.5 cm or so between pancakes. When bubbles form around the edges of the batter, gently lift and flip the pancakes with a flexible spatula. Cook on the other side until the pancakes are golden brown around the edges, about 2 minutes. Don't worry if the first one doesn't come out perfect—just adjust your heat as needed and nibble on the practice pancake while you stack up a plate of beauties. Repeat, adding more butter to the pan as needed until all the pancakes are cooked.

To serve, stack the pancakes as high as you dare, and garnish with butter or additional Greek yogurt and a generous ladle of Blackberry Crush. Serve hot and fresh.

P.S. *If you like light, evenly golden brown pancakes, go light on the butter in the pan, and keep the heat on your griddle nice and low. If you prefer a pancake with a crisper exterior and a golden rim, cook pancakes at slightly higher heat, using enough butter to sizzle and foam in the pan between each batch.*

STEEL-CUT OATS

serves 4

{that sustain} Steel-cut oats deliver such satisfaction and sustenance that you might just fall in love with oatmeal in a way you never thought possible. Cooked on the stovetop to a creamy and toothsome balance, they are heartier than their rolled-oat counterparts, and arguably healthier too. But it's the richer flavor you're likely to love most of all. To cut back on their cooking time, soak your grains in water in the pot the night before, and turn on the heat when you press the little go button on your coffee machine the next morning—guaranteed goodness, before you've finished the morning paper.

1 cup/155 g steel-cut oats

3 cups/720 ml water

¾ cup/180 ml whole milk, plus more as needed

Pinch of sea or kosher salt

1 cinnamon stick

⅓ cup/55 g raisins {optional}

1 tbsp unsalted butter

Agave nectar, honey, or brown sugar

Milk or buttermilk {optional}

Blueberries, shredded apple, sliced bananas, or pears

Combine the oats, water, whole milk, salt, cinnamon stick, and raisins {if using} in a large pot over medium heat. Bring to a simmer and immediately decrease the heat to medium-low. Keep the oatmeal at a low simmer until the oats are just tender, about 25 minutes. Add additional milk to thin to the consistency you prefer and stir for another 5 minutes. Stir in the butter.

Divide between individual bowls and top with your favorite sweetener, a drizzle of milk, and blueberries, shredded apple, sliced bananas, or pears.

P.S. *This makes enough for two people for 2 days. Pack leftovers in a container and store in the fridge. Reheat in the microwave the next morning on medium power for about 2 minutes and stir in a little additional milk to loosen.*

MONDAY MORNING MUESLI

serves 2 for 4 breakfasts {makes 6 cups/540 g}

{good to the grain} Move over sugary granola. Muesli's slow-burning energy is utterly packed with protein, fiber, and flavor. If you're new to muesli, the texture can take some getting used to, but it's so addictive you'll soon wish for it every morning. It delivers on whole grains, complex carbs, and fast protein without all the sweeteners commonly found in granola. Make big batches on the weekend and you'll always be ready to start your week out right. I've added a few of my favorite fruit garnishes, but you can make it your way.

MUESLI

4 cups/340 g rolled oats or rolled barley

2 cups/230 g walnuts, hazelnuts, or pecans, coarsely chopped

1 cup/130 g sunflower seeds

1 tbsp extra-virgin olive oil

½ tsp kosher salt

¼ tsp ground cinnamon

SERVE WITH

¼ cup/40 g plump raisins

1 crisp apple, grated

½ medium banana, sliced

1 cup/240 ml lowfat or nonfat yogurt or milk

Honey or molasses

Preheat the oven to 350°F/180°C/gas 4.

Toss together the oats, nuts, sunflower seeds, olive oil, salt, and cinnamon and spread in a thin layer on a baking sheet/tray. Toast until fragrant and slightly golden, 15 minutes. Cool.

Fill two bowls with ¾ cup muesli each. Garnish with raisins, grated apple, and sliced banana, and top with yogurt or milk. Stir together and eat, with a touch of honey or molasses.

RISE & SHINE MUFFINS

makes 12 large muffins

{a wholesome start} Sometimes you need a little morning magic. Start the day with one of these big beauties, bursting with everything you need to jumpstart your morning and keep you going until lunch. This muffin is hearty, slightly sweet, and so delicious you'll never complain about eating your vegetables again.

½ cup/85 g raisins

2 cups/255 g white whole-wheat/wholemeal flour or all-purpose/plain flour

1 cup/200 g packed dark brown sugar

2 tsp baking soda/bicarbonate of soda

2 tsp ground cinnamon

¼ tsp ground ginger

½ tsp salt

4 medium carrots, grated {about 2 cups/200 g}

½ medium zucchini/courgette, grated {about 1 cup/100 g}

½ cup pecans/55 g chopped, plus more for garnish

⅓ cup pine nuts/40 g, plus more for garnish

3 large eggs

⅔ cup/165 ml grapeseed or vegetable oil

⅓ cup/75 ml buttermilk

2 teaspoons pure vanilla extract

Butter or goat cheese

Preheat the oven to 375°F/190°C/gas 5. Lightly coat a standard 12-cup muffin tin with vegetable-oil cooking spray. Cut parchment/baking paper into twelve 6-by-6-in/15-by-15-cm squares and tuck into the muffin-tin cups with the edges sticking up {this little trick gives muffins more room to climb high, so they look more like bistro muffins when you serve them}, or line with paper cupcake liners. Put the raisins in a small bowl, cover with hot water, and set aside to plump.

Whisk together the flour, sugar, baking soda/bicarbonate of soda, cinnamon, ginger, and salt in a large bowl. Stir in the carrots, zucchini/courgette, pecans, and pine nuts. In a separate large bowl, add the eggs, oil, buttermilk, and vanilla and whisk until well combined.

Add the egg mixture to the flour mixture and stir together with a wooden spoon or spatula until just moistened. Drain the raisins and stir them in.

Drop about ½ cup/120 ml batter in each muffin cup, filling each cup a little over half way. Sprinkle a few pecans or pine nuts or both on the top of each muffin.

Bake until the muffins are evenly golden brown and spring back when touched lightly, about 25 minutes. Remove from the oven and cool in the tin until easy to handle, about 5 minutes. Turn out onto a rack.

Serve warm or at room temperature with butter or goat cheese. Peel back the paper and indulge! Keep extras covered in an airtight container overnight or wrapped well {after cooling completely} and stored in the freezer for a quick breakfast any day of the week.

OATMEAL SCONES
···· WITH ····
BROWN BUTTER GLAZE

makes 6 medium or 12 petite scones

{the art of brown butter} My journey to the perfect scone was a long one, but the reward so worth the effort. As I baked, batch after batch, they morphed in structure and shape. With the help of brown butter, a chef's best trick for nutty flavor without adding nuts, they became irresistible.

SCONES

8 tbsp/115 g unsalted butter

1½ cups/175 g white whole-wheat/ wholemeal flour

1 cup/85 g rolled oats or rolled barley, plus more for optional topping

⅓ cup/55 g packed dark brown sugar

2 tbsp granulated sugar

2 tsp baking powder

1¼ tsp fine sea salt

½ cup/120 ml half-and-half/half cream

1 large egg, beaten

1½ tsp pure vanilla extract

1 large ripe pear, nectarine, or peach, pitted, peeled, and chopped {1 cup/100 g}

BROWN BUTTER GLAZE

4 tbsp/55 grams unsalted butter

1 cup/100 g confectioners'/icing sugar

¾ tsp pure vanilla extract

2 tbsp cold half-and-half/half cream

TO MAKE THE SCONES: Melt the 8 tbsp/115 g butter in a wide saucepan over medium-low heat. Once the butter melts, continue to cook on low heat until the butter bubbles and foams, then snaps and sizzles. Continue cooking until there are brown bits along the surface of the butter and bottom of the pan and the butter smells like buttered toast, 8 to 10 minutes. Pour the brown butter into a shallow pan and freeze until it is completely solid.

Line two baking sheet/trays with parchment/baking paper, wax/greaseproof paper, or a silicone baking mat.

Whisk together the flour, rolled oats, sugars, baking powder, and salt in a medium bowl. Scoop spoonfuls of the chilled brown butter into the bowl and work into the dry ingredients with your hands, pinching the butter into the flour until the mixture resembles couscous with a few pea-size pieces remaining.

In a small bowl, whisk together the half-and-half/half cream, egg, and vanilla. Stir into the dry mixture with a fork until just combined, just a few strokes to make sure it doesn't get overworked. Gently stir in the fruit.

Turn the dough out onto a clean, lightly floured counter-top and fold it over itself about three times until the dough is a rough ball. Pat into a round about 1¼ in/3 cm thick and cut into six plump pie-shaped wedges {for mini scones, pat into two rounds and cut each into six pie-shaped wedges}.

Transfer the wedges to the prepared baking sheets/trays. Sprinkle the tops with additional rolled oats or barley {omit if you plan to glaze}. Chill in the fridge for 30 minutes. Preheat the oven to 350°F/180°C/gas 4 while the dough rests.

Bake the scones until evenly golden around the edges and a touch crisp, about 35 minutes. Remove and let cool slightly on a rack.

TO MAKE THE GLAZE: Brown the 4 tbsp/55 g butter as you did for the scones. Transfer to a small bowl and whisk in the confectioners'/icing sugar, vanilla, and cold half-and-half/half cream. When the scones are cool, spread or drizzle glaze over the top.

CHEDDAR-CORNMEAL BISCUITS

makes 10 biscuits

{more please} Buttery Cheddar biscuits are a tapestry of flavor, bursting with savory notes that make them hard to stop eating once you start. Try them at least once hot and slathered with sweet butter and tomato jam. Cooled, split open, and stuffed with ham or mortadella and arugula, they become easy brunch or supper sandwiches to pack for a picnic or perk up any party. The key to a flaky biscuit is to work the dough as little as possible, so use a gentle hand. Like all biscuits and scones, these are best eaten fresh the day they are baked.

1¾ cups/200 g all-purpose/plain flour

½ cup/70 g semolina flour or finely ground cornmeal

4 tsp baking powder

½ tsp freshly ground black pepper, plus more for sprinkling

¼ tsp fine sea salt

Dash cayenne pepper

1 cup/115 grams grated Cheddar cheese

10 tbsp/140 g cold unsalted butter, plus more for spreading

¾ cup/180 ml half-and-half/half cream

1 large egg, beaten

Coarse sea salt

10 thin slices of your favorite ham {optional}

1 bunch of arugula/rocket, torn {optional}

Line a baking sheet/tray with parchment/baking paper or a silicone baking mat.

Whisk together the flours, baking powder, ½ tsp black pepper, salt, and cayenne pepper in a large bowl. Stir in half of the grated Cheddar.

Cut the cold butter into little bits and work half into the flour mixture with your hands, pinching the butter into the flour until you have pea-size pieces. Add the remaining butter and continue to mix together until the mixture resembles couscous. Add the remaining Cheddar and toss together with a fork.

Add the half-and-half/half cream and mix with a fork until the dough just comes together with some dry bits remaining. It should not be sticky or tacky {if it gets to that point it's overmixed}. Rest in the fridge for 25 minutes.

Preheat the oven to 400°F/200°C/gas 6 while the dough rests.

Turn the chilled dough out onto a clean countertop, adding a thin dusting of flour only if necessary. Fold the dough over itself twice and then pat into a rectangle about ¾ in/2 cm thick. Cut into six biscuits using a 2-in/5-cm biscuit cutter or glass. Pat the dough scraps together and cut four more biscuits.

Transfer the dough rounds to the prepared baking sheet/tray and brush generously with the beaten egg. Sprinkle with additional black pepper and coarse sea salt. Bake until evenly golden around the edges, about 18 minutes. Remove and let cool slightly on a rack.

Serve warm with butter and tomato jam. To serve as sandwiches, cool completely, split open, spread with butter {to your taste}, and stuff with ham and a few leaves of fresh arugula, if desired.

SUNDAY BUTTERMILK BISCUITS & GRAVY

serves 4

{plus, The Big Nasty} Where I come from, one cannot keep a home without a proper house biscuit. My recipe is made with whole-wheat flour because I love the texture and flavor, but it bakes up hot and fluffy with white flour as well. With hot biscuits smothered in your homemade sausage gravy on the table, your house will start to smell like home in no time. If you're feeding a crowd, bring a second hot batch of biscuits to the table for smearing with butter and jam after the gravy is gone and watch all adoring eyes turn on you.

BUTTERMILK BISCUITS

1¾ cups/200 g white whole-wheat/wholemeal flour

2 tsp baking powder

½ tsp baking soda/bicarbonate of soda

¾ tsp salt

6 tbsp/85 g cold unsalted butter, cubed

¾ cup/180 ml buttermilk

SAUSAGE GRAVY

12 oz/340 g bulk breakfast sausage or sausage patties

¼ cup/30 g all-purpose/plain flour

3 to 4 cups/720 to 960 ml whole milk

Freshly ground black pepper

Kosher salt

Preheat the oven to 425°F/220°C/gas 7. Line two baking sheet/trays with parchment/baking paper or a silicone baking mat.

TO MAKE THE BISCUITS: Whisk together the flour, baking powder, baking soda/bicarbonate of soda, and salt in a medium bowl. Add the butter and blend into the flour with your fingers or a pastry cutter until the flour is coated with fat and it is mostly incorporated with some pea-size pieces remaining. Stir in the buttermilk with a fork until just combined.

Turn the dough onto a lightly floured surface and turn over itself about 8 times to form a cohesive dough. Pat into a round about ½ in/12 mm thick. Cut into biscuits with a 2-in/5-cm cookie or biscuit cutter or a thin-rimmed glass.

Transfer to the prepared baking sheets and set aside while you get the gravy started {so your biscuits and gravy can be hot and fresh at the same time}.

TO MAKE THE GRAVY: Cook the sausage in a medium skillet over medium heat until evenly browned and cooked through, about 8 minutes. Remove the sausage to a plate and cover with aluminum foil to keep warm. Remove the excess fat from the pan, leaving just enough to coat the bottom of the pan with a thin layer.

Put the biscuits in the oven and bake until lightly browned, about 12 to 15 minutes.

While the biscuits bake, sprinkle the ¼ cup/30 g flour over the fat in the pan and cook until toasted and brown, about 3 minutes. Gradually whisk in 3 cups/720 ml of the milk and stir until the liquid begins to bubble and thicken. Let the gravy bubble briefly over medium-low heat for a minute or two. Stir only occasionally, to keep it from scorching, until it thickens to a rich gravy consistency. Thin to your liking with more milk until the gravy just coats a spoon. Season generously with about ½ teaspoon black pepper and just a dash of salt.

Ladle over hot biscuits and serve with sausage patties on the side.

THE BIG NASTY: *Made famous at the Hominy Grill in Charleston, South Carolina, The Big Nasty is a big ol' mess of goodness in the form of tender biscuits, crispy chicken, and rich gravy. To make it yourself, stack a piece of fried chicken {white meat, no bones} on the bottom half of a fresh hot biscuit, drizzle with sausage gravy, then cover with the biscuit top. It's so bad, it's good.*

SAUSAGE SAVVY: Look for freshly ground breakfast sausage and form it into patties. Since it is harder to find these days, high-quality breakfast sausage links can be snipped from their cases and repacked into patties with clean hands. Vegetarians don't have to miss out. Soy sausage makes a fine substitution.

GOLDEN ZUCCHINI BREAD

makes 2 large loaves

{full of goodies} In July, when the garden is bursting with zucchini and the market is practically giving them away, make this slightly sweet bread with just enough veggies to make it good for you. This is divine eaten just a touch warm, with thick slabs of cream cheese spread on for the weekends. Farmer's cheese or fresh ricotta, both high in protein and much lower in fat, make this a go-to breakfast treat as easy for everyday as it is elegant for breakfast with friends.

4 tbsp/55 g unsalted butter, plus more for the pans, at room temperature

1 cup/200 g lightly packed dark brown sugar

⅔ cup/130 g granulated sugar

3 large eggs

½ cup/120 ml grapeseed or vegetable oil

2 tsp pure vanilla extract

3 cups/400 g white whole-wheat/wholemeal flour

1½ tsp baking soda/bicarbonate of soda

½ tsp baking powder

1 tsp fine sea salt

1 tsp ground cinnamon

1 large zucchini/courgette, grated {about 3 cups/720 ml}

1 firm Bartlett/Williams pear, cored and grated {about 1 cup/240 ml}

¾ cup/85 g chopped toasted walnuts {about 3 oz}, plus more for garnish

¼ cup/40 g golden raisins/sultanas

2 tbsp sesame seeds

½ cup/120 ml farmer's cheese, ricotta cheese, or cream cheese, for serving

Sliced pears or figs, for serving

Preheat the oven to 350°F/180°C/gas 4. Butter two 9-by-5-in/23-by-12-cm loaf pans/tins. Line them with parchment/baking paper, butter the parchment/baking paper, and set aside.

Beat the butter and sugars in a stand mixer with the paddle attachment, on medium speed until fluffy. Add the eggs, one at a time, beating between each addition. Add the oil and vanilla and stir to combine.

Whisk together the flour, baking soda/bicarbonate of soda, baking powder, salt, and cinnamon in a medium bowl. Mix half the dry ingredients into the butter mixture and stir together. Stir in the remaining dry ingredients with a spatula, along with the zucchini/courgette, pear, nuts, raisins, and sesame seeds.

Divide the batter between the prepared pans. Sprinkle with additional walnuts. Bake until the bread springs back when lightly touched, and a toothpick inserted into the center comes out dry with some crumbs, about 50 minutes. Cool on a rack 10 minutes. Remove from the pan, slice, and serve warm with a thick schmear of cheese and sliced pears or figs.

P.S. *This is the perfect bread to do ahead and keep on hand for fast weekday breakfasts and unexpected guests. Let the bread cool completely before you wrap it, and freeze the loaf whole for weekend guests and in halves or slices for quick on-the-run breakfasts and snacks.*

TWO BREAKFAST SANDWICHES

{to keep up your sleeve} With a little thought put into the details and the ingredients, these two breakfast sandwiches will serve you well for years to come.

{ THE PARISIAN }

serves 4

{a tartine} In Paris the finest breakfast is a fresh baguette, halved and slathered with hazelnut paste, served with a warm bowl of café au lait. You can change it up by substituting almond butter, fresh jam, or, when the mood strikes you, a chocolate-hazelnut spread. It is the easiest way to spoil your overnight guests without giving yourself any work, requiring just a twist of the wrist, and a trip to the local bakery for the freshest of baguettes. Serve with café au lait.

1 large fresh baguette

4 tbsp/55 g unsalted butter, at room temperature

Hazelnut paste, almond butter, jam,
or chocolate-hazelnut spread

Halve the baguette lengthwise, then crosswise. Spread each quarter with the butter and paste.

{ THE NEW YORKER }

serves 4 to 6

{a savory stack} The New York deli staple of bagels and lox is an even bigger treat served in the comfort of your own home. Where you can, taste before you buy your lox or smoked salmon. Like most things, the best one is purely a matter of personal taste. I prefer the buttery texture of nova lox, which is brined and then cold-smoked, or delicate gravlax, which is slightly more buttery than nova and just a touch sweet from its dry curing process in salt, sugar, and dill.

Very thinly sliced red onion {optional}

4 fresh bagels {salt, onion, sesame, poppy, or everything},
halved

8 to 12 oz/225 to 340 g cream cheese

6 oz/170 g thinly sliced smoked salmon or lox

2 tbsp capers or 8 caper berries

Fresh dill fronds, for garnish

Soak the red onion slices in a bowl of warm, salted water to wilt slightly. Meanwhile, toast the bagels. Spread bagels with the cream cheese, and layer with the lox, capers, and dill. Top with wilted red onions and serve.

WHOLE-GRAIN CROQUE MONSIEUR

makes 4 sandwiches

{hot ham & cheese} Leave it to the French to find a way to eat ham and cheese for breakfast, and give it an elegant name like *croque monsieur*. Add a fried or poached egg, and your monsieur becomes a madame. Either way, it's pure decadence. Serve warm, with or without an egg, And don't forget your greens dressed with a bracing mustard vinaigrette, bistro style.

6 tbsp/85 g unsalted butter

2 tbsp all-purpose/plain flour

1½ cups/360 ml low-fat milk

1 to 1½ tsp sea salt

Pinch of nutmeg

Freshly ground black pepper

12 oz/340 g Gruyère or Comté cheese, grated {about 3½ cups}

¼ cup/30 g freshly grated Parmigiano-Reggiano cheese

4 large slices hearty seven-grain or nutty whole-grain bread {about 12 oz/340 g}

2 tsp Dijon or whole-grain Dijon mustard

12 oz/340 g ham

Preheat the broiler/grill to medium-high.

Melt 2 tbsp of the butter in a small saucepan over low heat. Sprinkle the flour over the butter in the pan and cook until smooth but not toasted, about 2 minutes. Gradually add the milk, whisking constantly until the milk begins to thicken, about 8 minutes. Remove from the heat, add 1 tsp salt and the nutmeg. Taste, and season with salt and black pepper. Stir in ¼ cup/30 g of the Gruyère and the Parmigiano-Reggiano.

Melt the remaining 4 tbsp/55g butter. Lay the bread on a baking sheet/tray and brush with melted butter and mustard. Divide the ham among four of the bread slices and sprinkle with 1 cup/280 g Gruyère. Top with the remaining bread. Ladle the sauce over the sandwiches and sprinkle with the remaining Gruyère. Broil/grill until the sauce is bubbly and lightly browned, 3 to 5 minutes. Serve immediately.

MAKE IT MEATLESS: This sandwich is too good to hoard among carnivores. Lose the ham and add the egg for a Croque Les Ouef de Fromage!

LITTLE BEAUTY BAKED EGGS

serves 6

{serve with style} Baked eggs are the prettiest little things you ever served that require almost no work from you. Preheat your ramekins in a hot oven with butter and cream, crack in your eggs, and in 15 minutes you've got breakfast. Serve with a hearty salad and crusty bread.

⅓ cup/75 ml cream
or half-and-half/half cream, plus more for drizzling

3 tbsp/40 g unsalted butter

6 fresh whole farm-fresh or organic eggs

Sea salt

Freshly ground black pepper

1 small handful chopped mixed fresh herbs
such as basil, dill, chives, or parsley

Preheat the oven to 350°F/ 180°C /gas 4.

Arrange six 4-oz/120-ml ramekins in a 9-by-13-in/ 23-by-33-cm roasting pan/tray. Fill each ramekin with 1 tbsp of the cream and ½ tbsp butter. Transfer to the oven to heat the ramekins and melt the butter, about 5 minutes.

Remove the roasting pan from the oven and crack an egg into each ramekin. Sprinkle each with salt and pepper to season.

Fill the roasting pan with warm water that comes about halfway up the sides of the ramekins; return the pan to the oven. Bake until the eggs are just set around the outside but the yolks are still soft and slightly runny, about 15 minutes. Remove the pan from the oven and set aside; the eggs will continue cooking slightly in the hot ramekins so err on the side of runny.

Drizzle the eggs with a touch of cream and sprinkle with fresh herbs. Serve immediately.

WINTER GREENS & FONTINA OMELET

serves 2

{hearty & healthful} In the winter when the farmers' market is scarce, you can always count on finding hearty greens. Here's one exceptional way to serve them, seasoned simply with garlic and oil and tucked into a hefty cheese omelet. Mix and match your favorite greens or cheese, or stick to this winning combination, made with potent Fontina that melts to a mouthwatering finish. Serve with toast or salad.

1 small bunch Swiss chard, mustard greens, escarole, or a combination

2 tbsp olive oil

1 small onion, thinly sliced

1 clove garlic, smashed and chopped

Pinch red pepper flakes

5 eggs, lightly beaten

⅓ cup/40 g grated Fontina cheese

Sea salt

Freshly ground black pepper

Wash and strip the greens of their stems. Chop into thin strips.

Heat 2 tsp of the oil in a small nonstick 6-in/15 cm frying pan over medium-high heat. Add the onion and cook until soft and pale golden, about 6 minutes. Add the garlic, greens, and red pepper flakes and cook until the garlic is fragrant and the greens are just wilted, about 5 minutes {they will cook further inside the omelet}. Transfer the greens to a plate, leaving oil behind in the frying pan.

Add the remaining oil to the frying pan and heat until shimmering. Add the eggs and stir occasionally with a heat-proof spatula or wooden spoon until it begins to set. Use the spatula to lift the edges of the omelet and turn the skillet to let raw egg slip underneath and cook. When almost all of the egg is set, add the greens and cheese to the center of the omelet. Use the spatula to fold the omelet in half and cover to cook through, about 1 minute more.

Serve on a plate with two forks.

OVERNIGHT
EGG & CHEESE STRATA

serves 2

{for a small crowd} I grew up thinking strata was my mom's signature dish, until I realized every mother has her own version. You should know how to make it too, but {just between us}, yours can be a little more elegant than your mother's, especially when you make it in a small dish to serve two and pair it with a large salad.

Butter, for greasing the baking dish

4 thick slices hearty whole-wheat/wholemeal or multigrain artisan bread {about 4½ oz/130 g}

2 large eggs, lightly beaten

1 cup/240 ml whole milk

8 oz/225 g grated Fontina cheese {about 1 cup}

Sea salt

Freshly ground black pepper

6 to 8 asparagus stalks

4 thin slices mortadella or prosciutto {optional}

1 tbsp finely snipped chives

Preheat the oven to 350°F/180°C/gas 4. Butter a small 4-cup/960-ml ovenproof baking dish.

Remove the crusts from the bread. Lay the slices across the baking dish, slightly overlapping and allowing some edges to hang over the sides.

Whisk together the eggs and milk in a large bowl. Stir in half of the cheese and season with salt and pepper. Pour three-fourths of the egg mixture over the bread cubes.

Peel the bottom half of the asparagus and break off the stem ends where it snaps naturally. Discard any woody stems.

Layer the mortadella over the bread and top with asparagus spears. Pour the remaining egg mixture over the top and finish with the remaining cheese. At this point, you can bake the strata immediately, or cover with plastic wrap/cling film and refrigerate overnight for a surprise breakfast in bed.

Bake the strata until just set, 30 to 35 minutes. Let cool slightly, sprinkle the top with chopped chives, and serve in the baking dish.

P.S. *Double this recipe easily for a large crowd, and watch it disappear at every New Year's Brunch or potluck. Bake for 1 hour in a 9-by-13-in/23-by-33 cm pan.*

CHAPTER 4

LITTLE MEALS

Soups, Salads, Sandwiches & Lots of Elegant Eggs

Most of us have been conditioned to eat our biggest meal at the end of the day, but that's also the time we want to put up our feet and tuck into the couch together the most. Mustering up the gumption to pull out all the stops after everything you've tackled in your day is sometimes out of the question. The best thing about being grown-ups is that you get to make your own rules. There's no one there to insist that meat and potatoes is the most wholesome meal, and no matter who wrote your vows, they probably didn't include anything in the vein of "I promise to make a hot meal every night." This chapter is built on the philosophy that some nights all you need is a little meal, something like Lobster Rolls {page 107} or A Real Good Salad {page 87}. Something light and happy that's just enough to satisfy and settle your belly before you settle into bed.

Some of the best meals are prepared rather quickly, like sandwiches. And when I say sandwiches, I mean serious sandwiches with serious flavor, like Pan-Fried Striped Bass Sandwiches {page 104} with crisp cucumbers and Baguette BLTs with Spicy Moroccan Mayo {page 95}— sandwiches even a man is comfortable calling dinner {check out The Man Sandwich, page 103}.

If you don't subscribe to that philosophy {they are your rules to make and break}, use this chapter to play mix-and-match and turn two little meals into a feast. Alone, or in pairs, all of these meals would make a lunch to look forward to any day of the week, and with so many meatless choices,

those of you with mixed tastes like us {my hubby doesn't eat meat, I do} will find your common ground in these little meals for years to come.

The best part of this section is that all of these recipes are fast to prepare {give yourself about 30 minutes}, and are incredibly fresh. Most nights of the week you can throw something special together so fast you might amaze yourself. It is these meals, based on high-quality ingredients and simple preparations, that leave more time for enjoying the meal than it took to make it. They are full of the flavor-building principles from your stocked pantry, and are the perfect opportunity to show off your hard work in the garden or you latest trip to the greenmarket.

WINDOW BOX GREEN SALAD FOR TWO
&
CLASSIC VINAIGRETTE

serves 2

The secret to a good salad is variety and freshness. Before mesclun mix was introduced to grocery stores across America, European chefs and gardeners composed their own vibrant mixes of lettuces, baby greens, and herbs for salads so flavorful they barely needed a touch of accoutrement. Here's how to make your own, plus a basic dressing that goes with almost any salad very well.

SALAD

Handful of fresh arugula/rocket

Handful of watercress or mâche

Handful of baby Swiss chard

Handful of baby mizuna

Handful of fresh parsley or chervil

Snipped chives and/or chive blossoms

Fine sea salt

Freshly ground black pepper

A CLASSIC VINAIGRETTE

1 tsp Dijon or whole-grain Dijon mustard

2 tbsp red wine or apple cider vinegar or lemon juice

6 tbsp/90 ml best-quality extra-virgin olive oil

½ garlic cloves, pressed or minced {optional}

Fine sea salt

Freshly ground black pepper

TO MAKE THE SALAD: Toss all your greens and herbs together in a medium bowl. Season with salt and freshly ground black pepper before you add the dressing.

TO MAKE THE DRESSING: Whisk the mustard and vinegar or lemon juice together in a small bowl. Drizzle in the olive oil a drop at a time, and then in a slow, steady stream, whisking constantly to create a slightly thick and uniform dressing. Whisk in the garlic {if using}. Taste, and season lightly with a pinch of salt and freshly ground black pepper.

Pour about 2 tbsp dressing into a large bowl. Add your salad mix to the dressing {not the other way around} and toss with your hands or two forks to lightly coat. Add a touch more dressing if needed, but be careful not to overdress, which can ruin a salad very quickly.

Store excess dressing in the fridge for up to 1 week.

GROW YOUR OWN LETTUCE: Lettuces are about the most quickly rewarding greens to grow. They thrive well in small spaces like window boxes, big pots, or a patch of healthy backyard soil. Start with loose and fine organic starter soil. Sprinkle the seeds over the top and cover with ¼ in/6 mm of soil, or sow into neat rows. Mix and match varieties planting each in its own row. If you only have a tiny pot, opt for seeds labeled mesclun mix or cut-and-come-again lettuce that can be cut frequently and grows fast enough to fill your salad bowl for several spring months.

A REAL GOOD SALAD

serves 2

{worth repeating} They say you marry a man like your father. In my case, this is mostly true. Like my dad, my hubby loves history, movies, war stories, and a good {or bad} joke. They are both athletic and jovial. My dad's compliments to my mother's meals were not only verbal but physical as well. He would often lick and smack his lips wildly when he was truly enjoying something. In this, András is quite different. He's quiet at meal times, concentrating deeply on getting every bite into his mouth fast.

Like many men, András is not a big salad guy, so when I made this one night from the dredges of our CSA box, I didn't have high expectations for praise. But all of the flavors just sung. Within two bites, András raised his head and proclaimed it a *real good salad*, high praise in his book, and enough to make this a regular in our house.

4 small beets/beetroots
{1¾ to 2 lb/800 to 910 g}

1 large head red leaf lettuce

2 handfuls young arugula/rocket
or young mustard greens

1 small handful mixed herbs, such as basil, opal
basil, chives, chocolate mint, spearmint, or dill

1 shallot, thinly sliced

1 small handful raw green beans or haricots verts

4 large farm-fresh or organic eggs,
hard boiled

½ cup/55 g toasted walnut halves

Sea salt

Freshly ground black pepper

1 tbsp whole-grain mustard

1 tbsp red wine vinegar

3 tbsp/45 ml best-quality extra-virgin olive oil

Preheat the oven to 400°F/ 200°C /gas 6.

Wash the beets and trim the tops, leaving just a little at the top. Line a baking sheet/tray with aluminum foil and place the beets in the center. Wrap the foil to make a packet, poke a few holes in the foil, and roast until the beets are tender, about 1½ hours, depending on the size of the beets.

Remove the pan from the oven, open up the foil, and let the beets cool until you can handle them easily. Slip the skins off {if you have rubber gloves, use them or your hands will be stained for a day!}. Quarter the beets.

Divide the lettuces, herbs, shallot, green beans, beets, and walnuts between two large, deep bowls. Split the hard-boiled eggs in halves and add four halves to each salad. Season with salt and freshly ground pepper

Whisk together the mustard and vinegar in a medium bowl and drizzle in the olive oil, whisking constantly to make a smooth dressing. Season with salt and pepper. Dress the salads and toss at the table.

ARUGULA, GRAPEFRUIT & FENNEL SALAD

serves 2

This dish {pictured on page 281} is spectacular, from the pale pinks and shades of green to the clean, bright flavors of grapefruit and fennel to the buttery green castelvetrano olives that give the whole dish depth. It is a crisp complement to pork pâtés and salumi as a first course.

1 large ruby red grapefruit

1 small head fennel, quartered and cored

1 large bunch arugula/rocket

4 tbsp best-quality extra-virgin olive oil

Sea salt

Freshly ground black pepper

⅓ cup/55 g castelvetrano olives

2 to 4 oz/55 to 115 g Pecorino Romano cheese

Place your grapefruit on the cutting board and cut off a little bit of both ends to create a flat surface. Use a large, sharp knife to shave off the skin along the curve of the fruit. Squeeze any juices from the skin into a bowl. Use the knife to cut the segments between the membrane over the bowl to collect the juices and the fruit itself.

Shave the fennel into thin pieces using a mandoline or sharp knife. Toss together the arugula/rocket, olive oil, and salt and pepper. Toss in the grapefruit and juices with the greens and divide between the bowls. Top each bowl with shaved pecorino cheese, the olives, and season with a little sea salt.

CASTELVETRANO OLIVES are a meaty, mild, and buttery bright-green olive from Italy. You can find them at specialty food stores, gourmet shops, and grocers with great olive sections. If you don't want to splurge, skip the olives and give the salad a little extra love from your highest quality, fruity olive oil instead.

WATERMELON, PISTACHIO & BABY GREENS SALAD

serves 2 to 4

{so fresh} Watermelon is always bursting with life, and if you love it plain on a hot summer day with your legs swinging off a dock, you might agree it's best left as nature intended. This salad {pictured on pages 90–91} pays its respects to watermelon's best qualities, and complements its juice and sweetness with the salty crunch of pistachios. It makes an excellent first course or light lunch or dinner all on its own, and is the perfect place to show off a handful of spicy arugula and fresh herbs you grew yourself.

2 small heads butter lettuce, torn

Heaping handful of young arugula/rocket

Heaping handful of mâche, purslane, or watercress

½ medium seedless watermelon {about 4 lb/1.8 kg}, cut in wedges and rind removed

1 small handful fresh chocolate mint, peppermint, or spearmint leaves, torn

1 tsp snipped fresh chives

Coarse white, grey, or pink sea salt

Freshly ground black pepper

4 tbsp best-quality extra-virgin olive oil

2 to 4 oz/55 to 115 g tangy goat cheese, such as Selles-sur-Cher or Crottin if available, at room temperature

Divide the butter lettuce between two or four dinner plates or one large platter. Distribute the arugula/rocket and mâche between the plates, then arrange watermelon wedges on each plate. Garnish all the salads with torn mint and chives, and season liberally with sea salt and black pepper. Drizzle with your finest extra-virgin olive oil and top with pieces of fresh goat cheese. Serve straight from the garden, or crisp and cold from the crisper drawer.

SUMMER CORN SOUP

serves 4 to 6

{a breeze} There are so many delicious ways to eat corn when it is fresh and in season. At their peak, both the sweet kernels and the milky cobs are full of flavor. Use them to flavor this simple soup that highlights the sweetness of corn and the beautiful vegetables, like squash and tomatoes, that appear at the market about the same time.

6 ears fresh corn

1 tbsp kosher salt, plus more for seasoning

4 cups/960 ml water

Freshly ground black pepper

1 tbsp best-quality extra-virgin olive oil, plus more for drizzling

2 small yellow summer squash {about 12 oz/340 g}, diced

1 large yellow onion, diced

2 medium beefsteak tomatoes {about 1 lb/455 g}, diced

1½ cups/360 ml half-and-half/half cream

Handful of fresh small or baby basil leaves, torn or thinly sliced

2 tbsp fresh chervil leaves, snipped chives, or chopped dill

Trim the corn kernels from the cobs using a serrated knife and reserve the cobs. Add the kernels, salt, and the water to a wide, shallow pot. Use the back of the knife to scrape and "milk" the reserved corn cobs, scraping all the leftover kernels and milky white liquid into the pot, and then add the cobs. Bring to a simmer, season with pepper, and cook until the broth tastes of sweet corn, about 20 minutes. Keep warm on the lowest heat.

Meanwhile, heat the oil in a frying pan over medium heat. Add the summer squash and cook until golden but still a touch crisp, about 8 minutes. Remove to a plate. Add the onion and cook until soft and light brown in some parts, about 8 minutes. Set aside.

Season the tomatoes with salt, pepper, and a drizzle of your best olive oil and set aside.

Add the half-and-half/half cream to the pot with the corn. Remove the cobs with tongs and discard. Stir in the squash and onions and season with additional salt and pepper. Divide between soup bowls and spoon the seasoned tomatoes in the center of each bowl. Sprinkle with herbs. Serve warm or at room temperature.

BUTTERFLIED & BROILED LEMON SHRIMP

serves 4

{in their shells} In many cultures and restaurant kitchens, shrimp is cooked in its shell for maximum flavor. This dish is a good example of when that is a very good idea. Put your broiler to work in this simple, fast preparation and you'll enjoy the sweet, tender shrimp inside their shells twice as much.

3 lemons

¼ cup/50 g sugar

2 lb/910 g extra-large shrimp/prawns with shell and tail on, deveined

3 tbsp extra-virgin olive oil

Kosher salt

Cayenne pepper

1 bunch radishes, thinly sliced

1 handful fresh dill fronds

Preheat the oven to 450°F/230°C/gas 8.

Slice two of the lemons into thick rounds; discard the ends. Juice the third lemon into a medium bowl and set aside. Lay the slices in a 9-by-13-in/23-by-33-cm baking pan or large oval gratin dish and sprinkle with the sugar. Bake until the sugar dissolves and the lemons soften, about 10 minutes; remove from the oven. Turn on the broiler/grill.

Meanwhile, butterfly the shrimp/prawns with kitchen shears, leaving the shells and tails intact. Toss them in 1 tbsp of the olive oil. Place them shell-side down on top of the lemons and season with salt and cayenne. Broil the shrimp until their shells turn pink and start to crisp, about 8 minutes.

Toss the radish slices with the lemon juice, the remaining 2 tbsp olive oil, and the dill. Season with salt.

Serve the shrimp/prawns on a bed of lemons topped with the radish salad.

SUSTAINABLE SHRIMP: With shrimp/prawns, the texture and flavor is directly correlated to where and how it was raised or caught. Many farmed shrimp imported from Asia taste flat. Wild-caught domestic shrimp that are fished sustainably have a sweeter taste and firmer texture. If you're fortunate to live near the water, local shrimp is usually the best. If not, seek out one of the numerous good choices from the South Atlantic, Canadian Atlantic, or the waters of the Pacific Northwest. Look for something fresh or frozen labeled wild, sustainable, or farm-raised sustainably, such as Pacific white shrimp, pink shrimp, or spot prawns.

BAGUETTE BLTs
WITH
SPICY MOROCCAN MAYO

serves 4

{ classic, but better } All-American and all grown up, a BLT with fancy bacon and a harissa-based mayo is both filling and indulgent. This is inspired by my favorite brunch sandwich at Tbsp. in New York City. Use harissa, a sweet and spicy North African pepper paste to make the mayo on page 207, a complement to smoky bacon. Thick, juicy, in-season tomatoes, a key ingredient to the success of this sandwich, are at their peak in late summer, just in time to settle into a sandwich that requires little cooking at all.

8 to 12 slices thick-cut smoked bacon/streaky bacon

2 large beefsteak or heirloom tomatoes {about 2 lb/910 g}, cut in thick rounds

Sea salt

Freshly ground black pepper

1 fresh baguette

2 handfuls mixed greens such a mizuna, arugula/rocket, red oak, or mesclun mix

Spicy Mayo {page 207}

Preheat the oven to 425°F/220°C/gas 7. Arrange the bacon in a single layer on a wire rack set on top of a baking sheet/tray. Cook until the bacon is crisp, rotating the tray halfway through cooking, about 12 minutes total. Remove from the oven and set aside to cool.

Arrange the tomato slices on plates lined with paper towels/absorbent papers and season with salt and pepper. Let the tomatoes drain while you prepare the bread.

Halve the baguette lengthwise and then crosswise into four segments to make four large sandwiches. Spread both cut sides with mayo and layer with cooked bacon, mixed greens, and tomatoes. Serve immediately.

BACON BASICS: The same butcher that sells you the best pork and beef will likely have high-quality smoked bacon. If not, check Sources {page 293} for where to find bacon that is big on smoky flavor, low on nitrates, and void of antibiotics. Cooking bacon on a rack in the oven lets all the excess fat drip away and gives you the crispiest result.

CHEF'S SCRAMBLE CROSTINI

serves 2

{a fancy egg toast} **If** you grew up with big, fluffy scrambled eggs, then this custardy version will be as much of a revelation for you as it was for me. I learned how to make these from the line cooks at Café Boulud, in New York City, who would feed me eggs for lunch when I just couldn't stomach tripe stew for a family meal. The eggs get whisked constantly into velvety curds over steady heat, and make a lush topping for toast as breakfast or an appetizer before any seasonal meal. Switch out seasonal accompaniments to your liking. Below are my favorite five garnishes.

4 thick slices nutty whole-grain bread

4 farm-fresh or organic eggs

2 tbsp best-quality extra-virgin olive oil,
plus more for drizzling

2 tbsp unsalted butter

Sea salt

Freshly ground black pepper

Toast the bread lightly in a toaster or toaster oven. Arrange open-face on two serving plates or a small platter.

Crack the eggs into a medium bowl and whisk together to combine yolks and whites completely.

Heat the olive oil and 1 tbsp of the butter in a small non-stick frying pan over medium-high heat. Add the beaten eggs at all once, and season with salt and pepper. Immediately lower the heat to medium-low and stir constantly with a wooden spoon or a whisk until the eggs are creamy and just beginning to set into hundreds of little curds. If the eggs look dry and pull away from the pan, you've gone too far.

Quickly whisk in the remaining butter, immediately pull the pan from the heat, and spoon the eggs directly onto the toasted bread before they set. Garnish with your favorite herbs or greens. Drizzle with your finest olive oil and finish with freshly ground black pepper.

FIVE GORGEOUS GARNISHES
Watermelon radishes and sea salt
Pea shoots
Chives or chive blossoms
Heirloom tomatoes
Avocado and mâche, watercress, or mizuna

GRILLED CHEESE & TOMATO SLIDERS

serves 4

{thursday special} This is no ordinary grilled cheese. This is pure crispy, cheesy, oozy goodness.

2 small vine-ripened or
plum tomatoes, thinly sliced

Sea salt

8 fresh dinner rolls or fresh potato rolls, split

4 tbsp/55 g unsalted butter, at room temperature

2 to 3 tbsp Dijon or brown mustard

Four slices sharp Cheddar cheese
{about ½ oz/15 g each}

Four slices Muenster cheese {about ½ oz/15 g each}

Freshly ground black pepper

Arrange the tomato slices on paper towels/absorbent paper and salt lightly to extract some of the juices. Press with another layer of paper towels/absorbent paper.

Slather the outside crusts of both halves of the rolls with soft butter. Spread the mustard on the cut side of the bottom halves of the rolls. Top the mustard with a half a slice Muenster and a half a slice of Cheddar, followed by a tomato slice. Top with the remaining roll halves.

Heat a griddle or nonstick frying pan on medium heat. Add the sliders and press down lightly with a sandwich press or another clean frying pan. Cook until the cheese begins to melt and the bun is crisp and golden on the bottom. Flip and repeat until the second side is crispy and the cheese is melted and oozy. Sprinkle sea salt and freshly ground black pepper over the top. Serve hot and fast with extra napkins.

CHAMPS-ÉLYSÉES PÂTÉ & WATERCRESS SANDWICHES

serves 4

{go strolling} One bite of this sandwich and you'll feel like honeymooners strolling along the Champs-Élysées in Paris. This is the perfect sandwich for tucking into the basket of a bike for a long lazy ride, or turning into supper for movie night under the stars.

1 fresh baguette

2 tbsp butter, at room temperature {optional}

2 tbsp whole-grain or Dijon mustard

1 small cucumber, thinly sliced

Sea salt

1 bunch watercress

4 thick slices country pork pâté {6 to 8 oz/170 to 225 g}

Freshly ground black pepper

Begin with an immaculately fresh baguette. Halve it lengthwise and then crosswise into four segments to make four large sandwiches. Spread the bottom layer of each portion with a thin layer of the butter and the top layer with the mustard.

Lay out the cucumber slices on a plate lined with paper towels/absorbent papers; sprinkle with salt. Set aside for 5 minutes to let a little of the liquid drain out. This will keep your cucumbers crispy and your bread from getting soggy when it's all wrapped up.

Pick through the watercress and toss any woody stems in your compost bin. Layer the rest with the cucumbers and pâté on the bread, season with black pepper, close with the bread tops, and voilá, it's lunch!

MAKE IT MEATLESS: Veggie lovers, spread your sandwich with nut and lentil pâté instead of one made with pork.

OPEN-FACE SOFT-BOILED EGG SANDWICHES

serves 2

{welcome at any hour} Never underestimate the magnificence of a simple soft-boiled egg, particularly when the egg comes fresh from the farm. When it's split open to reveal its oozing golden yolk, it creates an indulgent topping for almost anything, including crusty toasted bread, herb mayo, and spicy arugula. You can morph this sandwich into your own personal favorite with spicy mayo, your favorite cheese, or anything else that suits your fancy.

4 farm-fresh or organic eggs

2 tbsp best-quality extra-virgin olive oil, plus more for drizzling

2 thick slices nutty whole-wheat/wholemeal bread

Plain mayonnaise or Herb Mayo {page 207}

½ bunch arugula/rocket, torn

Sea salt

Freshly ground black pepper

Sweet or smoked paprika

Place the eggs in a large bowl of warm water. Bring a small pot of water to a simmer over medium heat. Gently lower the eggs into the water, using a spoon. Set the timer for 6 minutes and keep eggs at a low simmer.

Meanwhile, heat a large frying pan over medium-high heat. Add the olive oil and the bread, toasting until golden on both sides, about 1 minute per side. Transfer to small plates.

When the timer goes off, immediately remove the eggs from the pan and rinse under cool water. Carefully remove the shell from all the eggs.

Spread the toasted bread with mayonnaise, then top with arugula. Split the eggs in half with a sharp knife and place the halves on top of the arugula/rocket. Season with salt and pepper, and add a pinch of smoked paprika for color and heat. Drizzle the whole thing with your finest extra-virgin olive oil and serve immediately.

GROW ARUGULA: Arugula/rocket is a great green-thumb starter. It grows well in pots, raised beds, or in the ground. Start seeds every 3 weeks from the last frost to early summer by sprinkling seeds in rows about 2 in/5 cm apart, ¼ in/6 mm below the soil. Cover with a thin layer of fine soil or compost. You'll see sprouts in about 1 week and will have mature leaves in 30 to 50 days. Cut out crowded baby leaves when they are about 2 in/5 cm long and toss them into salads. Let the rest mature, pulling leaves as you need them through the season. Arugula goes to seed quickly in hot summer months, so harvest often and early to create flavorful salads, sandwiches, or an incredibly pungent pesto {Green-On-Green Pesto, page 209}. Plant again in September and enjoy the robust leaves through Thanksgiving.

THE MAN SANDWICH

serves 2

{enough said} In the middle of July, the prolific garden zucchini beg your creativity. Turn this bounty into a man-sized sandwich grilled alongside a coil of spicy sausage and sweet spring onions. Stack the three together into a hearty sandwich that's a summer meal in every bite. This is guy food at its delicious best.

12-oz/340-g coil spicy beef
or lamb sausage, such as merguez,
or spicy Italian sausage

1 large zucchini/courgette, cut lengthwise into
¼-in/6-mm-thick slices

2 spring {bulb} onions, thickly sliced

¼ cup/60 ml extra-virgin olive oil

Sea salt

Freshly ground black pepper

4 slices whole-wheat/wholemeal
or seven-grain sandwich bread

Herb Mayo {page 207}

Preheat the grill/barbecue or a grill pan until hot. Lay the sausage on the hottest part of the grill/barbecue and cook until crisp, about 6 minutes. Turn the sausage and grill until cooked through, 8 to 10 minutes depending on thickness of the sausage. Remove to a platter to rest.

Meanwhile, drizzle the zucchini/courgette and onion slices with the olive oil and season generously with salt and pepper.

While the sausage cooks on the second side, add the vegetables to the grill. Cook until crisp-tender and lightly charred, about 4 minutes per side. Add the bread to the grill about 2 minutes before the veggies are finished and toast on both sides.

Spread Herb Mayo on two slices of the grilled bread. Slice the sausages and divide between the two sandwiches along with the grilled veggies. Top with the remaining bread. Serve warm with lots of napkins.

MAKE IT MEATLESS: I make these sandwiches for András without the sausage and add double doses of grilled zucchini/courgette and onions, plus a grilled portabella cap with melted muenster cheese. He raves about them for days and it turns out I love this version just as much, too.

PAN-FRIED STRIPED BASS SANDWICHES

serves 4

{no ordinary supper} A fresh fish sandwich is transformative, and this one just might rock your world. Bass is widely available and well suited for the heat of a piquant mayo. If you can't find black or striped bass, you can use your favorite local white, flaky fish, particularly if you live near the water. Serve this sandwich with Fried Zucchini {page 191} and a light lager or a good Italian white wine like pinot grigio or Orvieto.

1 fresh baguette,
or 4 Portuguese rolls, split

Melted unsalted butter, for brushing

½ medium bulb fennel, quartered and cored

Handful of sharp or spicy lettuce,
such as arugula/rocket

3 tbsp best-quality extra-virgin olive oil

Sea salt

Freshly ground black pepper

Four 6-oz/170 g black or striped bass fillets,
scaled and pin bones removed

1 tsp fennel seeds, crushed

Hearty pinch of red pepper flakes

Spicy Mayo {page 207}

1 medium cucumber, peeled and thinly sliced

Preheat the broiler/grill to high. Brush the cut sides of the bread with melted butter and set aside {you'll broil the bread just before you build your sandwich}.

Slice the fennel as thinly as possible with a sharp knife. Toss the lettuce and sliced fennel with 1 tbsp of the olive oil in a bowl and sprinkle with salt and freshly ground pepper. Set aside.

Lay the fish fillets on a cutting board, skin-side up. Pinch the skin lightly and score it diagonally about ¼ in/6 mm deep with a thin, sharp knife. Repeat about six times across the skin of the fish, which helps the flesh to cook evenly and keeps it from curling up in the pan. Sprinkle the fish on both sides with salt, pepper, fennel seeds, and red pepper flakes.

Heat the remaining 2 tbsp of the oil in your largest nonstick frying pan over medium-high heat. Add the fish, skin-side down, and cook until the skin is golden and crisp, about 4 minutes. Meanwhile, pop the bread under the broiler/grill for a few minutes until crisp and golden {don't forget it; it can burn quickly!} Using a flexible metal or fish spatula, gently turn the fish over and cook the flesh side until just cooked through, about 1 minute more. Remove from the pan and set on a plate.

Halve the baguette lengthwise and then crosswise into four segments to make four large sandwiches. Smother one cut side of the bread with the spicy mayo and layer on the fish, fennel salad, and cucumber slices. Top with the remaining bread and serve.

BASS—A BEST CHOICE FISH: Both farmed and wild striped bass from the United States is on the Seafood Watch's Best Choice List. It's a great choice for conscious consumers because it's fished in a way that supports conservation efforts.

LOBSTER ROLLS

serves 2 to 4

{worth it} I'm the first to admit that I cry a little when I have to kill a living creature in order to have dinner. But sometimes you fancy the taste of the sea, and lobster is just too good to leave off the menu. You'll want to eat and serve lobster at its best, and since it's one of the few fish or seafood you can buy alive, you can be assured of its freshness. Brave the task at home with a sharp quick knife to the back of the lobster's head, straight into the center of the small cross mark on its shell. This is arguably the most humane way to go about this. What follows is pure deliciousness.

One more thing: It's worth serving lobster salad on impeccably fresh bread. Make your own Dowry Dinner Rolls, or buy rolls fresh from a local baker. Serve with bread-and-butter pickles and ice cold lemonade.

One 1½-lb/680-g lobster	½ cup/120 ml olive-oil mayonnaise
Sea salt	1 inner stalk of celery with leaves, finely diced
Freshly ground black pepper	1 to 2 tbsp chopped fresh flat-leaf parsley
1 tsp finely grated lemon or orange zest	2 tsp freshly squeezed lemon juice
2 tbsp unsalted butter	Dowry Dinner Rolls {page 132}, or fresh bakery rolls, split

Halve the fresh lobster lengthwise down the middle with kitchen shears and remove the innards and roe. Lay both halves on a glass pie plate that fits inside a wide, deep saucepan. Sprinkle with sea salt, fresh black pepper, lemon zest, and a few dabs of the butter. Fill the saucepan with about 1 in/2.5 cm of water and set the pie plate in the pan, making sure the water is just below the lip of the plate. Cover the pot, and bring the water to a boil over medium-high heat.

Steam the lobster until it is evenly pink and just cooked through, 10 to 12 minutes depending on the size of the lobster.

Remove the lobster with tongs and set aside on a platter until just cooled enough to handle {lobster meat is sweetest and most tender when warm, and gets rubbery when chilled}. Meanwhile, mix together the mayonnaise, celery, parsley, and lemon juice in a large bowl.

Remove the steamed lobster from the shell. Start by twisting off the claws where they meet the body and use the back of a heavy knife to crack the shells just slightly. Pull out the meat in big pieces. Pull the tail meat out of the shell and chop on a cutting board into bite-size pieces {the claw meat will be the most tender and will fall apart easily; the tail meat can stay in slightly large pieces}. Put the warm, chopped lobster meat into the bowl with the mayonnaise mixture and toss to coat. Taste and season with more salt, pepper, or lemon juice as needed.

Spoon onto fresh rolls and serve immediately.

CHAPTER 5

SUPPER

Simple Meals for Well-Fed Couples

Welcome to your supper. "Dinner," whether eaten in the afternoon or evening, used to be the main event, but "supper" evokes something simpler—easy and enjoyable meals that bring you back to the table over and over again.

These meals can be eaten at noon or at night, and are based on small cuts of meat, fish, and meatless entrees that can be thrown together quickly {in about an hour} for nourishing meals after work, a workout, or an afternoon adventure. There are so many delicious recipes in this chapter I can hardly wait to tell you about them. But first, I need to talk to you about one thing: You won't find boneless, skinless chicken breasts in this chapter. I know, you love them. They are fast, cheap, and lean.

But, there are more exciting things on your menu now, like Monday Night Broiled Chicken with Scallion Pesto {page 117}, Pan-Seared Arctic Char with Sorrel {page 125}, and Baked Risotto with Roasted Vegetables {page 115}.

There is only one rule for this meal: Supper should satisfy. It should be full of flavor, and fill your soul. That is the nature of Skewered Lamb with Tomato Couscous {page 118}. That doesn't mean enormous portions or even the standard protein-plus-starch-plus-vegetable formula. It doesn't even have to be hot food {try the Brown Rice Bowl with Watercress, Walnuts & Winter Citrus, page 112}, but it should be warming food, food that fills the belly and soothes the brain in a way that inspires you to slow down and enjoy the person across the table from you.

That's sounds lovely, doesn't it? Let's begin.

{ FOOLPROOF BONELESS CHICKEN BREAST }

It only takes a few sentences to describe how to make an excellent chicken breast every time:

Preheat the oven to 375°F/190°C/gas 5. Season 2 boneless, skinless chicken breasts on both sides with kosher or sea salt, freshly ground black pepper, and some sort of nice spice blend. Heat 2 tablespoons olive oil in a medium ovenproof frying pan over high heat until shimmering. Add the chicken breasts to the pan and cook them until golden and they release easily from the pan, about 4 minutes. Flip and cook on the other side 2 to 3 minutes more. Transfer the chicken in the pan to the oven to finish cooking; bake until the internal temperature reads 165°F/74°C . Remove and let rest 5 minutes before serving.

See, easy! You can take this and add it to any of the sides or vegetables in the following chapters to create a scrumptious supper.

BROWN RICE BOWL
WITH
WATERCRESS, WALNUTS
& WINTER CITRUS

serves 4

{a healthful treat} If you've relegated brown rice to the obligatory healthful option to accompany Chinese takeout, you're about to get a whole new peek into its versatility with this winter salad. Warm, filling brown rice becomes incredibly exciting when paired with crunchy walnuts, crispy watercress, and bright winter citrus. A study in contrasts between warm and cold, soft and crunchy, this meal in a bowl is bursting with flavor.

1 cup/215 g brown rice

1 tsp kosher salt

2 or 3 tbsp unsalted butter

1 bunch watercress, woody stems removed

1 avocado, peeled, pitted, and sliced

⅓ cup/30 g toasted walnuts {1 small handful}, coarsely chopped

¼ cup/30 g toasted cashews {1 small handful}, coarsely chopped

2 sweet navel oranges or clementines, peeled and cut into rounds

3 tbsp best-quality extra-virgin olive oil

Smoked or coarse finishing sea salt

Freshly ground black pepper

Rinse the rice in a strainer under cold running water until the water runs clear, about 45 seconds. Bring 8 cups of water and the 1 tsp kosher salt to a boil in a large pot with a lid over high heat. Add the rice and stir. Boil, uncovered, for 30 minutes. Strain the rice. Return the rice to the pot, put the lid on, and set aside for the rice to steam, about 10 minutes. Stir in the butter and fluff with a fork.

Divide the cooked rice among four deep bowls. Arrange the watercress, avocado, toasted nuts, and oranges around the outside. Drizzle with the olive oil, salt, and pepper. Serve just warm or at room temperature, tossing together in the bowl with chopsticks or a fork as you eat.

SAVE TIME: When I make brown rice, I almost always make extra. It's great to have on hand for Kitchen Sink Fried Rice {facing page}, to stuff into veggie burritos, or to stir into your morning oatmeal for added texture and whole grains. Cook it like pasta in a big pot of boiling water {as above} for a perfect, fluffy texture every time.

KITCHEN SINK
FRIED RICE

serves 2

{stir it all in} It's time to dip into your well-stocked pantry and reward yourself with a one-dish meal that requires very little planning. Fried rice is completely unfussy and makes good use of whatever's on hand, including a mismatched harvest from the garden, which means you'll never make the same fried rice twice. The best part is when you're done, you'll have only a few dishes to wash—your wok or frying pan, two bowls and a couple sets of chopsticks! Don't panic if you're missing anything on this list. There are so many opportunities for flavor {soy, Sriracha, scallion, ginger} that one won't be missed.

3 tbsp toasted sesame oil,
plus more for seasoning

3 tbsp peanut oil

1 tbsp sesame seeds

2 garlic cloves, finely chopped

1-in/2.5-cm piece fresh ginger, peeled and chopped

4 scallions/spring onions
{white and green parts}, chopped,

2 handfuls vegetables {such as carrots, turnips, shiitake mushroom caps}, cut in small pieces

4 cups/960 ml cold, leftover
cooked short-grain or regular brown rice

4 large eggs, lightly beaten

2 tbsp soy sauce

1 to 3 tsp Sriracha sauce or sambal oelek

4 to 6 cornichon pickles, chopped

Handful of sugar snap peas, halved on the bias, or fresh pea shoots

½ lime, cut in wedges

Heat the largest frying pan or wok you have over medium heat. Add the sesame oil and 1 tbsp of the peanut oil and heat until shimmering. Drop in the sesame seeds and toast lightly until pale golden. Add the garlic and ginger and stir quickly until fragrant, about 1 minute, keeping everything moving so it doesn't burn. Add the white parts of the scallions/spring onions and the vegetables, starting with those that take the longest to cook like carrots or turnips, followed by the mushrooms. Cook until the veggies are just tender.

Push the veggies to the side of the pan. Add the remaining peanut oil and the cold rice. Cook over medium heat, tossing until all the grains are coated with oil. Increase the heat to medium-high and cook until rice is toasty with some crispy brown bits, moving it around occasionally to keep it

from sticking together, about 8 minutes. Once you start seeing crispy brown bits all along the bottom, scrape everything off the bottom with a rigid spatula and push to the sides of the pan.

Add the eggs and let them set a few seconds to begin to cook. Stir the rice into the eggs to coat and cook, moving occasionally, until some parts are crispy. Let the rice sit in the hot pan until crisp and brown, stirring only occasionally, 5 minutes more.

Stir in the scallion/spring onion greens, soy, Sriracha, and cornichons and season with additional sesame oil. Stir in the sugar snaps or pea shoots until they are just warmed, about 2 minutes. Serve hot with chopsticks, lime wedges, and more Sriracha or sambal on the side.

BAKED RISOTTO
· · · · WITH · · · ·
ROASTED VEGETABLES

serves 2

Soft, creamy risotto topped with warm roasted vegetables makes a complete meal in a bowl. If you don't like the idea of standing at the stove and stirring risotto to a perfect consistency, this is the method is for you. Thirty minutes in the oven and this risotto comes out cooked to perfection while you and your beloved wind down from your day.

If you've made Roasted Winter Vegetables earlier in the week, you can reheat leftovers as a topping here. If not, roast a favorite combination {mine is winter squash, yellow onion, and tomato} in the oven with your risotto.

Roasted Winter Vegetables {page 193}

1 tbsp extra-virgin olive oil

½ onion, finely chopped

¾ cup/150 g Arborio rice

¼ cup/60 ml dry white wine

2 to 2¼ cups/480 to 540 ml hot water, homemade or packaged organic chicken broth, or a mix

¾ tsp kosher salt

Pinch of freshly ground black pepper

1 to 2 tbsp unsalted butter

¼ cup/30 g freshly grated Parmigiano-Reggiano cheese, plus more for garnish

Preheat the oven to 400°F/200°C/gas 6. Roast the vegetables on a single baking sheet/tray on the top rack of the oven {the risotto will bake on the bottom rack}.

Meanwhile, heat the olive oil in an ovenproof saucepan or Dutch oven over medium-high heat. Add the onion and cook, stirring, until it is soft and translucent, about 3 minutes. Add the rice and stir to coat with the oil. Stir in the wine and cook until the wine has evaporated, 1 minute more. Stir in 2 cups/480 ml of the hot water, salt, and pepper, and bring

to a boil. Cover and transfer to the oven. Bake on the bottom rack during the last 25 minutes of roasting time for the vegetables. After 25 minutes, check the risotto. Most of the liquid should be absorbed and the rice just cooked.

Remove the risotto from the oven and stir in another ½ cup/120 ml hot water, the butter, and cheese.

Serve topped with roasted vegetables with thin shavings of Parmigiano-Reggiano.

CURRIED CHICKPEAS & SQUASH

serves 4

{filling & flavorful} This is a beginner's curry, both in technique and intensity, using curry powder to get you started on your way. The mildly spicy, deeply soothing flavors of curry blend beautifully with chickpeas and squash. There is a richness to curries that satisfies vegetarians and carnivores alike. The dish reheats beautifully over low heat on the stove, so save those leftovers!

2 tbsp canola or grapeseed oil

1 yellow onion, chopped

2 garlic cloves, smashed and minced

1-in/2.5-cm piece of fresh ginger, grated

1 small hot green chile {such as Thai bird chile or serrano, seeded and minced

2 to 3 tsp Madras curry powder

1 small squash {such as butternut, kabocha, or pumpkin {about 1 lb/455 g}, peeled and cubed

1 large beefsteak tomato or 2 plum tomatoes {about 1 lb/455 g}, chopped

One 13.5-oz/400-ml can coconut milk

One 15-oz/439-g can chickpeas, drained and rinsed

2 handfuls of fresh Swiss chard or spinach leaves, stemmed

½ lemon

Sea salt

Freshly ground black pepper

1½ cups/360 ml plain whole-milk yogurt

Handful of cilantro/fresh coriander leaves, chopped

Warm rice or naan, for serving

Heat the oil in a medium frying pan over medium-high heat. Add the onion and cook until soft and translucent, about 3 minutes. Add the garlic, ginger, and chile and continue cooking until fragrant, about 1 minute. Add the curry powder and squash and stir to coat in the spices. Add the tomato, coconut milk, and 1 full coconut–milk can of water and bring to a simmer. Reduce heat to medium-low. Cook until the squash is fork-tender. Add the chickpeas and chard and stir to warm the chickpeas and wilt the chard. Squeeze the lemon over the curry and stir in the juice, tasting as you add, to brighten the sauce. Season with salt and pepper.

Divide between two or four bowls, dollop yogurt over the top, and garnish with fresh cilantro/fresh coriander leaves. Serve warm over rice or warmed naan bread.

MONDAY NIGHT BROILED CHICKEN
WITH
SCALLION PESTO

serves 2 to 4

{a go-to meal} Let me introduce you to the fast and fabulous broiled chicken. It delivers all of the things you love about roast chicken: crispy skin, juicy meat, real chicken flavor, but it comes together considerably faster, and easier. It's the perfect quick meal for a Monday night when you get home from work. The addition of pesto made with scallions, a distant cousin to Green-On-Green Pesto {page 209}, might make this your new favorite chicken dish.

SCALLION PESTO

6 scallions/spring onions {white and green parts}, washed and coarsely chopped

½ bunch cilantro/fresh coriander leaves and stems

2 teaspoons grated fresh ginger

1 garlic clove

¼ cup/60 ml extra-virgin olive oil or grapeseed oil

CHICKEN

4 bone-in, skin-on chicken breast halves {10 to 12 oz/280 to 340 g each}, preferably free-range

¼ cup/60 ml extra-virgin olive oil

½ lemon, sliced

Sea salt

Freshly ground black pepper

Grilled Flatbread {page 280}

MAKE THE PESTO: Combine the scallions/spring onions, cilantro/fresh coriander, ginger, and garlic in a mini food processor or finely chop them all and stir together in a medium bowl. Pulse or whisk together, adding oil gradually, until the ingredients come together in a smooth green paste. Set aside.

MAKE THE CHICKEN: Preheat the broiler/grill to medium-high with the oven rack about 6 in/15 cm from the broiler flame. Line a broiler/grill pan with aluminum foil and preheat it in the oven.

Pat the chicken pieces dry and toss them with the olive oil and sliced lemons in a large bowl. Coat and season the chicken generously with the sea salt and freshly ground black pepper. Carefully remove the broiler pan from the oven and place the chicken skin-side down on the pan. Arrange the lemon slices around the chicken.

Return to the oven and broil about 6 minutes. Flip the chicken to skin-side up {tongs make this easy} and continue broiling until the skin is golden and crisp, the chicken is cooked through, and any juices run clear, 6 to 8 minutes more, depending on the size of the chicken pieces. Remove the chicken from the oven and let it rest about 5 minutes before serving.

Serve the chicken with the pesto and flatbread.

EAT GREEN: Chicken raised in pens are often tasteless, and lead a pretty tragic life. The flavor of a free-range bird benefits from the grass, nuts, seeds, and fruit they eat on the farms where they roam. Splurge on the best chicken your budget can afford; you'll taste the difference.

SKEWERED LAMB
· · · · WITH · · · ·
TOMATO COUSCOUS

serves 4

{a feast} There are many things to love about lamb. For starters, compared to beef or chicken, it's easier to find wonderful pasture-fed lamb raised on a smaller farm. Lamb is also fairly lean but still full of flavor and it loves the grill, grill pan, or frying pan equally. Couscous, which takes only 5 minutes to make, garnished with pan-roasted tomatoes, quickly rounds out the meal and makes it a go-to dinner that will fool your hubby into thinking you spent all day at the stove.

1 lemon

1 lb/455 g boneless lamb sirloin, cubed

¼ cup/60 ml extra-virgin olive oil

1 tsp za'atar or a pinch each dried thyme, parsley, and oregano

Sea salt

Freshly ground black pepper

TOMATO COUSCOUS

1 lb/455 g campari or small tomatoes-on-the-vine, halved

1 small garlic clove, crushed

1 tbsp extra-virgin olive oil

1 cup/168 g plain or whole-wheat/ wholemeal couscous

1⅓ cups/315 ml chicken stock or water

3 tbsp/40 g cold, unsalted butter

¼ tsp sea salt

Freshly ground black pepper

Handful of fresh parsley, coarsely chopped, for garnish

Tsatsiki {optional, page 210}

Have ready metal skewers or wooden skewers soaked in water for 30 minutes.

Halve the lemon; reserve one half and cut the other half crosswise into half moons. Toss lamb with the olive oil, lemon slices, and za'atar in a medium bowl; season with salt and pepper. Cover and set aside at room temperature for 30 minutes or in the fridge up to overnight.

Toss the tomatoes, garlic, and olive oil together in a medium bowl. Cook the tomato mixture in a small skillet over medium-high heat until the tomatoes soften and give up their water as if melting. Squeeze the reserved half lemon over the top, discarding any seeds, and remove from the heat, swirling to bring the juices together. Set aside.

Heat a grill pan or grill to medium-high heat. Thread four lamb cubes and two lemon slices alternately on each skewer. Grill until marked by the hot grates and cooked, about 5 minutes. Flip and rotate on all three remaining sides with long tongs until well marked and cooked to medium-rare, about 3 minutes every quarter turn.

MAKE THE COUSCOUS: Put the couscous in a medium bowl. Bring the stock to a boil and pour over the couscous. Add the butter, salt, and pepper, cover the bowl, and set aside for 5 minutes. Fluff with a fork.

To serve, transfer the couscous to a serving bowl, and spoon the tomatoes and their juices over the top. Sprinkle with parsley. Serve with grilled lamb and Tsatsiki.

GROW TOMATOES: The best tomatoes you'll ever taste are the ones you grow yourself and pick just hours before eating. Red, yellow, or deep purple heirloom tomatoes make exceptional sandwiches, soups, and instant salads.

Tomatoes do very well in big pots or planted directly in the soil. Pick out a spot that gets 8 hours of full sunlight. Buy the healthiest looking tomato starters you can find from a nursery you trust or your favorite farmer at the market, and ask them plenty of questions about what varieties grow best in your climate and how they grow the most flavorful tomatoes. Dig a deep, wide trench for your tomato plants, splash a little water in the hole, and plant the tomatoes so that the first 2 in/5 cm of stem is underground. Cover the stems with compost and dark, loose soil and plant a tall, sturdy stake about 1 in/2.5 cm from the root. Use twist ties or twine to secure the stem to the stake. Keep tomatoes well watered at their roots, but avoid wetting their leaves. Let the sunshine do the work, and if you hit any rough patches, head back to the farmer or nursery with a leaf or tomato for troubleshooting.

BETTER BEEF BURGERS
···· WITH ····
QUICK PICKLED ONIONS

serves 4 {makes 4 large burgers or 8 sliders}

Sometimes you just want a burger. When you do, make it special out of grass-fed beef on an über-fresh bun, stacked to the heavens with homemade fixings. A grass-fed beef burger deserves a better cheese, too. Give it a few thin slices of something sharp, smoky, or slightly sweet from aging, like clothbound Cheddar, aged or smoked gouda, or asiago.

This recipe makes four big burgers, which use standard rolls, or eight sliders, the perfect size to stuff inside your own homemade Dowry Dinner Rolls {page 132}.

QUICK PICKLED RED ONIONS

2 red onions, peeled and sliced {about 1 lb/455 g}

3 cups/720 ml red wine vinegar

1½ cups/300 g sugar

4 black peppercorns

1 bay leaf

BURGERS

2 lb/910 g grass-fed ground/minced chuck

Kosher salt

Freshly ground black pepper

8 oz/225 g aged gouda, Manchego, or sharp white Cheddar cheese, thinly sliced

4 fresh rolls, split and lightly toasted

4 thick slices beefsteak tomato {1 large tomato}

4 crunchy lettuce leaves, such as butter, Bibb, or romaine/Cos lettuce

Bread-and-butter pickles

Everything's Better with Aioli {page 208}

Herb Mayo {page 207}

Spicy Mayo {page 207}

Ketchup/tomato sauce

Mustard

MAKE THE PICKLED ONIONS: Put the onions in a large bowl. Heat the vinegar, sugar, peppercorns, and bay leaf in the microwave or on the stovetop until the sugar dissolves, about 2 minutes. Pour the pickling liquid over the sliced onions and set aside for 5 minutes. Remove the onions from the pickling liquid while they are still crisp and let them cool on a plate. Let the pickling liquid cool to room temperature and then return the onions to the mixture. Pour the onions and the liquid into pretty jars or containers and store in the fridge until you're ready to use them, up to 1 week.

MAKE THE BURGERS: Preheat a charcoal or gas grill until the coals are a deep red or the grill grates are evenly hot {this takes about 20 minutes on a charcoal grill}.

Divide the meat into four equal portions and shape gently into patties about 1 in/2.5 cm thick {eight 1-in/2.5-cm portions for sliders}. Season both sides generously with salt and pepper.

Place the burgers on the grill and cook them without moving until the outside browns deeply, about 5 minutes for standard burgers, 3 to 4 minutes for sliders. When the patties slide easily on the grill grates, flip them over {flipping them too early can cause burgers to break apart and all the good juices to disappear into your grill!}. Lay the cheese on top of the burgers during the last 2 minutes of cooking and close the lid to let the cheese melt. Cook 3 minutes for medium-rare, 5 minutes for medium, and slightly less for sliders.

Place the burgers on the toasted rolls. Build your own burgers to order with your favorite garnishes.

EAT GREEN: Grass-fed beef is lower in saturated fat, higher in omega-3 fatty acids, and higher in vitamins A and E than beef fed on corn and soybeans. And, grass-fed farms are a healthier environment for the animals too! Factory-farmed beef causes more greenhouse emissions in our country than cars. Choosing grass-fed beef, on the other hand, has the power to help reduce greenhouse gases by reducing the need for large factory farms to grow and ship grains in increasingly large quantities to support the grain-fed cattle industry. And, since a cow's stomach is made to digest grass, not grain, we can bet that's what's best for them, too.

LINGUINE WITH SAUSAGE
AND
AN EASY EGG SAUCE

serves 2 to 4

If you like sweet or spicy sausages, a pound of them in the fridge is as good as dinner on the table. Whip together fresh linguine and a simple {and oh-so-satisfying} egg sauce, and supper is served.

1 lb/455 g high-quality sweet or spicy Italian sausages

2 tbsp extra-virgin olive oil

Sea salt

Freshly ground black pepper

1 lb/455 g linguine pasta, fresh or dried

4 large organic egg yolks

½ cup/120 ml whole milk or half-and-half/half cream

¾ cup/85 g freshly grated Parmigiano-Reggiano cheese

Grated zest of 1 lemon

Handful of fresh chives or flat-leaf parsley, chopped

Cut or slice the skins of the sausage, and peel back the skins. Cut the sausage into little blunt-edged meatballs.

Heat the olive oil in a large frying pan over medium-high heat and fry the sausages until golden brown all over, about 5 minutes.

Meanwhile, cook the linguine in boiling salted water until it is just al dente, 3 to 5 minutes for fresh and 10 to 12 minutes for dried.

Whisk together the egg yolks, milk, half the grated cheese, pepper, and the lemon zest. Drain the pasta and reserve about ½ cup/120 ml cooking liquid. Add the pasta back to the pot along with the egg mixture. Add the hot sausage, toss it all together, and let the heat from the pot and the linguine cook and thicken the egg to a silky sauce. Add ¼ to ½ cup/60 to 120 ml of the reserved pasta water to loosen. Toss with the remaining cheese and chives or parsley and serve fresh from the stove in shallow bowls or plates.

PAN-SEARED ARCTIC CHAR
WITH
SORREL

serves 4

{rustic, but special} I fell in love with bright, lemony sorrel while working as a private chef in St. Tropez where it grew in the family garden. Now it grows in mine. I serve it raw, chopped, and stirred with nuts and olive oil as a rustic pesto over fish, steak, lamb, and seafood. These clean, boisterous flavors are particularly well matched to the healthful fats found in arctic char or wild-caught salmon. It is the easiest little supper for two. And with a side of fresh corn on the cob or tomato salad, this may be the fastest meal you'll have all week.

SORREL PESTO

2 handfuls {1 small bunch} of fresh sorrel, stemmed

1 small handful {½ bunch} of fresh basil or parsley leaves, or a mix, coarsely chopped

½ cup/55 g walnuts or pecans {or a combination}), coarsely chopped

½ garlic clove, peeled and finely chopped

1 lemon

¼ cup/60 ml best-quality extra-virgin olive oil

Sea salt

Freshly ground black pepper

FISH

2 tbsp extra-virgin olive oil

Two 6-oz/170-g pieces arctic char or wild-caught salmon, skin on

½ tsp kosher salt

¼ tsp freshly ground black pepper

MAKE THE PESTO: Stack several sorrel leaves on top of each other on the cutting board. Slice into thin strips and transfer to a bowl; repeat with the remaining leaves.

Add the sorrel to the chopped herbs and nuts along with the garlic. Zest the lemon and add to the sauce with the olive oil. Halve the lemon, and squeeze a bit of juice into the bowl. Toss all together and season with salt and pepper.

COOK THE FISH: Heat the olive oil in a large nonstick or stainless-steel frying pan over medium-high heat. Season the fish with the salt and pepper and add it to the pan, skin-side down. Cook until the skin is crispy and pulls away from the pan easily and the fish is about halfway cooked through {you'll know when the translucent pink flesh turns to a pale opaque pink around the sides and edges and is still shiny in the thickest part}, about 5 minutes. Using a flexible spatula, flip the fish onto the flesh side, and cook until the fish is just cooked through, but still slightly shiny pink inside, about 4 minutes more. If this makes you nervous, simply cover the pan with the lid and cook until just pink throughout but still a touch translucent.

Transfer the fish to two plates, spoon the pesto over the top, and serve.

EAT GREEN: If you like the idea of salmon but wish for something with a milder taste, you'll love artic char. Most of it comes from the United States, Canada, Norway, or Ireland and is farmed in low-eco-impact tanks that prevent escape into the wild. If you can't find it in your area, choose wild or line-caught salmon or lake trout from Lake Superior {rather than Lake Huron or Michigan}, which also has a mild, fatty pink flesh.

CHAPTER 6

COMFORT FOOD

Classic Recipes for Cozy Meals

At the advice of parents and married friends we admired, András and I took a marriage prep course before we walked down the aisle. One of the most eye-opening exercises in the whole session was "name five things your fiancé does that make you feel the most loved." Top on András's list was "when she makes me Hungarian food," meaning food from home.

In this, I don't have the home court advantage. Most of the foods we grew up with {he in Hungary, and I in the United States} are different, but I learned quickly that comfort food comes in many forms, and I made it a point to know what foods from his homeland or mine made him feel really happy and loved.

The best comfort food of all will soon become those that you prepare for your beloved when a little extra TLC is needed, and those are the foods on which you'll build your own traditions. Whether you grew up with Southern Shrimp & Grits {page 151} or French Onion Soup {page 134}, get ready to adopt these recipes as your own for those long, hard weeks when you need something to melt away the cares of the world.

Most of these dishes, like Grown-Up Mac 'n' Cheese {page 135} and Pan-Fried Pork Chops {page 146}, are not everyday foods. Many of them require a little extra time and a willing diversion from counting calories. I believe that Buttermilk Fried Chicken {page 140} and Skillet Corn Bread {page 130}, when enjoyed on occasion, pose no threat in the balance of an overall healthy lifestyle. Made at home with pure, wholesome ingredients, these meals inspire pleasure and well being, which are as important to our health as vitamins or exercise. And besides, you've just signed on for a lifetime workout partner. You're in this together.

There is no such cozy combination as man and wife. —Menader

SKILLET CORN BREAD

serves 6 to 8

Even a basic boxed corn bread mix is pretty good, but imagine how much better corn bread can get when you make it fresh with buttermilk and real butter, and baked in a cast-iron skillet until it's just set on the outside and tender and almost wobbly at its core. This one is good hot or cold, plain or drenched in butter, and honey or molasses. The best and worst part about it is that it's so fast and easy you'll be tempted to make it over and over again. If you don't have a cast-iron skillet, make this cornbread in a regular 8-in/20-cm skillet or 8-in/20-cm round cake pan/tin.

2 cups/280 g fine yellow cornmeal

3 tbsp sugar

1 tsp fine sea salt

½ tsp baking soda/bicarbonate of soda

2 large eggs, beaten

2 cups/480 ml buttermilk

6 tbsp/85 g unsalted butter, plus more for serving

Cool butter, for serving

Molasses or honey, for serving

Preheat the oven to 400°F/200°C/gas 6.

Whisk together the cornmeal, sugar, salt, and baking soda/bicarbonate of soda in a large bowl. Make a well in the center. Crack in the eggs, add the buttermilk, and combine with a fork, starting in the middle to break up the eggs and then bring the dry ingredients into the wet to make a smooth batter.

Melt the butter in the cast-iron skillet over low heat {if you're using a cake pan/tin, melt the butter separately in the microwave}. Turn off the heat and pour the butter from the pan into the batter. Stir together with the fork.

Pour the batter back into the warm skillet and bake in the middle of the oven until the corn bread is lightly golden brown and slightly wet looking in the center, 22 to 25 minutes. {It's essential to remove it from the oven before it's completely set, at which point the texture changes from custard to more traditional cornbread.} It should pull away from the sides of the skillet just slightly once it comes out of the oven.

Bring the hot skillet directly to the table, slice, and serve warm with cool butter and honey or molasses.

DOWRY DINNER ROLLS

serves many {20 rolls}

{that puff like pillows} There is arguably nothing more comforting than rolls still warm from the oven with a shimmer of warm butter. Sure, making fresh bread for just two seems like a luxury, but it's one you both deserve. Make time to learn how to make fresh, pillowy dinner rolls from scratch for those nights that you or your beloved need a little something soft and sure in your world. Potatoes are the secret to these pillowy buns, and are prepped in the same way for the Don't-You-Dare Mashed Potatoes {page 187}. The next time you make them, cook up an extra potato and give these rolls a head start.

1 large Idaho or russet potato {about 12 oz/340 g}

½ cup/120 ml whole milk

⅔ cup sugar

2¼ tsp active dry yeast

1½ cups whole-wheat/wholemeal or white whole-wheat/wholemeal flour

3 cups/885 g bread or all-purpose/plain flour

2 large eggs

¾ tsp fine sea salt

8 tbsp/115 g unsalted butter {plus more for buttering the bowl and brushing and serving}, at room temperature

Maldon or coarse sea salt, for garnish

In a medium saucepan, boil the potato with the skin on over medium-high heat until you can squeeze it easily between your hands, about 30 minutes. While still warm, cut open the potato and scoop out the flesh. Pass the potato flesh through a ricer or food mill to get 1 cup/240 ml of fluffy, light potato puree. Set aside.

Heat the milk and sugar in a saucepan over medium heat until the sugar dissolves. Bring just to a simmer and then transfer the liquid to a large bowl or the bowl of your stand mixer if you have one. Test the temperature with an instant-read thermometer: when it is between 105°F/40°C and 110°F/45°C, add the yeast.

In a large bowl, combine the potato puree, the whole-wheat/wholemeal flour, ½ cup of the bread flour, eggs, and salt and stir together to create a sticky dough about the consistency of cooked oatmeal. Cover and let the bowl stand in a warm place until the mixture has doubled, about 2 hours.

When the dough has doubled, turn it into the bowl of a stand mixer, and with the paddle attachment gradually blend in the softened butter. Beat together on medium speed to create a sticky dough, about 1 minute. Switch to the dough hook and add another 2 cups/255 g bread flour, ½ cup/60 g at a time, and continue beating until the dough pulls away from the bowl. Knead with the dough hook or on a lightly floured surface until it is soft and a touch tacky, about 4 minutes. Continue kneading until it is a smooth and supple ball that doesn't stick to your hands or the board or bowl, adding the remaining flour as needed.

Brush a large bowl with additional soft butter. Turn the dough around in the butter to coat and set in the bowl. Wrap the top tightly with plastic wrap/cling film and let it rise at room temperature until it has doubled and is soft and full of air, about 1½ hours.

Butter a 9-by-13-in/23-by-33-cm baking pan or dish. Turn the dough gently over into the middle of the baking dish and gently stretch the dough to fill evenly to all four corners. At this point it might have deflated slightly but it should still be about ½ in/12 mm high. Use a metal bench {pastry} scraper or sharp knife to score the dough all the way down to the pan bottom into five rows lengthwise, followed by four rows crosswise to make twenty square rolls.

Gently brush the tops of the rolls with additional soft butter without deflating the dough further, and sprinkle with flakes of sea salt. Cover loosely with plastic wrap/cling film and set in a warm {but not hot} place until the rolls are puffed to almost double their original size, about 1 hour.

During the last 30 minutes of rising time, preheat the oven to 400°F/200°C/gas 6. Bake the rolls, uncovered, until they are evenly golden brown and spring back lightly when touched, about 20 minutes.

Serve warm in the pan, and encourage guests to pull off their rolls as they wish.

P.S. *These freeze beautifully. Reheat them in a hot oven for easy assurance on any old night. Keep extras for Lobster Rolls {page 107} or Grilled Cheese & Tomatoes Sliders {page 98}. Cool the fresh rolls completely before wrapping them tightly in plastic wrap/cling film for the next day, or freeze for up to 2 weeks.*

GET YEAST SMART: If you've never worked with yeast before, or if you don't have a thermometer to test the temperature of the water, try this: Dip your finger in the warm water. It should be slightly warmer than your body temperature, or in other words, about like a very hot bath. To double check your judgment, sprinkle just a few grains of yeast over the water. If they soften and puff into the water, the temperature is likely just right. Add the remaining yeast and set aside until foamy {like shaving cream} and softened, about 5 minutes.

FRENCH ONION SOUP

serves 6

{a classic} The brilliance of French onion soup is its ability to turn the humblest of ingredients, the onion, into a spectacularly seductive meal. Traditionally made with caramelized onions and a touch of port, it is best served hot and bubbling from the oven, capped off with melting alpine cheese. Since I don't regularly keep port in the house, and don't like to splurge on such a small amount, I use a heady red wine with a pinch of sugar instead, which does the trick every time. Use the tastiest broth or stock you can get your hands on, best of all is one you make at home {see Better Broth, page 13}.

¼ cup/60 ml extra-virgin olive oil

1 tbsp unsalted butter

4 large yellow or Vidalia onions {about 2 lb/910 kg}, thinly sliced

A few sprigs of thyme

1 garlic clove, smashed

1 bay leaf

Kosher salt

Freshly ground black pepper

¾ cup/180 ml dry white wine

8 cups/1.4 L chicken broth or stock

6 thick slices country bread or baguette

⅓ cup/75 ml red wine

Pinch of sugar

12 oz/340 g grated Gruyère or Comté cheese

Heat the olive oil and butter in a large Dutch oven or other heavy pot over medium heat. Add the onions and thyme and cook, stirring occasionally, until the onions are deep brown and caramelized, about 40 minutes. Add the garlic and bay leaf and continue to cook another 8 minutes, seasoning with the salt {up to 1 tbsp} and pepper as you go.

Increase the heat to medium-high and add the white wine. Bring the wine to a boil and cook until about half evaporates, about 3 minutes. Add the broth and decrease the heat to medium. Simmer the soup until it is fragrant and just a touch thickened, about 40 minutes.

During the last 10 minutes of cooking the soup, preheat the broiler/grill to medium-low and toast the bread slices. Pull the thyme and bay leaf out of the pot and stir in the red wine and pinch of sugar.

Arrange six ovenproof bowls on one or two rimmed baking sheets/trays. Divide the soup among the bowls. Top each bowl of soup with a slice of toasted bread and sprinkle the Gruyère over the top. Place the baking sheet/tray with the bowls on the top oven rack about 6 in/15 cm from the broiler/grill element. Broil/grill until the cheese is melted and starting to turn golden brown, about 3 minutes. {Don't broil them too long or the fat will separate out of the cheese and become oily.} Carefully transfer the bowls onto plates and serve bubbling hot.

GROWN-UP MAC 'N' CHEESE

serves 4 to 6

{three cheers for cheese!} **Though it takes a little more foresight to make mac 'n' cheese from scratch, you'll be so glad you did. This one is baked stovetop and finished under the broiler for a bubbly top without all the fuss.**

For a small crowd of good buddies, we make this in a cast-iron frying pan. Smother the top with Muenster cheese, broil it, and bring it right to the table with four spoons and a stack of bowls. Watch them ooh and ah and dip back in for seconds while you sit back and enjoy their company. Serve with a large green salad tossed with a crisp, mustardy dressing.

Fine sea salt

10 oz/280 g regular or whole-wheat/wholemeal rigatoni, gemelli, ziti, or macaroni pasta

4 tbsp/55 g unsalted butter

2 tsp white whole-wheat/wholemeal or all-purpose/plain flour

1½ tsp dry mustard

1 tsp warm water

1½ cups/360 ml whole, 2-percent, or 1-percent milk

2 large eggs, lightly beaten

¼ tsp cayenne pepper

1½ cups/170 g grated sharp Cheddar cheese

1½ cups/170 g grated Gruyère or Comté cheese

3 slices Muenster cheese {about 2½ oz/70 g}

Freshly ground black pepper

Bring a large pot of water to a boil over medium-high heat. Salt generously and cook the pasta until al dente, 10 to 12 minutes depending on the shape. Drain the pasta and set aside.

In the same pot, melt the butter. Add the flour and cook until lightly toasted. Meanwhile, dissolve the mustard powder in the warm water. Add the milk and mustard to the pot and whisk until smooth. Cook over medium-low heat until the sauce thickens slightly. Whisk in the eggs, ½ teaspoon salt, and the cayenne and stir constantly with a flat-edged wooden spoon, trailing the bottom of the pan to make sure it

doesn't curdle, until the sauce thickens, about 5 minutes. Stir in the Cheddar and Gruyère cheeses over low heat. Remove from the heat as soon as about half the cheese is melted. Continue stirring off the heat until all the cheese melts. Add the cooked pasta and stir to coat.

Preheat the broiler/grill to high.

Transfer the macaroni to a 1-qt/1-L ovenproof baking dish and lay the Muenster cheese over the top. Broil/grill on the top rack of the oven until golden and bubbly, about 2 minutes. Top with freshly ground pepper. Serve immediately.

MAKE-AHEAD LASAGNA

serves 8 to 10 {or 2, with leftovers}

{easier than you thought} Lasagna is the kind of food that can keep a man happy for many nights in a row. The very best thing about it is that you can prepare the whole thing a day before, and store it in the fridge overnight to bake up fresh right before dinner. Bring it out for cold rainy nights and serve up leftovers that get better for days.

This one is light and lively, and won't derail you from your pact to help each other stay fit and trim. The secret is in the sauce {marinara}, simple and homemade by you with just 30 minutes of simmering on the stovetop. There's something mystical about homemade sauce. It's the subtle natural sweetness of stewed tomatoes that shine, especially when they aren't overloaded with too many spices or sugar. If you're in a rush, let yourself off the hook with a jar of your favorite store-bought sauce, but check the ingredients first since too sweet a sauce {sugar should be low down on the list} can overpower the savory satisfaction of the whole meal. Serve with a big green salad.

MARINARA

¼ cup/60 ml extra-virgin olive oil

4 garlic cloves, smashed

Two 32-oz cans whole, peeled San Marzano tomatoes, with juice

2 bay leaves

Pinch of dried thyme or basil {optional}

2 or 3 sprigs of fresh basil

1 tsp sea salt

Freshly ground black pepper

LASAGNA

Iodized salt

8 oz/225 g dried lasagna noodles

1 lb/455 g ground grass-fed beef

One 16-oz/455-g container organic, whole-milk cottage cheese

2 large eggs, beaten

½ cup/60 g freshly grated Parmigiano-Reggiano cheese

Freshly ground black pepper

8 oz/225 g fresh mozzarella cheese

8 oz/225 g shredded mozzarella cheese

MAKE THE MARINARA: Heat the oil in a large pot over medium heat. Add the garlic and cook until fragrant, 3 minutes. Add the tomatoes, crushing through your fingers as you pour them in the pan. Add the bay leaves, dried thyme, and basil and cook until the sauce thickens, about 30 minutes, crushing the tomatoes further with a wooden spoon to help them break down. Season with the salt and pepper. Pull out and discard the bay leaves and basil. You should have about 4 cups/960 ml of sauce. Reserve 2½ cups/600 ml of sauce for the lasagna, and freeze the remaining 1½ cups/360 ml of sauce for your next pasta dinner.

CONTINUED

MAKE THE LASAGNA: Preheat the oven to 350°F/180°C/ gas 4.

Bring a large pot of salted water to a boil. Cook the lasagna noodles until al dente, about 12 minutes. Drain.

Heat a large skillet over medium heat and add the beef. Cook, stirring occasionally, until browned through. Transfer to a bowl with a slotted spoon, leaving excess fat behind.

In a medium bowl, mix together the cottage cheese, eggs, and ¼ cup/30 g of the Parmigiano-Reggiano, and season with a pinch of salt and a few grinds of black pepper.

Slice the fresh mozzarella as thin as possible with a sharp knife, season lightly with salt, and drain on paper towels/absorbent paper.

Lightly brush a 9-by-13-in/23-by-33-cm ovenproof pan with olive oil. Line the bottom with drained noodles. Add a third of the sauce, and half the cottage cheese mixture. Sprinkle on half of the meat and top with a layer of shredded mozzarella. Repeat with remaining noodles, another third of the sauce, and the rest of the cottage cheese mixture and meat. Finish with any remaining sauce and finally the slices of fresh mozzarella, sprinkling on the remaining Parmigiano-Reggiano cheese.

Cover with aluminum foil and bake for 20 minutes. Remove the foil and continue baking until the cheese bubbles and the lasagna is warmed through, 20 minutes more. Remove from the oven and let cool about 15 minutes before slicing. Serve immediately.

P.S. *You can use no-boil lasagna noodles to save yourself a step. Keep the lasagna covered for the first 30 minutes of cooking so the steam can soften and cook the noodles.*

MAKE IT MEATLESS: This lasagna is light and delicious with sliced zucchini/courgette instead of the meat. Slice 1 large zucchini/courgette into long, thick slices. Salt them well and drain between layers of paper towels/absorbent paper to release the moisture for at least 30 minutes. Layer into the lasagna along with the cheese mixture and top with regular {not fresh or buffalo, since it will make the zucchini version too wet} mozzarella. Bake as instructed in the regular recipe.

SUCCULENT BARBECUED CHICKEN

serves 4

{what's your secret?} There are hundreds of ways to make barbecue sauce. Depending on what part of the country you're from, it can be a topic for hot debate. In my opinion, good barbecue is all about the sweet and the tang and only gets better with a little heat. This one gets its sweet from maple syrup, its tang from cider vinegar, and its heat from Sriracha Thai hot sauce. Slather it all over juicy cage-free chicken and you just might win the neighborhood barbecue crown.

The cardinal mistake of a barbecue novice {including me, until my baby bro clued me in} is putting the sauce on the bird too early, which can burn the sauce and give it a bitter taste. Put the sauce on at the last 5 minutes of cooking to preserve all of that lip-smacking succulence.

BARBECUE SAUCE

4 tbsp/55 g unsalted butter

1 yellow onion, chopped

¾ cup/180 ml apple cider vinegar

¾ cup/180 ml water

2 tbsp tomato paste

⅓ to ½ cup/75 to 120 ml maple syrup

¼ cup/60 ml anejo tequila or bourbon {optional}

2 tbsp Worcestershire sauce

1 tbsp Dijon or spicy brown mustard

1 to 3 tbsp Sriracha sauce

Freshly ground black pepper

CHICKEN

Vegetable oil

8 free-range or organic chicken pieces {white, dark, or a mix}, about 3 lb/1.4 kg

Kosher salt

Freshly ground black pepper

MAKE THE SAUCE: Melt the butter in a medium saucepan over low heat. Add the onion and cook until soft, about 4 minutes. Add the vinegar, the water, tomato paste, maple syrup, tequila {if using}, Worcestershire sauce, mustard, and Sriracha sauce {start with the smaller amounts of both maple syrup and Sriracha}. Increase the heat to medium-low and simmer until the onions are incredibly soft and the sauce is slightly thickened, about 20 minutes. Taste and add additional maple syrup if needed, and all the remaining Sriracha you can stand if you like heat. Puree in a blender or with an immersion blender until completely smooth. Season with black pepper.

While the barbecue sauce simmers, bring your chicken to room temperature about 30 minutes before cooking.

PREPARE THE CHICKEN: Preheat the grill until the grates are hot but the hickory or coals or gas flame is medium-low. Brush the grill grates with oil.

Pat the chicken skin dry with paper towels/absorbent papers and rub all over lightly with oil. Season the chicken all over with salt and pepper.

Arrange the chicken on the grill and cook on one side until the skin is beginning to crisp and the chicken is halfway cooked through, about 20 minutes. Turn the chicken over and cook until it is golden, about 15 minutes. Brush all the chicken pieces generously with barbecue sauce and continue cooking until crisp, 5 minutes more. Serve hot off the grill.

BUTTERMILK
FRIED CHICKEN

serves 6

Fried chicken can make a mess of your kitchen. But there are many captivating reasons to go for it. The first is the crispiest buttermilk coating imaginable, full of salty satisfaction. The second is the flavor of a high-quality, well-raised chicken whose juices are sealed inside by their minutes in simmering hot oil. There's nothing like it.

The secret to the best fried chicken is to put lots of flavor in your buttermilk soak. I like to get heat from a heaping tablespoon of freshly ground black pepper and a bit of cayenne. Many people use dried onion powder and garlic powder in their coating to make sure it's also full of flavor {just a little pinch of each}, but you can glam yours up with za'atar, fresh thyme, or whatever herb or spice you find the most exciting.

For the very best texture, put your chicken in the buttermilk brine to tenderize the minute you get home from the market and let it soak until you're ready to cook, even up to overnight. This will save you some time and increase the flavor every hour it soaks.

BUTTERMILK BRINE	COATING
3 cups/720 ml buttermilk	2 cups all-purpose/plain flour
2 tbsp kosher salt	1 tbsp za'atar or 1 tsp chopped fresh thyme or oregano leaves {optional}
1 tbsp freshly ground black pepper	
1 tsp cayenne pepper	1 tsp kosher salt
	1 tsp freshly ground black pepper
4 lb/1.8 kg organic chicken pieces {wings, thighs, drumsticks, and breasts}	Vegetable oil, for frying

MAKE THE BRINE: Whisk together the buttermilk, salt, black pepper, and cayenne in a large bowl.

Cut any chicken breasts in half crosswise with a sharp knife. Add the chicken parts to the buttermilk mixture and stir to coat all the pieces. Cover with plastic wrap/cling film and let sit at room temperature for 2 hours or refrigerate up to overnight.

MAKE THE COATING: Mix the flour, za'atar or other spices, salt, and black pepper in a large, sturdy plastic bag; set aside.

Meanwhile, heat 1 in/2.5 cm of vegetable oil in a large, deep frying pan over medium heat until it reaches 350°F/180°C/gas 4 on a deep-fat thermometer; keep steady on low heat. While the oil preheats, organize what you'll need and keep it handy so you're not forced to run around the kitchen like a chicken with your head cut off when there's hot oil on the stove.

Set a baking rack on a baking sheet/tray {to hold the coated, uncooked chicken pieces}. Set up a second rack on a baking sheet/tray lined with paper towels/absorbent paper {to hold the fried chicken pieces}.

Pull your chicken pieces, one at a time, from the soak and shake a little to let the excess drip off. Add one piece of soaked chicken to the bag of coating at a time and shake to coat it completely. Transfer it to the first rack to sit as you dredge all the pieces {the longer you let them sit, the crispier your chicken will be; 20 minutes is about right}.

Check the oil temperature again. It should read just under 350°F/180°C/gas 4 and will drop slightly, to about 320°F/165°C as you add chicken pieces. This is the perfect temp for frying. Fry the chicken a few pieces at a time until golden brown and an instant-read meat thermometer inserted into the thickest part of the chicken reads 165°F/74°C, about 15 minutes. If your new set of pots and pans came with a splatter screen, use it, as the chicken tends to pop and sizzle enthusiastically. Transfer to the second rack and let stand as you prepare the remaining chicken.

Serve sizzling with a stack of napkins.

ZA'ATAR, a Mediterranean dried herb blend that you can buy in specialty stores and ethnic markets, is mixed with ground sesame seeds, salt, thyme, and sumac. It's a quick fix of flavor that perks up chicken, lamb, and small cuts of beef or chicken equally. If you can't find it, a mix of fresh or dried chopped thyme, oregano, and parsley will do the trick. Use leftovers to spice up Buttermilk Fried Chicken, or toss with Roasted Winter Vegetables {page 193}.

DOUBLE-DIP ROAST CHICKEN

serves 2 {with leftovers} or 4

{no basting required} No matter how many elaborate things you master in the kitchen, few things will make you more unabashedly proud than a crisp, golden roast chicken. It's hard to say what is the very best thing about roast chicken: The smell of the lemons, chicken, and herbs wafting through the house? The crispy skin? Or picking apart the juicy, lukewarm leftovers for chicken salad for lunch the next day? One thing is for sure, a properly roasted chicken is so good you'll want to dip back into it to more than once.

This chicken uses the same ingredients to flavor the meat as in the Gremolata in Big-Flavor Braised Short Ribs {page 178}, so plan to make the chicken and short ribs the same week when you'll already have most of the herbs and aromatics you'll need. Start with the healthiest bird you can find {I recommend free-range, organic, or kosher}. Best of all, there is no basting, which keeps the heat inside the oven where it will do its work creating golden, crispy skin. Check out all the brown, crispy drippings in the pan. Sop them up with some crusty bread and serve it alongside the meat with Don't-You-Dare Mashed Potatoes {page 187} and a big green salad.

1 small roasting chicken
{about 3 to 3½ lb/1.4 to 1.6 kg}

1 lemon

⅓ cup coarsely chopped fresh flat-leaf parsley

1 tbsp extra-virgin olive oil

Kosher salt

Freshly ground black pepper

½ small onion or 1 shallot

2 or 3 garlic cloves

4 tbsp/55 g unsalted butter, melted

Preheat the oven to 500°F/260°C/gas 10. While the oven preheats, pat the chicken dry and remove anything from the cavity. Let it sit at room temp while the oven preheats.

Use a vegetable peeler to strip two or three long pieces of lemon zest from the lemon. Slice the zest strips as thinly as possible with a sharp knife {reserving the lemon} and stir together with the parsley and olive oil in a medium bowl. Season the lemon mixture with a pinch of salt and black pepper. Gently separate the skin from the breast of the chicken by sliding your fingers between the skin and flesh of the chicken. Spread this herb-lemon mixture under the skin next to the breast.

Quarter the zested lemon and stuff two quarters into the cavity of the bird along with the onion and as many garlic cloves as you see fit. Generously season the bird all over with salt and black pepper, and set it breast-side up on a roasting rack or wire rack set on a rimmed baking sheet/tray. Tie the legs together with kitchen twine and pour the melted butter over the breast and legs.

CONTINUED

Roast until the bird just starts to brown all over, about 25 minutes. Cover the breast of the bird with a double sheet of aluminum foil folded in a triangle like a tent. Decrease the oven temperature to 300°F/150°C/gas 2 and continue roasting until the bird is plump and golden and cooked through, about 35 minutes more. To test the chicken for doneness, tilt the pan and watch the juices that run out of the cavity of the chicken; if they are clear with a few streaks of red, the chicken is cooked through. If the juices are cloudy and pink, let the chicken cook 5 to 10 minutes more. If the juices are perfectly clear, pull the chicken out immediately, the chicken may be slightly overcooked {but don't worry, with all that flavor it will still be delicious}. If you have an instant-read thermometer, stick it into the bird between the thigh and the breast. It should read 165°F/74°C when done.

When just cooked through, remove the bird from the oven and let it rest 20 minutes before serving to let the juices soak into the meat before carving. Don't skip this part or you'll loose all the good flavor into the grooves of your cutting board.

P.S. *To make chicken salad, pick every juicy morsel from the bones and stir together with 1 chopped apple or rib of celery, a handful of chopped onion or scallions, and ¹⁄₂ cup/120 ml mayo or Greek yogurt. Season with salt and pepper, and slather on soft bread.*

{ EASY ROAST VEGETABLES }

{make it a meal} Make roast chicken into a meal in no time flat, letting the flavor and aromatics for the chicken drip down to flavor the veggies. Or use roasted vegetables, especially roasted tomatoes, as a quick garnish for Baked Risotto {page 115} or Iron-Skillet Steak {page 176}. Swap in any other small, favorite roasting vegetable.

Several cloves of garlic

6 baby potatoes, halved

1 onion, quartered

3 carrots, cut into chunks

2 parsnips, cut into chunks

1 pint sweet cherry tomatoes

Olive oil for tossing

Salt and pepper

If not roasting with the Double-Dip Roast Chicken, preheat the oven to 500°F/260°C/gas 10.

In a large bowl, toss the garlic and vegetables with olive oil and season with salt and pepper. Spread the mixture on a baking sheet {or arrange the vegetables under the chicken's roasting rack} and roast for about 45 minutes, until they are browned and tender when pierced with a fork. Give the pan a good shake halfway through cooking, after about 20 minutes, to turn the vegetables around for even cooking.

Serve immediately.

PAN-FRIED PORK CHOPS

serves 2

{blue plate special} This recipe is old school, but if your hubby is a meat eater, this is sure to make him happy. Thick-cut pork chops, lightly breaded and fried, are a juicy and tender mess of meat that requires some buttery Don't-You-Dare Mashed Potatoes {page 187} for sopping it all up. Serve with green beans and a big salad.

2 thick-cut pork loin chops
{2 lb/910 g, about 1½ in/4 cm thick}

1 large egg

½ teaspoon kosher salt, plus more for seasoning

½ teaspoon freshly ground black pepper, plus more for seasoning

½ cup/60 g all-purpose/plain flour

½ tsp baking powder

Pinch of cayenne pepper

Vegetable oil

Preheat the oven to 325°F/165°C/gas 3. Line a baking pan with a wire rack. Pat the chops dry on all sides with a paper towel/absorbent paper and discard the towel. Beat the egg in a shallow dish and season with a little salt and pepper.

Combine the flour, salt, black pepper, baking powder, and cayenne in another shallow dish. Dip both sides of the chops into the beaten egg. Add the pork chops to the flour mixture and turn to coat both sides. Pat the pork chops to shake off excess until they are evenly coated.

Heat a large frying pan over medium heat and fill with just enough oil to cover by about ¼ in/6mm. Increase the heat to medium-high and heat the oil until it shimmers. Add the pork chops and cook until golden brown and crisp on one side, about 5 minutes. Flip and repeat on the other side.

Put the pork chops on the wire rack in the baking pan and bake until the chops are cooked through and the internal temperature registers 160°F/65°C on an instant-read ther-mometer, about 8 minutes.

Remove and let rest 5 to 8 minutes before serving.

PORK PRIMER: The "other white meat" is full of iron, magnesium, thiamin, vitamins B_{12} and B_6, and zinc, so even though cured, fatty cuts like bacon have given pork a bad rap, chops are a pretty delicious part of a balanced diet.

These days, haute-pork producers are sending their Berkshire and Mangalista pigs to butcher, which means better chops, ham, and prosciutto for the rest of us if you're into seeking out the extra good stuff. No matter where your pork comes from, it is best with a thin layer of fat for flavor.

If and when you decide to go a healthier route, leaner cuts of pork like pork loin and tenderloin all benefit from a little brine. Here's a good starting point:

{ BASIC BRINE FOR PORK }

for one 2 to 3 lb/1 to 1.4 kg pork loin
or two pork tenderloins

5 cups/1.2 L water, at room temperature

6 tbsp/35 g sugar

3½ tbsp kosher salt

2 bay leaves

5 whole black peppercorns

Combine 1 cup/240 ml of the water, the sugar, salt, bay leaves, and peppercorns in a medium saucepan. Bring to a simmer over medium-high heat and simmer until the sugar dissolves. Remove from the heat, let cool, and add the remaining 4 cups/2 L water. Rinse the pork and pat dry, and add it to the brine in the pot. Fully submerge the pork with a plate on top to hold it under the liquid, and refrigerate for 2 days for tenderloin and up to 3 days for loin. Remove the pork from the brine, rinse under cold water, and pat very dry with paper towels/absorbent paper.

Rub the tenderloin with olive oil, season with salt and pepper, and cook as desired.

PLENTY OF POT ROAST

serves 6 to 8

{*make leftovers count*} One of the best things about pot roast is all of the tender, juicy carrots and potatoes that cook alongside the meat, flavored with the cooking liquid. But there is rarely enough. This pot roast is bursting with flavor and veggies, plenty to savor and serve for several nights or turn into a sandwich for dipping in the flavorful juice.

One 5-lb/2.3-kg chuck roast, tied	1 bunch fresh parsley
Sea salt	1 bay leaf
Freshly ground black pepper	1 large bunch of carrots {about 1 lb/455 g}, peeled and cut into chunks
2 to 4 tbsp/30 to 60 ml extra-virgin olive oil or canola oil	2 stalks celery, cut into chunks
2 large yellow onions, cut into wedges	20 small new potatoes {about 1¼ lb/570 g}, halved
Splash of apple cider vinegar	Pinch of crushed celery seeds
4 cups/960 ml {or more} water	

Season meat generously all over with salt and freshly ground pepper and set it aside for 30 minutes.

Preheat the oven to 325°F/165°C/gas 3.

Heat the oil in a large Dutch oven or other heavy ovenproof pot over medium-high heat. Brown the meat on all sides until deep brown, about 15 minutes. Add the onions and brown, nestled between the roast and the sides of the pan. Add the splash of vinegar and scrape the brown bits off the bottom of the pan. Turn off the heat and add just enough water to cover the meat half way {about 4 cups}.

Tear the stems off the parsley and reserve the leaves. Tie the stems together with a bay leaf using kitchen twine and tuck into the water with the onions. Cover the pot and transfer to the oven. Cook about 1 hour.

Remove the pot roast from the oven and add the carrots, celery, and potatoes and stir to distribute the vegetables evenly. Sprinkle the celery seeds over the veggies. Cover and return to the oven and cook until the meat is tender and vegetables are just cooked through, 1½ hours more.

Remove from the oven and transfer the meat to a cutting board to rest 10 minutes.

Place the roast on a cutting board so the longest part is lying from left to right {this should be the same direction that the fibers of the meat run}. Slice just enough meat as needed, perpendicular to the roast, using a very sharp knife, cutting against the grain, making slices about ¼ in/6 mm thick. Serve with the veggies on a platter with sloped sides to catch the juices. Strain the jus into a pitcher or gravy boat, pour a little over the meat, and serve the rest on the side. Wrap up any leftovers, keeping the extra meat in one large portion, and pour extra jus over the top to help preserve its juiciness until you dip back into it.

A WELL-SEASONED ROAST: Before you start a roast of any kind, bring your meat completely to room temperature. Season it well on all sides, cover, and leave it at room temperature. If you have the time, pre-season the meat about an hour or so before cooking; it's your best head start to a tender, juicy piece of meat.

FRENCH DIP

serves 4

One of the best things about pot roast is the leftovers, and all the flavorful meat jus. Slice and serve it up on a warm baguette *au jus* {with juice}, warmed, for dipping.

1 fresh baguette

4 tbsp/55 g melted butter

¼ cup/60 ml prepared horseradish

1 lb/455 g leftover Plenty of Pot Roast {facing page} or fresh roast beef

2 cups/480 ml leftover jus from the pot roast, warmed through

Preheat oven to 400°F/200°C/gas 6.

Halve the baguette lengthwise and then crosswise into four segments to make four large sandwiches. Brush both cut sides of the bread with melted butter and toast in the oven on the rack or on a tray until just warm, about 4 minutes. Spread on a generous layer of horseradish.

Slice the leftover pot roast very thinly against the grain using a sharp carving knife. Microwave the meat and jus to just warm through, about 2 minutes, before stacking the meat on the bread. Or divide the sliced meat evenly between the bread and return to it to the oven to warm through. Meanwhile, heat the jus on the stovetop. Serve warm sandwiches with jus in small bowls on the side, for dipping.

SOUTHERN SHRIMP & GRITS

serves 4

{homey goodness} If you haven't yet learned to love grits, get yourselves to a Southern establishment. Or better yet, learn to make them for yourself at home. Comforting, filling, and full of pleasure, grits are like a soothing Southern version of polenta with the same sweet corn flavor that makes cornbread a hit in most homes. This is fill-your-belly food that's even easy to fancy-up a little for company.

GRITS

2 cups/480 ml whole milk

1 cup/240 ml water

2 tbsp/30 g unsalted butter

½ tsp salt

¾ cup/135 g quick-cooking grits

SHRIMP/PRAWNS

1 lb/455 g wild-caught or sustainably-raised shrimp/prawns, shelled and deveined

3 tbsp extra-virgin olive oil

Kosher salt

Freshly ground black pepper

½ lemon

2 oz/55 g sharp white Cheddar or Manchego cheese, grated

TO MAKE THE GRITS: Combine the milk with the water, butter, and salt in a large saucepan over medium-high heat. Bring to a roaring boil and slowly whisk in the grits. Decrease the heat to medium low. Continue whisking until no lumps remain, about 12 minutes. Decrease the heat to low. Cover the pan, and let the grits simmer while you finish the other component.

TO PREPARE THE SHRIMP/PRAWNS: Heat a medium pan over medium-high heat. Toss the seafood together with the oil in a small bowl and season lightly with salt and pepper.

Add the shrimp to the hot pan and cook, stirring, until each one is just pink throughout, 2 to 4 minutes, depending on the size of the shellfish. Turn off the heat, squeeze the lemon over the top to release all the good bits from the pan, and make a light, flavorful sauce.

To serve, remove the grits from the heat and stir in the cheese. Spoon into four shallow bowls and spoon on the shrimp and pan sauce. Serve hot.

P.S. *Grits can stand on their own as good eating any time of the day, and make a fine addition to an Easter ham or Passover lamb.*

CHAPTER 7

DATE NIGHT

Romantic Meals for Each Other

Okay hubs, this chapter is for you. You've heard that you should never stop dating your wife right? Even the most stoic among us secretly likes a little romance. Tonight's the night to put in a little extra effort. Make gnocchi from scratch {I guarantee she will love coming to your rescue if you find yourself in a floury mess}, or splurge on that steak you've been dreaming of {I'll show you how to make it look like it's just for her}.

Ladies, if your hubby has been cooking for you all week, it's your turn to show him a little extra love. You can create all the seduction and surprise you've been wishing for at your own table. And I bet you anything that with a bottle of wine and big bowl of Moroccan Couscous {page 170} between you, he'll be much more inspired about that trip to North Africa.

Some date nights are even better when you're both in on the anticipation. These meals, like Swirls of Spaghetti with Sweet Corn & Chanterelles {page 165}, are fun to shop for, prep for, and make together. Set the table and open that bottle of wine you've been saving for a special occasion. This is the special occasion, a meal made especially for and with the one you love.

When you're choosing a wine to cook with, use something good enough to drink, which will make a huge difference in the final outcome of your dish.

BOTTLE OF RED, BOTTLE OF WHITE

There's something about date night that makes it seem like a good idea to open a bottle of wine. Sometimes the best part of the date is going to a wine store to pick out the wine together. You shouldn't need to take out a second mortgage to have a good pour. Here are a few words of wisdom on how to choose and what to look for.

- The best wine experts will tell you there is no direct equation between a wine's cost and the pleasure it can provide. Save extravagant splurges for your anniversary. For the dinner at hand, simply ask the expert at your wine shop {or the sommelier if you're dining out} what modest treasures lie within your reach.
- Don't be fooled by flashy labels. Some are cheeky and playful enough to warrant a taste {tasting, if you can, before buying is always good!}, but sometimes the most unassuming packages conceal a coveted wine.
- Like with food, what grows together goes together. Consider the meal and its origin and look for a wine with similar roots.
- Learn how to describe what you like using, whatever flavors and textures come to mind, then find a wine merchant you can trust, and one whose tastes most closely match your own.
- Don't allow wine to intimidate you. There are thousands of wines to learn about and enjoy, but the best wine is always the empty bottle sitting between you and the one you love.

{ SIX GRAPES TO LOVE }

In addition to the well known chardonnay, pinot grigio, pinot noir, syrah, cabernet sauvignon, and merlot grapes, here are five grapes to look for and love.

GRENACHE {RED}: This is a generous, easy-going cousin to syrah, with a richer fruit profile. Subtle pepper, herb, and wild berry notes.

MOURVÈDRE {RED}: The tall, dark, and handsome of grapes. Black, inky, and easy to fall for.

TEMPRANILLO {RED}: The infallible food wine. Easy to drink and on the rise, but remains a good value.

SANGIOVESE {RED}: An excellent food-pairing wine from Italy. Balanced mouth-watering acidity and bright red fruit.

SAUVIGNON BLANC {WHITE}: Snappy and breezy. Pairs well with most lighter meals {gazpacho is its classic pairing}.

CHENIN BLANC {WHITE}: Slightly sweet. Something for everyone and every dish, from pizza to peach pie.

When you're choosing a wine to cook with, use something good enough to drink, which will make a huge difference in the final outcome of your dish.

SPLURGE: For special occasions, don't forget to break out the bubbly and splurge on something that might normally be out of the question. You never get to relive your first anniversary, the big promotion, or the day you saw the two little pink lines on the pregnancy test. Find your own ways to commemorate the moment. Save your cork or wine labels, snap a photo of this special meal, or write down the menu in your prettiest script and tuck it away for a rainy day game of "remember when."

TWO-FOR-TWO CHEESE SOUFFLÉ

serves 2

{*don't miss this*} There is nothing cozier than a cheese soufflé for two. Light a candle, bring the dish to the table with two forks and an herb-y salad for two, and let the world melt away.

Sip: An American brown ale

½ cup/60 g finely grated aged Parmigiano-Reggiano cheese, plus 2 tbsp for topping

1 tbsp unsalted butter, at room temperature, plus more for buttering and brushing

2 tbsp all-purpose/plain flour

Pinch of nutmeg

¾ tsp kosher salt

¾ cup/180 ml whole milk

½ small garlic clove, minced or pressed

¾ cup/85 g finely grated semihard cheese such as Manchego, Gruyère, or Comté, or a blend

3 large eggs, separated

½ tsp freshly squeezed lemon juice

Preheat the oven to 375°F/190°C/gas 5 with the rack in the middle of the oven. Butter an 8-cup/2-L soufflé mold and sprinkle with Parmigiano-Reggiano to coat completely all the way to the top. Shake any excess cheese out into a bowl. Put the mold in the freezer to chill.

Melt the butter in a medium saucepan over low heat. Whisk in the flour, nutmeg, and salt. Whisking constantly, cook the flour without browning, about 5 minutes. Whisk in the milk and garlic and continue to cook, whisking, at a low simmer until the mixture is smooth and thick like pudding, about 5 minutes.

Stir in the Manchego and any Parmigiano-Reggiano left over from coating the molds and cook, stirring, until the cheese melts. Remove from the heat and stir in the egg yolks, one at a time. Continue stirring vigorously with a rubber spatula to cool.

Whisk the egg whites and lemon juice in a spotless medium bowl with an electric mixer on medium-high until they just hold a soft peak. The key is to not overwhip the whites, which would give your soufflé a cloudy instead of creamy consistency.

Fold one-fourth of the egg whites into the cheese mixture with a rubber spatula, carefully turning the bowl and mixing gently until the whites are streaked throughout. Add the remaining whites and fold in but don't overmix, which can deflate the whites.

Transfer the batter to the chilled mold and scatter the 2 tbsp Parmigiano-Reggiano over the top. Place the dish on a baking sheet/tray and set in the oven, decrease the oven temperature to 325°F/165°C/gas 3, and bake until the soufflé is golden, puffed, and set but just a touch wobbly inside, 30 to 40 minutes. Serve immediately.

CHEESE PRIMER: A cheese soufflé is the sexiest way imaginable to use up leftover cheese since it benefits from a blend of different kinds. I like to use Spanish Manchego for the soufflé's tender insides, and a well-aged Parmigiano-Reggiano for a crisp, golden crust. Other cheeses like Gruyère or Comté, semihard alpine cheeses that age slightly sweet and buttery, are classic and excellent choices for a soufflé as well.

GARDENER'S PIZZA

 *makes enough dough for a double date;*
or two date nights {4 pizzas or 2 large ones}

{sauceless} When we found out our friends Katie and Parker got engaged, we packed up our pizza dough and big bag of greens from our garden and headed to their place for an impromptu celebration that's become a tradition in both our homes. Though the best pizza dough takes a little preparation, a pizza topped with little more than fresh farmers' market finds can be thrown together on the fly like a grand game of Twister, with everyone's arms cutting, slicing, patting, and rolling in a tangle that is soon to become a very good dinner.

Sip: Snappy and crisp sauvignon blanc from New Zealand

PIZZA DOUGH

Generous pinch of sugar

1¼ cups/300 ml warm water {about 110°F/45°C}

One ¼-oz/7-g package active dry yeast

2 tbsp extra-virgin olive oil, plus more for drizzling

2 cups/255 g bread/strong flour

1 to 1¼ cups/175 to 200 g whole-wheat/wholemeal or white whole-wheat/wholemeal flour

1 tsp fine sea salt

Cornmeal or semolina flour

4 to 6 oz/115 to 170 g cheese, such as shredded or fresh mozzarella, burrata, or fresh ricotta

2 garlic cloves, very thinly sliced

2 to 4 handfuls fresh veggies such as sliced tomatoes, arugula/rocket, sorrel, shaved zucchini/courgette, kale, Swiss chard, corn, or mushrooms {see toppings page 276}

Handful of fresh herbs, such as basil, opal basil

Parmigiano-Reggiano cheese

Extra-virgin olive oil

Fine sea salt

Freshly ground black pepper

MAKE THE DOUGH: Whisk the pinch of sugar into the warm water in a small bowl and sprinkle the yeast over the top {yeast feeds on sugar so this helps to wake it up and get it going}.

Stir 3 cups/385 g of the flours and salt together in a large bowl or the bowl of a stand mixer to combine {reserving ¼ cup/30 g of the flour for later}. Make a well in the center and pour in the yeast mixture. Stir with a fork or the dough hook to make a shaggy dough. If making the dough by hand, stir vigorously with a wooden spoon to work the gluten for about 5 minutes until the dough is smooth. Then turn onto a lightly floured countertop and knead until the dough is smooth and elastic, about 5 minutes, adding small sprinkles of flour as needed to just keep it from sticking. If you're using a stand mixer fitted with the dough hook, beat on high speed until the dough comes together and slaps the side of the bowl, about 5 minutes, adding up to ¼ cup/30 grams of the remaining flour as needed to create a cohesive ball.

CONTINUED

Divide the dough in half {for large pizzas} or quarters {for small pizzas} and form into balls. Place each ball of dough in a lightly oiled plastic bag, seal, and refrigerate overnight {it gets more supple as it sits overnight} or up to 3 days {or freeze for up to 1 week}.

Remove the dough from the fridge 2 hours before you plan to cook. Oil two or four bowls {depending on whether you are making two large or four individual pizzas}. Turn each dough ball in the bowl to coat in oil; cover the bowl tightly with plastic wrap/cling film. Draw a circle around the top to mark where the dough is now, so you can watch it expand. Set aside in a warm place until doubled, about 2 hours.

Position a pizza stone on the bottom rack of your oven. Preheat the oven to 475°F/240°C/gas 9 at least 45 minutes before you plan to bake the pizzas.

Lightly dust a clean countertop and the dough with flour. Press and pat each ball of dough into a rectangle or round. Once you have the basic shape you want, stretch the dough by draping it over the back of your hands and wrists, letting it hang down so gravity does the work. For larger pizzas, aim for a 7-by-12-in/17-by-30.5-cm rectangle or a 12-inch/30.5-cm round; for individual pizzas, aim for a 6-to-9-in/15-to-23-cm round or rectangle for smaller pizzas and flatbreads, depending on how thick you like your dough. {Don't worry if it's misshapen.} Cover the dough with a towel until baking.

Generously dust a pizza peel or baking sheet/tray with cornmeal and lay on the dough, shaking the peel or sheet/tray back and forth a little to make sure the dough slides easily.

Chop or slice all the vegetables into small pieces that will cook quickly in the hot oven. Top the pizzas with any topping that needs to be cooked or melted, like cheese, sliced

garlic, mushrooms, and small pieces of vegetables that need to be cooked through {the key is to use a light hand here, since overtopped pizzas tend to turn soggy}, dividing the toppings between all the dough.

Slide the pizza onto the stone {or cook directly on the baking sheet} and bake larger pizzas one at a time, smaller ones two at a time, until puffed, crisp, and evenly baked through, about 8 to 10 minutes.

Remove and top with fresh and raw ingredients like shaved corn, sliced tomatoes, fresh basil, arugula/rocket, or sorrel. Shave or grate fresh Parmigiano-Reggiano over the top, drizzle with your best olive oil, and season with salt and black pepper.

HOMEMADE GNOCCHI
· · · · WITH · · · ·
SUMMER BEANS

serves 2 to 4

{toss with herb butter} It's time to roll up your sleeves. Grab your guy or gal, pluck some fresh baby beans from the garden, and get busy rolling your own little pillows of pasta. Gnocchi made fresh at home with pureed potatoes and flour, is a lighter, more luxurious version of the hearty dish most of us think of. This one is ethereal and bright with the snappy fresh beans and herbs and is worth every precious minute you two spend in the kitchen together. Once you become the accomplished pasta maker you always aspired to be, invite friends for a DIY double date.

Sip: Pinot gris or Aglianico

GNOCCHI DOUGH	
4 medium russet or Idaho potatoes, scrubbed {about 2½ lb/1.2 kg}	Sea salt
1 large egg, beaten	8 oz/225 g fresh green or yellow beans or haricots verts, trimmed
2 tbsp unsalted butter	2 tbsp butter
½ cup/60 g freshly grated Parmigiano-Reggiano cheese, plus more for garnish	2 tbsp fresh tarragon leaves
1¼ to 1⅓ cups/140 to 155 g all-purpose/plain flour	¼ tsp freshly ground black pepper
1 tsp sea salt	¾ cup/180 ml chicken broth or water
	2 tbsp torn or chopped fresh mint leaves, for garnish

Preheat the oven to 425°F/220°C/gas 7.

MAKE THE GNOCCHI DOUGH: Prick the potatoes all over with a fork and place on a rack in the center of the oven. Bake until the flesh is soft in the middle {can be squeezed easily with a kitchen towel} and the skin is crisp, about 1 hour. Remove from the oven.

Cool the potatoes until they are still warm but cool enough to handle. Halve them lengthwise and scoop the potato flesh into a bowl. Pass through a potato ricer, food mill, or smush through a coarse sieve to make a fine, fluffy pulp. Add the egg, butter, Parmigiano-Reggiano, 1 cup/115 g of the flour, and salt and stir together gently with a fork,

using a light touch, until the dough comes together in a soft, slightly sticky ball.

Turn the dough onto a clean, lightly floured surface and knead until it forms a soft dough, about 1 minute. Add ¼ cup/30g of the remaining flour.

Divide the dough into four pieces. Halve each piece so that you have eight small balls of dough. Roll each piece into a long rope about 12 in/30.5 cm long. Divide each rope into ¾-in/2-cm pieces using a pastry cutter or a knife. Transfer the pieces to a lightly floured plate or baking sheet/tray and cover with a dry towel until you're ready to cook them.

CONTINUED

Bring a large pot of water to a roaring boil over medium-high heat. Salt the water generously with sea salt. Add the beans and cook until bright green and crisp tender, about 6 minutes. Remove with a slotted spoon and transfer to a bowl of ice water to stop the cooking. Drain and set aside.

Return the water to a rapid boil. Add the gnocchi to the boiling water and cook until they float to the top and are firm, about 3 minutes. Drain and reserve the gnocchi in about ½ cup/120 ml of the cooking liquid to keep them warm and moist.

Melt the butter with the tarragon in a large saucepan over medium-low heat and swirl to melt and flavor the butter. Add the gnocchi, reserved cooking liquid, and green beans and toss to coat. Loosen with chicken broth {or water, if you're cooking for a vegetarian} and cook until the sauce coats the gnocchi with a glimmering sheen. Taste and season with salt and pepper.

To serve, divide the gnocchi and beans among four bowls and grate fresh Parmigiano-Reggiano over the top. Season with salt and pepper and top with mint. Serve immediately.

GREEN THUMB: Fresh beans are your first chance to give your green thumb a go. They grow like gangbusters and make you feel like a proud parent. Beans agree with almost any reasonably good garden soil. Plant directly in the ground in early spring and give them room to grow {check the seeds to see if they are bush beans, which grow wide, or pole greens, which grow tall} with a stake, post, or trellis for them to climb on. Pick beans early and often to keep them producing, and save a handful of the healthiest looking ones for next year's crop.

SWIRLS OF SPAGHETTI
· · · · WITH · · · ·
SWEET CORN & CHANTERELLES

serves 2 to 4

{dare to share} On a weekend trip to Vermont one July, we had the good fortune to go mushroom foraging with a local expert. Just off the trail, we found two handfuls of tiny, golden chanterelles that had popped up after the previous week's rain. We headed home that day, but not before stopping at a farm stand for a half-dozen ears of the sweetest corn I'd ever tasted. I can't remember ever driving so fast, rushing home to cook them both when they were still just hours old. The simple meal that followed, late in the afternoon that Sunday, was one of the best we'd ever shared—earthy mushrooms enriched with just a touch of creamy goodness, tangled up in a heavenly swirl of noodles. You don't need to know a forager to enjoy this meal for yourself, just the good instinct to head to the farmers' market in the short season when these two treasures overlap.

Sip: A beautiful white Burgundy

8 oz/225 g whole-wheat/wholemeal or plain spaghetti or bucatini pasta

2 fresh ears sweet corn

1 small zucchini/courgette

1 tbsp unsalted butter

1 to 2 tbsp extra-virgin oil

2 garlic cloves, thinly sliced

8 oz/225 g chanterelle mushrooms, cleaned and halved

Sea salt

Freshly ground black pepper

1 cup/240 ml half-and-half/half cream

Opal basil or young basil leaves for garnish {optional}

Bring a large pot of salted water to a roaring boil over medium-high heat. Add the pasta and cook until al dente, 10 to 12 minutes {bucatini will need to cook slightly longer than spaghetti}.

Meanwhile, shave off the corn kernels from the cobs in large slabs onto a cutting board using a serrated knife. Rub the cobs with the back of the knife to get all the juicy corn milk off as well {chefs call this "milking" the cob} and scrape into a bowl. Using a vegetable peeler, shave long, thin ribbons of zucchini/courgette into the bowl with the corn and set aside.

Combine the butter and olive oil in a large frying pan over medium-high heat. Add the garlic and chanterelles and cook, stirring occasionally, until the mushrooms are golden and just cooked through, 5 to 6 minutes. Taste a mushroom and adjust seasoning with salt and pepper. Don't be afraid to add a touch more salt; mushrooms need to be well seasoned to appreciate their flavor.

Add the half-and-half/half cream, decrease the heat to low, and stir until it thickens slightly and coats the mushrooms, about 2 minutes.

CONTINUED

Strain the pasta and reserve about 2 tbsp of the cooking liquid. Add the corn and zucchini/courgette to the pan with the sauce and toss over medium-high heat for about 1 minute. Add the pasta and use two forks or tongs to toss together. Add up to 2 tbsp reserved pasta cooking liquid to bring it all together and coat the pasta.

Taste and adjust the seasoning with salt and pepper {mushrooms soak up a lot of salt, so don't be surprised if you need more than you think}. Garnish with fresh basil and serve immediately.

GROW BABY BASIL: This dish is the perfect reason to grow your own basil, because you can grow many varieties and pick it while it's young, tender, and slightly sweet. Opal basil makes a beautiful garnish for this dish, but young baby basil or basil flowers are also delicious. Big, bunchy basil can overpower with anise, so use it only with a very light hand.

FRESH PAPPARDELLE
WITH
PORK RAGU

serves 2 {with lots of lunch leftovers}

{simmered seduction} In the middle of winter, there's nothing more satisfying than a plate of fresh pasta with a rich, meaty ragu. Buying prepared fresh pasta sheets frees you up to concentrate on your pork ragu and the one you love. Traditionally, ragu is made with equal parts beef and pork. I make mine with more pork for a slightly leaner sauce with all the same satisfying flavor. This recipe makes enough sauce to serve two for date night, plus loving heaps of leftovers that only improve with time.

Sip: Fresh, light red wine like barbera or dolcetto.

RAGU

3 tbsp extra-virgin olive oil

1½ lb/680 g organic ground/minced pork

½ lb/225 g organic ground/minced beef

½ large yellow onion, diced

1 stalk celery, finely chopped

1 large carrot, shredded

1 tsp kosher salt

1¼ tsp freshly ground black pepper, plus more for seasoning

3 large garlic cloves, smashed and chopped fine, or crushed

2 tbsp tomato paste

1½ cups/360 ml dry white or red wine

2 bay leaves

2 large sprigs of rosemary

1 tbsp minced fresh thyme leaves

4 cups/960 ml low-sodium or homemade chicken broth

One 28-oz/794-g can San Marzano or plum tomatoes in juice

PASTA

1 tbsp extra-virgin olive oil, plus more for drizzling

½ lb/225 g fresh egg pasta sheets for every 2 cups/480 ml of sauce

Kosher salt

TO SERVE

Parmigiano-Reggiano cheese, fresh ricotta cheese, or mascarpone cheese

A few small mint leaves

MAKE THE RAGU: Heat the oil in a large Dutch oven {or other heavy pot} or straight-sided pot {for braising} over medium heat. Add the ground/minced pork and beef and brown evenly over medium-high heat until they release their juices and fat. Scoot the meat to the side of the pan with a wooden spoon and add the onion, celery, and carrot to the pan. Cook until the vegetables are tender, 5 to 7 minutes.

Using a sturdy wooden spoon, mix the meat into the vegetables; season with about half of the salt and ¼ tsp of the pepper.

Add the garlic and tomato paste and cook to brown, 1 minute more, until the liquid has almost evaporated off the bottom of the pan. Add the wine and stir together, scraping the bottom of the pan to get all the good brown bits {this is called deglazing}. Cook until the sauce thickens slightly {or reduces}, about 5 minutes.

Add the bay leaves, rosemary, thyme, and 2 cups/ 480 ml of the chicken broth. Add the tomatoes and their juices, passing them through clean hands on the way to the pot to crush them. Cook to reduce the liquid slightly, about 15 minutes.

Add the remaining 2 cups/280 ml broth and cook, uncovered, at a slow, steady simmer with small bubbles popping up all over the surface of the sauce, for about 1½ hours. The meat should be suspended in a thick sauce. Season with the remaining black pepper and salt.

COOK THE PASTA: When the ragu is just about finished cooking, bring a large pot of generously salted water to a boil over high heat. Add the olive oil. Cut the pasta sheets with a pizza cutter or a sharp knife into 1-in-/2.5-cm-wide strips.

Drop the pasta strips, a few pieces at a time, into the boiling water. Stir after you add each bit to keep the strips from sticking to each other. Cook the pasta until al dente, 3 or 4 minutes. Drain well, saving about ½ cup/120 ml of the pasta cooking water. Drizzle the pasta with olive oil and salt.

Remove two-thirds of the sauce and cool to store for lunches and fast dinners. Add the cooked pasta to the remaining sauce and toss gently to coat.

SERVE: Divide the pasta among two shallow bowls and shave large strips of Parmigiano-Reggiano cheese over the top, or dollop with fresh ricotta or mascarpone cheese. Season with pepper and sprinkle with baby mint leaves.

P.S. *If you've got extra time and the hankering for getting your hands dirty together, this ragu goes beautifully with the Homemade Gnocchi {page 162}. It's also excellent served over Melted Polenta {page 175} for a really homey, hearty dish.*

MOROCCAN COUSCOUS

serves 2 {with leftovers}

{piled with vegetables} The aroma of a rich couscous cooking in the house inspires wanderlust for Morocco. This dish is both exotic and heart-warmingly familiar. As sophisticated as it is when it all comes together, it gets its start from a humble bunch of vegetables, giving you great return on your small investment at the market and plenty left in your budget for a beautiful bottle of something to sip.

*Sip: A crisp, refreshing Belgian saison beer or a rich,
firmly structured merlot that can hold up to harissa's heat.*

1 yellow onion, cut in large pieces

4 plum tomatoes, halved

½ lb/225 g carrots, cut in bite-size pieces,
or 1 bunch heirloom baby carrots, trimmed

1 bunch baby turnips {about 1 lb/455 g},
trimmed, peeled, and halved

1 medium zucchini/courgette

½ lb/225 g winter squash {such as butternut},
peeled and cut in thin half moons

¼ cup/60 ml extra-virgin olive oil,
plus more for drizzling

2 tsp sweet paprika

1 cinnamon stick

½ tsp ground anise seeds

2 tsp ground coriander

One 15-oz/439-g can chickpeas, rinsed and drained

½ cup/85 g golden raisins/sultanas

Kosher salt

Freshly ground black pepper

One 7-oz/200-g box plain or whole-wheat/
wholemeal couscous

1 cup/240 ml vegetable broth or chicken broth

½ cup/120 ml warm water

Handful of cilantro/fresh coriander leaves

Harissa

Soak onion, tomatoes, carrots, turnips, zucchini/courgette, and squash in cold water while you set up and measure your remaining ingredients {this helps the veggies keep their shape as they cook}.

Heat 3 tbsp of the olive oil in a large straight-sided frying pan over medium heat. Add the onion, stir to combine, and cook to soften, about 5 minutes. Add the paprika and stir to coat the onion pieces. Add half of the tomatoes, carrots, and turnips and cook to soften, about 10 minutes. Add the zucchini/courgette, 2 cups/480 ml of water, the cinnamon stick, anise, and coriander and bring to a simmer. Add the squash and continue cooking until all the vegetables are just tender but still holding their shape, about 6 minutes. Stir in

the chickpeas and raisins and stir together until the raisins plump and the chickpeas are just warmed through, about 2 minutes. Season with ¾ tsp salt and pepper.

Put the couscous in a medium bowl and ladle over 1 cup/240 ml of the vegetable broth and the ½ cup/120 ml warm water. Cover the top of the bowl with plastic wrap/cling film and set aside to steam for 5 minutes. Remove the plastic, fluff with a fork, and season with ¼ tsp salt and the remaining olive oil.

Serve the couscous in deep bowls heaped with steaming vegetables, a few cilantro/fresh coriander leaves, and harissa on the side.

SHRIMP SAGANAKI

serves 2 to 4

{one-dish dinner} It only takes a pound of fresh shrimp, salty feta, a few ripe tomatoes and 12 minutes in the sauté pan to transport you to the Greek Isles for the night. Fennel gives this Greek classic an herbaceous note that sings with the pan-roasted shrimp and sends the whole dish soaring. Serve with crusty bread.

Sip: A crisp white, such as pinot grigio

1½ lb/680 g peeled and deveined {tail on} large shrimp/prawns

2 tbsp extra-virgin olive oil

1 large bulb fennel or 1 large onion, thinly sliced

6 small vine-ripened or plum tomatoes, chopped

Kosher salt

Pinch of red pepper flakes

3 oz/85 g Greek or Bulgarian feta

1 small handful parsley, coarsely chopped

Freshly ground black pepper

Use a small pairing knife, slit the shrimp/prawns down the seam/vein about halfway through so that they open up but remain intact. Swish them in salty water {like sea water} and drain.

Heat the oil in a large frying pan until shimmering. Add the fennel and cook over medium-high heat until it is soft, stirring occasionally, about 5 minutes. Add the tomatoes, salt, and red pepper flakes and cook until the tomatoes are

soft and start to release their juices, about 5 minutes. Add the shellfish and cook, stirring occasionally until they are pink throughout, about 3 minutes. Add most of the feta and stir to heat, about 1 minute.

Transfer to shallow bowls or deep plates and top with the remaining feta and the parsley and season with freshly ground black pepper. Serve hot.

SEARED HALIBUT
WITH
CORIANDER & CARROTS

serves 2

{flirt with flavor} Season after season, I continue to be captured by the multicolored array of carrots that can be found at the farmers' market in all shapes and sizes, and am always looking for new ways to make them shine. Coriander and carrots make music together as a complement for meaty halibut. Dip your toe into the exotic flavors of Indian spices like coriander and turmeric with this lively, colorful spring supper so pretty you'll want to bring out your finest platter and pour some wine for two.

Sip: Torrontes, Sylvaner or Cabernet Franc

HALIBUT

1 tsp coriander seeds

1 tsp fennel seeds

1 tsp ground turmeric

Pinch of cayenne pepper

Two 6-oz/170-g Alaskan or Pacific halibut fillets

Sea salt

Freshly ground black pepper

2 tbsp extra-virgin olive oil

CARROTS

2 small bunches orange, red, or yellow baby carrots, trimmed and peeled

2 tbsp extra-virgin olive oil

Sea salt

1 shallot, thinly sliced

YOGURT SAUCE

¾ tsp mustard seeds

¾ cup/180 ml whole-milk yogurt

1 tsp extra-virgin olive oil

½ tsp grated fresh ginger

Sea salt

Freshly ground black pepper

2 tbsp coarsely chopped fresh parsley

CONTINUED

PREPARE THE HALIBUT: Toast the coriander and fennel seeds in a small frying pan over medium heat until fragrant, about 2 minutes. Remove from the heat and crush with a mortar and pestle, or transfer to a clean spice grinder. Grind to a fine powder. Add the turmeric and cayenne. Set aside ¼ tsp of the spice blend; reserve the remaining spice blend.

Lay out the halibut on a baking sheet/tray and season with the salt and pepper. Brush or drizzle with 1 tbsp of the olive oil and rub the remaining spice mixture over the fish on both sides. Cover and refrigerate for 1 hour.

PREPARE THE CARROTS: While the fish rests, bring a large pot of salted water to a boil. Meanwhile, fill another bowl with ice and water to create an ice bath. When the water boils, add the carrots and cook until crisp-tender, about 2 minutes. Transfer them to the ice bath with a slotted spoon. Pull them out after about 2 minutes and set aside.

MAKE THE YOGURT SAUCE: Toast the mustard seeds in a pan the same way you did with the coriander and fennel seeds. Crush or grind and stir together with the yogurt, olive oil, and grated ginger. Season with salt and pepper. Transfer to a small bowl.

When the table is set, heat a large nonstick frying pan over medium-high heat. Add the remaining 1 tbsp olive oil and heat until shimmering. Add the halibut fillets to the pan and cook untouched until they begin to release easily from the pan, about 4 minutes. Gently flip and cook the other side until the fish is just cooked through but still slightly translucent in the center. Remove the fish to the platter.

Heat the 2 tbsp olive oil in the skillet over medium-low heat. Add the carrots and toss to coat. Season with salt. Add the shallot and cook until just beginning to soften but still purple, about 2 minutes. Pull from the heat and transfer the carrots to a plate or platter. Add the ¼ teaspoon reserved spice blend to the residual oil in the pan. Spoon the flavored oil over the carrots and finish with the parsley.

Serve fish and carrots on two pretty plates or one platter with carrots. Drizzle with yogurt sauce or serve the sauce in a small bowl alongside.

WHY HALIBUT? Look for U.S. Pacific or Alaskan {Canadian Pacific} hook-and-line or wild-caught halibut. Also, check Monterey Bay Aquarium Seafood Watch for the latest news about the best choices.

GRILLED LAMB CHOPS
· · · · WITH · · · ·
MELTED POLENTA

serves 2 {with leftover polenta for lunch}

{*luscious*} Lamb chops have won my favor for their neat little packets of meat, fat, and bone that cook up with as much flavor as a T-bone in usually half the time {or price}. Melted polenta, simple and rich, is the most satisfying of savory foods and a buttery, blissful addition to any meal.

Sip: Oregon pinot, Cahors, Carbieres or an American Amber, such as Full Sail or Abita

MELTED POLENTA

3 cups/720 ml water

1 cup/140 g polenta

1 tsp salt

1¼ cups/300 ml milk

2 tbsp unsalted butter

¼ cup/30 g aged or smoked gouda cheese, grated

CHOPS

4 lamb rib or loin chops
{about 1 to 1¼ lb/570 g}

Kosher salt

Freshly ground black pepper

2 to 4 large sprigs of rosemary or tarragon

MAKE THE POLENTA: Bring the water to a boil in a medium saucepan over medium-high heat. Slowly add the polenta and stir with a wooden spoon. Season with the salt. Decrease the heat to medium and cook, stirring occasionally, until the polenta is tender and cooked through, about 20 minutes. Add the milk, butter, and cheese to the polenta and stir together over medium-low heat until just warmed through and just soft enough to drop easily from a spoon.

COOK THE LAMB CHOPS: Preheat a grill/barbecue or grill pan to medium-high, letting the flames die down if you're grilling over charcoal. Lightly oil the grill/barbecue grates. Season the lamb chops generously on both sides with

salt and pepper. Lay the rosemary on the grill and top with the lamb chops. Grill until crispy brown, about 3 to 6 minutes, depending on the thickness of the chops {loin chops are generally thicker}. Flip the chops, cover the grill {on an outdoor grill}, and cook until the meat is just marked and gives lightly to pressure from your finger, about 3 to 5 minutes more for medium-rare. Pull from the grill and let the chops rest a few minutes.

To serve, spoon the polenta among two plates {leave a little behind for a second serving or leftovers for lunch tomorrow} and top each with the chops. Serve immediately.

IRON SKILLET STEAK
···· WITH ····
THYME BUTTER

serves 2

My baby brother loves his steak almost as much as he loves his girl. And he loves to spoil his girl, too. One year for Christmas I gave him a well-seasoned cast-iron skillet along with all of the goodies he would need to pull off "Steak Night for Your Girl," including an elegant set of steak knives, linen napkins, and a James Brown CD. The crux of the whole meal is the steak itself, so I included a handwritten card with my recipe and tips for the ultimate steak. Here it is.

Guys, here's your chance to splurge on your lady, and spoil yourself in the process {you know you've been eyeing that T-bone!}. Serve with Oven-Roasted Tomatoes {page 193}.

Sip: A rich Aussie shiraz, a classic French Bordeaux or Spanish Ribera del Duero

1½ lb/680 g Porterhouse or T-Bone steak, preferably grass-fed or organic

Kosher salt

Freshly ground black pepper

4 tbsp/55 g unsalted butter

2 sprigs of thyme

Remove your steak from the fridge about 30 minutes before you begin cooking. Preheat the oven to 425°F/220°C/gas 7.

Season the steak generously on both sides with salt and lots of pepper. Heat a well-seasoned cast-iron skillet over medium-high heat until almost smoking. Add 2 tbsp of the butter to the pan. When the butter foams, lay the steak in the pan and watch it sizzle. Let the steak cook, without touching it, about 4 minutes. The steak will contract and should come away from the pan easily. Flip the steak {admiring your deep golden sear as you do}, and continue cooking on the other side, 4 minutes more.

Add the remaining 2 tbsp butter and the thyme to the pan and heat until the butter melts and sizzles. Tilt the pan so that the butter pools near the edge of the pan. Using a large metal spoon, scoop the flavored butter and pour it over the steak, repeating to baste the steak with flavor. Transfer the pan and steak to the oven to finish cooking, about 4 minutes for medium-rare, or 6 minutes for medium.

Remove the steak from the heat and transfer to a cutting board to rest for 10 minutes. Slice the steak against the grain and drizzle over with the warm thyme butter.

STEAK, YOUR WAY: HOW TO KNOW IT'S DONE Please do not cut into your pretty steak to see if it's done. If you're a steak novice, stick a meat thermometer into the center of your steak to test for doneness. It should read 120°F/48°C for medium-rare. If this isn't your first steak {or even if it is}, it's time to learn the chef's trick for testing steak for doneness: Hold your hand palm-side up. Press on the fleshy part below your thumb with your opposite pointer finger. That's how a rare steak should feel. Now join your thumb and pointer finger and, with your other hand, feel in the same area. That is how a medium-rare steak should feel. Join your thumb and third finger and feel again, that is a medium steak.

BIG-FLAVOR BRAISED SHORT RIBS
WITH
HERB GREMOLATA

serves 4

{melt his heart} Close your eyes and imagine the soft flavors of tender beef with punchy bursts of lemon and parsley. Don't-You-Dare Mashed Potatoes {page 187} or Melted Polenta {page 175} are consummate companions to this big, bold dish. Impress your honey with this hearty date-night dish.

Sip: Deserving of a bold, big-flavor red wine or a chilled glass of Belgian beer {like Chimayo}

SHORT RIBS

1 bay leaf

1 sprig of thyme

1 garlic clove

5 whole black peppercorns

2½ lb/1.2 kg beef short ribs {about 8 pieces}

2 tsp kosher salt

½ tsp freshly ground black pepper

2 tbsp extra-virgin olive oil

¼ cup/60 ml dry white wine {such as sauvignon blanc}

3 cups/720 ml low-sodium beef or chicken broth

1 large onion, chopped

2 large carrots, cut in 2-in/5-cm chunks

2 stalks celery, cut in 2-in/5-cm chunks

GREMOLATA

1 lemon

⅓ cup coarsely chopped fresh flat-leaf parsley

1 tbsp extra-virgin olive oil

Kosher salt, to taste

Freshly ground black pepper

MAKE THE SHORT RIBS: Preheat the oven to 300°F/150°C /gas 2. Wrap the bay leaf, thyme, garlic, and peppercorns in cheesecloth and tie with kitchen string to make an herb sachet.

Place the ribs on a piece of parchment/baking paper and season generously on all sides with the salt and pepper.

Heat the oil in a large Dutch oven or other wide, heavy ovenproof pot with a lid over medium-high heat. Add the ribs and cook to a deep brown on all sides, about 2 minutes per side. Transfer the ribs to a plate.

Add the white wine to the pan and scrape with a wooden spoon to loosen the brown bits. Add the broth and return the ribs to the pan along with the onion, carrots, celery, and herb sachet. Cover and bring to a simmer over medium-high heat; as soon as it reaches a constant simmer, transfer to the oven and cook until the meat is tender and falling off the bone, about 2½ hours, stirring once to make sure that all sides of the ribs are immersed in the cooking liquid.

Remove the ribs and large vegetables to a plate, leaving any small or delicate bits of vegetables behind. Cover the meat with aluminum foil to keep warm. Place the Dutch oven on the stove over medium-high heat; skim any excess fat off the broth with a large shallow spoon. Simmer the liquid over medium heat until it has thickened slightly and reduced to about 1¾ cups/420 ml of sauce, about 20 minutes.

MEANWHILE, MAKE THE GREMOLATA: Use a vegetable peeler to strip two or three long pieces of lemon zest from the lemon. Slice the zest as thinly as possible with a sharp knife and stir together with the parsley and olive oil. Season with a pinch of salt and black pepper.

Serve two ribs per person on top of a bed of melted polenta or mashed potatoes in shallow bowls or plates. Spoon the cooked carrots around the sides. Top the ribs with a generous heap of the Gremolata. Serve with the cooking liquid to spoon over.

CHAPTER 8

VEGETABLES

To Pass and Please

In our house, vegetables reign. This is partly because only one of us eats meat, and mostly because the things we pull out of our garden are so darn good it would be a crime to shove them to the side. Vegetables picked fresh and carefully cared for can be so delicious you'll want to praise and pass them for decades to come.

If you think of veggies as an obligatory afterthought to an otherwise exciting meal, read on. This chapter covers all the seasons and methods that make those vegetables you brought home from the market steal the show. You've never had green beans until you've had them with crisp, buttery bread crumbs and little cherry tomatoes bursting with natural sugars {Green Beans with Tomatoes & Bread Crumbs, page 199}, or slender shaved zucchini/courgette that yields to the bright juices of fresh lemon {Shaved Zucchini with Ricotta & Walnuts, page 192}. If you like mashed potatoes, how about a batch so rich you want to dive in head first, but so satisfying it takes just a spoonful to stop time {Don't-You-Dare Mashed Potatoes, page 187}? Do I exaggerate? You be the judge.

BOILED BABY POTATOES
WITH
GARDEN CHIVES

serves 4

{gardener's pride} The creamy texture of baby potatoes boiled in their skin and dressed simply with sea salt, olive oil, and fresh herbs can't be beat. These get their buttery texture from the young summer potatoes themselves, which makes the lightness of the olive oil that much more luxurious. This is a great opportunity to show off your windowsill herb garden. Sprinkle on chives alone, or mix chives, mint, dill, chervil, or basil.

1 tbsp sea salt,
plus more for seasoning

1 lb/455 g baby potatoes
{the smaller the better}

2 tbsp best-quality
extra-virgin olive oil

Handful of chopped chives, mint,
dill, chervil, or basil

Bring a medium pot of water to a boil over medium-high heat. Add the sea salt and the potatoes and cook until the skins start to burst and the potatoes can be pierced easily with a fork, 20 to 25 minutes. You may need to remove smaller potatoes with a slotted spoon a few minutes before larger ones.

Put the oil and herbs in your serving bowl. Drain the potatoes and toss in the oil to coat. Taste the potatoes, which should be perfectly seasoned from the salty water. Adjust seasoning with additional salt. Serve warm.

MIX AND MASH: Leftover potatoes smash beautifully with a little milk and/or sour cream for smashed potatoes, or quarter cooled potatoes and toss with mayo and Greek yogurt for a quick, flavorful picnic potato salad.

POTATOES RÖSTI

serves 4

{like his mother made} Rösti or hash browns done well are potatoes perfected. I learned this from my husband's mother in Hungary, but you'll find similar versions that are the pride of many a mother and a young bride in homes all over Central Europe. In our home, few things raise bigger enthusiasm than the smell of rösti cooking when András walks through the door. You'll love them for brunch or dinner, or a whole meal {vegetarians take note} with a poached egg and chopped herbs. Add in rosemary and you've got a really heady, flavorful substitute for French fries with your steak dinner.

The key to a crispy outside and soft inside not laden with oil is to get the oil very hot before you add the potatoes, in which case they will absorb very little of it and leave nothing but flavor and crunch for you to devour the instant they hit the plate.

2 medium baking potatoes {Idaho or russet}, peeled {1¼ lb/570 g}

2 tbsp unsalted butter

Extra-virgin olive oil

Sea salt

Freshly ground black pepper

2 tbsp rosemary leaves {optional}

Preheat the oven to 400°F/200°C/gas 6.

Cut the potatoes into thin matchsticks using a julienne attachment on a mandoline or food processor. Or, cut them into thin rounds and use a sharp knife to cut the rounds into strips {more time consuming, but it works!}

Heat the butter and olive oil in an 8-in/20-cm oven-proof cast-iron or non-stick frying pan, over medium heat. Add the rosemary to the potatoes, and season with salt and pepper. Increase the heat to medium-high and cook, stirring occasionally, until the potatoes are soft and a few pieces are brown. At this point, the potatoes should have settled into a round, flat pancake.

Transfer the potatoes in the skillet to the hot oven to bake until the top and bottom are golden and crispy and the center is soft but cooked through, about 30 minutes. Remove from the oven and slide out of the pan onto paper towels/absorbent paper. Slide onto a baking sheet/tray and continue until the top and bottom are cooked to a deep golden brown, about 10 minutes more. Serve in wedges or whole on a plate in the middle of the table for breaking and nibbling.

PUT YOUR MANDOLINE TO WORK: Hand-grating potatoes, as is often tradition in potato pancakes, release liquid and starch from the potatoes and can make your rösti gummy. Instead, use the grater on your food processor or a mandoline fit with the julienne attachment for thin, matchstick strips.

DON'T-YOU-DARE
MASHED POTATOES

serves 4 to 6

{decadent} At an elegant French restaurant in Chicago, attentive waiters serve rich mashed potatoes by the tiny spoonful, dolloped with panache tableside. Once, during dinner with my family, the server caught the look in my dad's eyes after he served the tiny portion and said, "And don't you dare ask for more." We all laughed, because that's exactly what Dad did, and you will too once you taste them.

What makes restaurant mashed potatoes stand out is their cooking method. Their potatoes are usually baked or boiled whole with skin on so the pure potato flavor prevails rather than being lost into a pot of water. Passed through a ricer, these take on a smooth, luxurious texture, heightened by the addition of butter, crème fraîche, and milk or even a splash of half-and-half depending on what diet you do {or don't} subscribe to.

6 medium Idaho or russet potatoes, scrubbed {about 4¼ lb/1.9 kg}

Sea salt

4 tbsp/55 g unsalted butter

1 cup/240 ml warm whole milk

¼ cup/60 ml crème fraîche or Greek yogurt

Freshly ground black pepper

Bring the potatoes and just enough water to cover them to a boil in a large pot over medium-high heat. Salt the water generously, cover, and simmer until the skins start to burst and the potatoes give easily to a fork, about 25 minutes.

Drain the liquid and peel back the skins, allowing the fluffy potato flesh to drop into a large bowl. Pass the flesh through a food mill or ricer into a second bowl while still warm, adding the butter as you go to melt into the potatoes. Stir in the warm milk with a wooden spoon or spatula and finally the crème fraîche, whipping to a light purée. Taste and season with salt and pepper. Don't be surprised if the potatoes require at least ¾ tsp salt.

Spoon into a warmed bowl and serve hot and fresh.

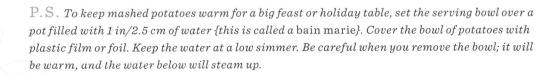

P.S. *To keep mashed potatoes warm for a big feast or holiday table, set the serving bowl over a pot filled with 1 in/2.5 cm of water {this is called a* bain marie}*. Cover the bowl of potatoes with plastic film or foil. Keep the water at a low simmer. Be careful when you remove the bowl; it will be warm, and the water below will steam up.*

PUMPKIN MASH

serves 4 to 6

{fall for it} Pure, homemade pumpkin puree is so warming and delicious. Transform it into an elegant accompaniment to seared fish or your Thanksgiving spread by mashing it with butter or olive oil and salt.

1 medium sugar pumpkin
or butternut, delicata, or acorn squash
{about 1 lb/455 g}

2 cups chicken broth or water

2 tbsp unsalted butter or best-quality extra-virgin olive oil, plus more for finishing

Kosher salt

Using a large, heavy knife, cut the root and stem end off the pumpkin so it has two flat ends. Place it on your cutting board flat-side down; peel using a Y-peeler or standard vegetable peeler. Divide it in half, remove the seeds, and cut the flesh into 2-in/5-cm chunks.

Transfer the pumpkin pieces to a medium saucepan and add just enough of the broth to cover the pumpkin halfway. {Chicken broth boosts the flavor for meat eaters, but you can use water for vegetarians.}

Bring the liquid to a simmer over medium-high heat and cook until the pumpkin is soft and falls apart easily when pierced with a fork, about 20 minutes.

Drain the liquid and transfer the pumpkin to a food professor and pulse to make a smooth puree; or use a potato masher or ricer to get a smooth mash. Pulse or stir in the butter and season with a pinch of salt. Transfer the pumpkin to a bowl and give it an additional dollop of butter or a drizzle of your finest olive oil. Serve warm.

SAVE TIME: Use plain, unseasoned pumpkin mash, made with water instead of broth, as a substitute for pureed carrots in Carrot Cake Bars {page 250}. Transfer the pureed pumpkin to a fine mesh strainer set over a bowl and leave to cool and let excess liquid drip out before packing it up or using it to bake.

MINT & CHILE
MARINATED CUKES

serves 4

{cold and crisp} This spicy-clean condiment is at home with just about any meal from Better Beef Burgers {page 120} to Succulent Barbecued Chicken {page 139}.

1-in/2.5-cm piece of fresh ginger

4 Kirby or small garden/heirloom cucumbers

Sea salt

Freshly ground black pepper

1 tsp fish sauce

1 garlic clove, thinly sliced

1 tbsp raw or turbinado sugar

1 small green chile
{such as Thai or serrano}, cut into thin rings

Juice of 2 limes {1½ tbsp juice}

Small handful of fresh mint leaves, thinly sliced

Small handful of fresh basil leaves, thinly sliced

2 scallions/spring onions
{white and green parts}, thinly sliced

Use a spoon to peel the skin from the ginger and grate the flesh on a microplane. Scrape the ginger pulp and juice into a medium bowl.

Peel the cucumbers if you prefer {it depends on the thickness of the skin, if fresh from the garden or market, they most likely won't need peeling}. Cut your cukes into spears lengthwise and remove any large seeds. Season with salt and pepper and toss together in the bowl with the ginger; add the fish sauce, garlic, sugar, chile, and lime juice, and toss to mix. Refrigerate until crisp.

Before serving, sprinkle with the mint, basil, and scallions/spring onions.

P.S. *If you like heat, leave the seeds inside your chile rings. Otherwise, push them out. They are the hottest part of the pepper.*

FRIED ZUCCHINI

serves 6 to 8

{light and crisp} In the heart of the summer when markets are practically giving zucchini away, buy a bunch and transform them into summer fries that could turn the heads of even the strictest potato devotees. These zucchini get their light and crispy skin from a beer batter. Use a beer you'd enjoy drinking. Eat them fresh and hot from the fryer dipped in harissa-spiked Spicy Mayo.

Vegetable oil, for frying

2 medium-large firm zucchini/courgette, scrubbed and cut into 2-in-/5 cm-long sticks

1 large egg, beaten

½ cup/120 ml cold full-flavored wheat beer

¾ cup/90 g all-purpose/plain flour

Sea salt

Spicy Mayo {page 207}

Before you begin, have everything you'll need handy so you can concentrate when you're working with hot oil on the stove. Set up a wire rack on a baking sheet/tray lined with paper towels/absorbent paper.

In a large, deep frying pan, heat 1 in/2.5 cm vegetable oil over medium-high heat until it reaches 350°F/180°C/gas 4 on a deep-fat thermometer. Decrease the heat to medium-low to keep the oil temperature steady.

Whisk together the egg and beer in a large bowl. Gradually whisk in the flour to make a thin batter.

Check the oil temperature again. It should read just under 350°F/180°C/gas 4 and will drop slightly, to about 325°F/165°C/gas 3 as you add the zucchini/courgette pieces. This is the perfect temperature for frying.

Dip vegetable pieces in the batter a few at a time to coat and let the excess drip off before carefully lowering them into the hot oil. Fry until the batter puffs and is crisp and golden, about 2 minutes. Turn over with a slotted spoon and continue cooking 1 minute more. Be sure to cover the pan with a splatter guard to protect yourself as the zucchini/courgette pops and sizzles enthusiastically {it's full of water}. Remove with a slotted spoon and drain on the rack. Sprinkle with salt while it's still warm. Continue until all the squash is fried.

Serve hot and fresh with Spicy Mayo or all on their own in a basket lined with paper towels/absorbent paper.

P.S. *This batter keeps well overnight in the fridge. Use any leftovers to fry up okra or onions.*

SHAVED ZUCCHINI
WITH
RICOTTA & WALNUTS

serves 2 to 4

{slender satisfaction} Until you've tasted zucchini raw, you haven't experienced its true potential. It's irresistible tossed with olive oil, lemon juice, and a hint of creamy ricotta and crunchy walnuts, lively enough to brighten any summer meal.

1 large, firm zucchini/courgette
or 2 small zucchini/courgette
or yellow summer squash

Juice of ½ lemon {3 tbsp}

3 tbsp best-quality extra-virgin olive oil

Kosher salt

Freshly ground black pepper

¼ cup/60 ml fresh ricotta

½ cup/55 g toasted walnuts,
broken in pieces

Using a vegetable peeler, peel the zucchini/courgette lengthwise into long, thin strips. Toss in a medium bowl with the lemon juice and olive oil, and season with salt and pepper.

Transfer to a serving bowl and dollop the ricotta over the top. Sprinkle with the toasted nuts and finish with a light drizzle of olive oil, and a sprinkling of salt and pepper.

GROW ZUCCHINI: Summer squash are heat-lovers who like long sunny days. All you need is one or two healthy, prolific zucchini/courgette plants to keep you in squash for weeks. Plant extras for their flowers, which are great deep-fried or as a topping for pizza {Gardener's Pizza, page 158}.

Plant seeds outdoors directly in rich soil fed well with organic compost, after any danger of frost has passed {squash and cucumber plants don't do well with transplanting}, about 2 in/5 cm below the soil. Leave at least 2 ft/60 cm between your two zucchini/courgette plants and give them lots of room to creep and grow. Water them well, only at the roots, and avoid wetting the leaves themselves. Trim any leaves at the first sign of disease, white spots, or mildew, but leave all healthy leaves on to shade the growing fruit.

When you can, pick the fruit the day you plan to use it, since it looses moisture quickly off the vine.

ROASTED WINTER VEGETABLES

serves 4 to 6

{*sweet and toothsome*} Roasting is a no-fuss way to put a lot of vegetables on the table. Roasting brings out the natural sweetness in fall root veggies and winter squash. Roast them in big batches to top Baked Risotto {page 115}, and throw them into fall and winter salads.

2 lb/910 kg winter squash
or pumpkin, parsnips, carrots, beets/beetroots,
or a mix

2 medium red or yellow onions, quartered

Extra-virgin olive oil

Kosher salt

Freshly ground black pepper

Handful of fresh parsley, coarsely chopped,
for garnish

Preheat the oven to 400°F/200°C/gas 6. Peel and cut the vegetables into equal sized pieces, about 1-in/2.5-cm chunks. Toss the vegetables and onions in olive oil in a large bowl and season generously with salt and pepper.

Spread the pieces out in a single layer on one or two roasting pans/trays so that the vegetables don't touch. Roast until the veggies are lightly browned and just tender, 45 minutes to 1 hour, depending on the vegetable. Remove and toss with additional olive oil. Season with salt and pepper and garnish with parsley before serving.

P.S. *Oven-Roasted Tomatoes: Baked tomatoes make a quick garnish or side to anything from Baked Risotto {page 115} to Iron Skillet Steak {page 176}. Replace the vegetables with 2 lb/910 kg halved plum tomatoes or small tomatoes on the vine and roast until they are just soft, about 30 minutes.*

ROASTED BEETS
WITH
PISTACHIOS

serves 4 to 6

{jewels on a plate} Good looks and powerful nutrients? What more could you wish for from a vegetable? You won't be thinking about how good this dish {pictured on page 281} is for you when you're eating it, just how smart you are for putting it all together.

2 large beets/beetroots or 1 bunch baby beets/beetroots {about 1¼ lb/570 g}, tops trimmed	2 cara cara, navel, or blood oranges, peeled and cut in thick rounds
Extra-virgin olive oil	¼ cup/35 g shelled Sicilian pistachios or regular pistachios {about 1¼ oz}
Sea salt	4 oz/115 g ricotta salata cheese
Freshly ground black pepper	Small handful of fresh mint leaves, for garnish

Preheat the oven to 450°F/230°C/gas 8. Trim the beet/beetroot tops to 1 in/2.5 cm and scrub the skins. Drizzle the beets generously with the olive oil, sprinkle with salt and pepper, and put them in a small roasting pan with ¼ in/6mm of water. Cover the pan loosely with aluminum foil.

Roast until the beets are just fork tender, 30 to 45 minutes, depending on the size. Set aside until cool enough to handle; cut off the root and stem ends and scrape off the skins {they should slip off easily} with a knife.

Quarter large beets or halve smaller ones and toss with additional olive oil just to coat, and salt and pepper.

Arrange them on a plate with the oranges, pistachios, and thin shavings of ricotta salata cheese. Drizzle with olive oil and garnish with the fresh mint.

P.S. *This is the same method for roasting beets/beetroots needed for A Real Good Salad {page 87}. Make the beets for both at once. They keep wrapped in the fridge for 1 week.*

CARROTS
· · · · WITH · · · ·
CARAWAY SOUR CREAM

serves 6 to 8

{an earthy delight} Carrots can be overlooked as a humble vegetable, particularly since they've been whittled down to nubs in grocery stores. But farmers' markets across the country have restored carrots to their glorious roots, displaying them in colors from brilliant orange to deep purple to pale yellow, which beg you to discover their earthy flavor and natural sweetness. This recipe, which I created for our wedding feast, makes the most of any carrot, and turns them into something spectacular.

¼ cup/60 ml extra-virgin olive oil

1 large red onion, diced

4 garlic cloves, smashed

1 tbsp sweet Hungarian paprika,
plus more for garnish

2½ tsp kosher salt

4 cups/960 ml water

10 medium carrots,
peeled and cut in large chunks on the bias

Freshly ground black pepper

¼ tsp caraway

1 large handful of parsley leaves, coarsely chopped

¾ cup/180 ml sour cream

Heat 3 tbsp of the olive oil in a medium-heavy pot or Dutch oven over medium heat. Add the onion and garlic, and cook until soft and glistening, about 6 minutes, stirring occasionally. Add the paprika and about half of the salt and cook until the oil turns a deep red, about 1 minute. Whisk in the water and add the carrots and remaining salt.

Bring the liquid to a gentle simmer, cover, and cook until the carrots are tender, about 20 minutes. Season with pepper and hold in the broth.

Heat the remaining oil in a small frying pan over medium heat. Add the caraway and toast until it smells fragrant, about 1 minute. Stir about half the parsley into the sour cream, and season with salt and pepper. Transfer to a serving bowl and drizzle the flavored caraway oil over the top of the sour cream. Strain the carrots into a large bowl or platter {reserving the broth to make soup}, and scatter the remaining parsley. Serve with caraway sour cream.

LOVE YOUR LEFTOVERS *Save your carrot-paprika broth for a light vegetable broth, or puree with the leftover carrots to make a quick carrot soup. Drizzle the soup with caraway sour cream and serve with chunky peasant bread for a fast feast.*

MARINATED AVOCADOS

serves 6

{almost guacamole} Lemon and chiles are all that's needed to make the creamy flavor of a ripe avocado explode onto the palate. This is one dish to make right before you're ready to eat to keep the avocados fresh and a pretty green. Serve with fresh tortillas and salt for an easy afternoon snack. Smash, and you've got guacamole.

4 firm, ripe avocados

2 tbsp extra-virgin olive oil

1 tbsp freshly squeezed lemon juice

1 splash green hot sauce

1 small green chile, cut into thin rounds and seeded

1 or 2 scallions/spring onions {white and green parts}, thinly sliced

Handful of cilantro/fresh coriander sprigs or leaves

Sea salt

Freshly ground black pepper

Halve the avocados around the pit and twist to separate the halves. Lay the avocado halves on a board and with a sharp knife, give the pit a gentle whack until the knife sticks into the pit. Twist slightly to loosen the pit and discard.

Scoop out the flesh into gently curved pieces with a big flat spoon. Arrange the pieces on a platter or shallow bowl and drizzle over the olive oil, lemon juice, hot sauce, chile, scallions/spring onions, cilantro/fresh coriander, salt, and pepper. Serve at room temperature.

GREEN BEANS
WITH
TOMATOES & BREAD CRUMBS

serves 4

{crispy, buttery, crunchy, good} It's not easy to get a bunch of fresh green beans from the market to the table without munching them straight from your hands. But try if you can, they are so good cooked with a bit of snap, sprinkled with crispy, buttery bread crumbs and bursting cherry tomatoes. So good in fact, you almost feel guilty going for seconds.

Salt

½ dry baguette or rustic bread loaf such as ciabatta or pugliese, crusts removed

2 large handfuls fresh green beans, ends snipped {about 12 oz/340 g}

¼ cup/60 ml extra-virgin olive oil, plus a drizzle

2 tbsp unsalted butter

Freshly ground black pepper

8 small Campari tomatoes, halved, or 1 pint mixed cherry tomatoes

¼ cup/30 g freshly grated Parmigiano-Reggiano or Manchego cheese

Bring a large pot of salted water to a boil over medium-high heat. Prepare a bowl with salted ice water and set it nearby.

Cut the bread into large pieces and pulse in the food processor to make coarse crumbs {you should have about 2 cups/110 g}.

Drop the green beans into the boiling water and cook until bright green and crisp-tender, 4 to 6 minutes. Pull the green beans from the water and shock them in salted, ice-cold water for a few seconds. Remove them, pat them dry, and toss with a drizzle of olive oil and salt. Set aside on a platter.

Meanwhile, heat 2 tbsp of the olive oil and the butter in a medium frying pan over medium-high heat. Add the bread crumbs and toast until evenly golden and crisp. Season with salt and pepper. Transfer the bread crumbs to a medium bowl with a slotted spoon, leaving any oil behind. Add the tomatoes and the remaining 2 tbsp olive oil to the frying pan and cook, tossing occasionally to flip on all sides, until they are golden and soft and release some of their juices. Season with salt and pepper. Toss together with the bread crumbs.

Spoon the tomatoes and bread crumbs over the green beans. Sprinkle with grated cheese and serve warm.

P.S. *With or without tomatoes, these green beans make a splendid side for the Thanksgiving table. Consider it a fresher, fancier version of green bean casserole.*

FRESH & PRETTY PEAS
WITH
RADISHES

serves 4

Oh joy, spring has arrived and with it barrels of peas and bunches of radishes. Both grow super easily in small plots and raised beds, and are abundant and often cheap at the farmers' market. There *is* the work of shelling the peas. But the reward, oh, the reward. Putting them together with crunchy walnuts and creamy ricotta as in this dish {pictured on page 281} makes for a refreshing first course or side.

2 cups fresh shelled peas
{from 2 lb/910 kg unshelled peas}

¼ cup/60 ml extra-virgin olive oil

Sea salt

Freshly ground black pepper

1 bunch globe or breakfast radishes,
trimmed and thinly sliced

¼ cup/30 g toasted walnuts, in pieces

2 tbsp fresh mint leaves, torn

2 tbsp finely snipped fresh dill

⅓ cup/75 ml fresh whole-milk ricotta

Bring a large pot of salted water to a boil over medium-high heat. Drop in the peas and cook until they turn bright green, about 1 minute. Drain into a colander and rinse the peas immediately in cold water to cool them to room temperature. Pat them dry, drizzle them with the best olive oil, and season with salt and pepper. Toss them together with the radishes, walnuts, mint leaves, and dill. Transfer to a serving bowl and top with fresh ricotta. Season with salt and pepper before serving.

GROW RADISHES: Radishes are about the first and easiest thing to grow each spring. Start with globe or French breakfast radish seeds. Make two or three lines in fresh soil just after the last frost, about April in most climates. Sow seeds ½ in/12 mm deep, about 1 in/2.5 cm apart, and wait for tender tops to appear. Pull when tiny for bright, brassy punch in salads, or let them grow to full maturity and serve on ice with good butter and fresh sea salt. Pull them before they get too large and the weather turns hot, when radishes turn spongy.

EMBELLISHMENTS

Snacks, Sauces & Sips to Enlighten the Table

When it comes to food, there is the kind of lovely, balanced flavor that comes from a good grasp of how to use salt, pepper, and acid, and then there is all-out gutsy flavor that is born of reckless enthusiasm for garlic and spice, herbs by the handful, smooth silky spreads, and sauces that bring a table to life.

That is the art of irresistible cooking—the special sauce, the layering of flavors, the little finishing touches. This chapter is full of the flavor-building sauces and snacks that take sandwiches from simple to sublime and turn a meal into a party. Some of these old tricks, like mashing up creamy egg yolks with a bit of kick for Little Deviled Eggs {page 221}, will be familiar. Others, like dressing up fresh ricotta {A Beautiful Bowl of Ricotta, page 213}, and turning black-eyed peas and a Spanish Manchego into a stylish spin on hummus {see page 212}, will help you surprise and delight your guests {and your spouse} and make sure your meals never get boring.

MAYO, TWO WAYS

{ HERB MAYO }

makes about
1 cup/240 ml

{tempting} **Life really picks up when you add**
this green mayo to sandwiches and serve it as a
dipping sauce for fries or fresh veggies. Its green
comes from fresh herbs {use your favorites, in any
combination} and its body from Greek yogurt,
with a touch of a store-bought mayo for creamy
sweetness.

1 packed cup fresh parsley,
dill, mint, basil, or chive leaves,
coarsely chopped

⅓ cup/75 ml Greek yogurt

3 tbsp/45 ml olive-oil mayonnaise
or regular mayonnaise

1 tbsp extra-virgin olive oil

2 to 3 tsp freshly squeezed lemon juice

Sea salt

Freshly ground black pepper

Blend the herbs, yogurt, mayo, and olive oil in a mini
food processor or blender until smooth and flecked with
green. Pulse in the lemon juice, adding just enough to
give it the right balance for you. Taste and season with
salt and pepper. Store in the fridge for up to 4 days.

{ SPICY MAYO }

makes about
½ cup/120 ml

{from any country} **Creamy mayonnaise mixed**
with Greek yogurt is the perfect, luscious base
to tame the feisty heat of a hot red pepper paste.
Stir in North African harissa, Hungarian hot red
pepper paste, Southeast Asian sambal oelek, or
Sriracha sauce to add a fiery streak to your favorite snack or supper.

¼ cup/60 ml Greek yogurt

¼ cup/60 ml olive-oil,mayonnaise or regular mayonnaise

2 to 3 tbsp hot pepper sauce or paste

Pinch of fine sea salt

Freshly ground black pepper

Mix together the yogurt, mayonnaise, and enough hot
pepper paste to make you sweat. Season to taste with
salt and pepper. Serve on everything your heart desires,
especially Baguette BLTs with Spicy Moroccan Mayo
{page 95}. Store in the fridge for up to 4 days.

SPUNK UP EGG SALAD: To make a zippy Green Eggs, Hold the Ham Sandwich {also known as
egg salad}, mix ½ cup/120 ml of green mayo with six chopped hard-boiled eggs and spread between two slices of
your favorite bread.

EVERYTHING'S BETTER WITH AIOLI

makes 2 cups/480 ml

{make it yourself} Whether you like mayo from a jar or not is irrelevant. Once you make it yourself and add a bit of garlic, you may be surprised by just how many things you'll find yourself dipping into it: Easier-Than-Pie Oven Fries {page 219}, St. Tropez Crudités {page 215}, or just about anything that needs a bit of spark. Now is the time to use your good olive oil and very fresh garlic—the flavors will come through.

½ to 1 garlic clove

1½ tsp salt

2 egg yolks {preferably organic}

1¼ cups/300 ml grapeseed or canola oil

½ cup/120 ml best-quality extra-virgin olive oil

1 tsp water {optional}

½ tsp red wine vinegar

1 tsp freshly squeezed lemon juice

Freshly ground black pepper

Smash the garlic clove on a wooden board with your fist or the flat part of a knife. Chop it coarsely, then sprinkle it with about half the salt. Use the flat part of your knife to mash the garlic into a fine pulp. If you have a mortar and pestle, use it.

Whisk together the egg yolks in a medium bowl. Combine the grapeside oil and the olive oil and drizzle the oil, one drop at a time, into the egg yolks, whisking constantly to make a thick mayo. {This is the perfect time to recruit your honey to drizzle while you whisk.} Thin the mayo slightly with the water if you're using this as a dipping sauce. Add a bit of the smashed garlic, the vinegar, lemon juice, and pepper. Taste. If you love garlic {and garlic breath}, add the rest of the garlic, but keep in mind that the aioli will intensify as it sits, so consider your guest audience before you go overboard.

Serve immediately, or store extra covered in the fridge for up to 5 days.

GREEN-ON-GREEN PESTO

makes about 1½ cups/360 ml

{timeless} Consider this pesto the little black dress of your kitchen {only green}. Simple changes, like arugula instead of basil, give it a whole new look and feel, and it's equally at home at a cocktail party or a picnic. And like your black dress, it never goes out of style.

It gets its green from whatever is thriving in the garden or at the market, like arugula, parsley, or mustard greens. Make enough for supper and then some. You'll be happy to find extra in your fridge for stirring into Baked Risotto {page 115}, spreading on sandwiches, or serving alongside chicken, fish, or seafood.

⅓ cup/50 g pine nuts or walnuts

1 tiny garlic clove {or ¼ regular clove}, chopped

3 handfuls fresh basil leaves, arugula/rocket, parsley, mustard leaves, or a combination

½ cup/60 g freshly grated Parmigiano-Reggiano cheese

⅓ cup/75 ml extra-virgin olive oil, plus more for topping

Sea salt

Freshly ground black pepper

Pulse together the nuts, garlic, greens, and about half of the Parmigiano-Reggiano cheese in a food processor until the greens are finely chopped. Pulse in the olive oil to make a smooth paste and continue until the pesto is evenly combined. {If you don't have a food processor, finely chop the nuts, garlic, and greens on your cutting board before stirring together in a bowl with the cheese and olive oil.} Season with salt and pepper. Taste the sauce. You may want to add the remaining cheese, or a little more oil, or extra salt or pepper. This is your sauce, and it's worth learning how to make it the way you like it.

You may want it thick enough to stuff into a fish fillet or thin enough to toss on your favorite pasta. If you prefer it thinner and plan to use it immediately, add 1 to 2 tbsp of warm water. If you aren't using it immediately, cover the surface with additional olive oil and plastic wrap/cling film and refrigerate until ready to use. Pesto stores well for about a week in the fridge, but make sure to top it off with extra oil every time you use it so the vibrant green doesn't discolor

GROW HERBS: Herbs and greens are easy to grow and offer huge rewards, both for your palate and your pocket book. Start herbs like basil and parsley from plants {easy to find at the farmers' market, nursery, or garden center}, in pots or window boxes. Set them in full sun and keep the soil moist. Keeping them in pots allows you to bring them indoors during cold winter months. You'll need the leaves from about two mature basil plants to make one batch of pesto. Greens like arugula/rocket and mustard are easy to start from seed, in pots or directly in the ground once the danger of frost has passed. These fast bloomers will delight you with endless pungent flavor.

TSATSIKI

serves 4 to 6

{a Greek's relish} In Greece, you'll find this garlicky and refreshing garnish at nearly every meal. It is excellent with Potatoes Rösti {page 186}, Skewered Lamb with Tomato Couscous {page 118}, or any meaty sandwich that needs a little sauce.

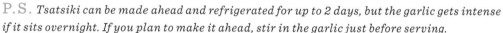

1 large English/hothouse cucumber
or 2 Kirby cucumbers, seeded

¾ tsp kosher salt, plus more for seasoning

1 cup/240 ml whole-milk Greek or plain yogurt

1 garlic clove, pressed or minced

Juice of 1 lemon {about ¼ cup/60 ml}

2 tbsp chopped fresh parsley

2 tbsp snipped fresh dill

Freshly ground black pepper

Lightly peel the cucumber, leaving some green skin. Grate on a box grater into a medium bowl and add the salt. Transfer to a mesh strainer set over another bowl, and let sit at room temperature until the liquid drains out, about 15 minutes. Press out excess liquid with a paper towel/absorbent paper.

Stir the drained cucumber into the yogurt, and add the garlic, lemon juice, parsley, and dill. Season with salt and pepper, and transfer to a serving bowl. Serve at room temperature.

P.S. *Tsatsiki can be made ahead and refrigerated for up to 2 days, but the garlic gets intense if it sits overnight. If you plan to make it ahead, stir in the garlic just before serving.*

BABAGHANEWLYWEDS

serves 6

{smoky eggplant dip} **There's a story behind every quirky recipe title.** This smoky eggplant dip is the very first thing I ever made for my beloved. We ate it the day we met, and again on our first few dates {there are lots of Middle Eastern restaurants in New York City} and served it at our wedding. But this is a dip for all newlyweds to love. Look for eggplant that is firm and smooth, with an even, shiny purple skin, and no big scratches, bruising, or soft spots.

2 large ripe, firm eggplant/
aubergines {about 3 lb/1.4 kg}

2 garlic cloves

Sea salt

1 cup/240 ml canned white beans,
drained and rinsed

⅓ cup/75 ml best-quality
extra-virgin olive oil

1 tbsp tahini

¼ cup/60 ml freshly squeezed lemon juice

Freshly ground black pepper

Small handful of flat-leaf parsley, chopped

Grilled bread or flatbread {page 280}, for serving

Preheat your grill/barbecue or grill pan over medium-high heat. Cook the whole eggplant/aubergines until the skins are well charred and the flesh is soft, almost melting, about 15 to 25 minutes, depending on the heat of your grill.

Meanwhile, smash the garlic cloves on a wooden board with your fist or the flat part of a knife. Chop the garlic coarsely, then sprinkle it with salt. Use the flat part of your knife to mash the garlic into a fine pulp. If you have a mortar and pestle, use it.

Remove the skin and cap {stem end} from the eggplant and add the flesh to the bowl of a food processor along with the garlic, beans, olive oil, tahini, and lemon juice. Pulse to a thick puree, and season with salt and pepper. Or, chop the eggplant, beans, and garlic together to a fine pulp on a cutting board, then stir together in a bowl with olive oil, tahini, and lemon juice. Sprinkle with chopped parsley and serve with warm grilled bread or flatbread.

BLACK-EYED PEA
& MANCHEGO DIP

makes about 1½ cups/360 ml

{chic & cheap} Black-eyed peas are sweet little suckers with a creamy texture. They pair well with cheese when they're pureed like hummus into a lush dip. Start with canned or frozen black-eyed peas, and you'll find half the work is done for you.

One 15.5-oz/439-g can
black-eyed peas, drained

¼ cup/30 g finely grated Manchego cheese

¼ cup/60 ml best-quality extra-virgin olive oil,
plus more for drizzling

1 tbsp freshly squeezed lemon juice,
plus more for seasoning

½ tsp fine sea salt

Freshly ground black pepper

¼ cup/60 ml warm water

Pinch of red pepper flakes

Puree the black-eyed peas and Manchego cheese in a food processor, gradually adding in the oil and lemon juice and processing until completely smooth. Season lightly with salt and pepper and pulse in the warm water to thin to the desired consistency. Spoon into a shallow bowl and use a spoon to swirl the dip into a bit of a pattern. Drizzle additional olive oil to pool in the creases and sprinkle with red pepper flakes.

Bean dips are the most flavorful when slightly warm or at room temperature. If you plan to make this ahead, store in the fridge and let it stand at room temperature before serving. Swirl in a bit more warm water to loosen and season again, if necessary, with additional oil or lemon juice.

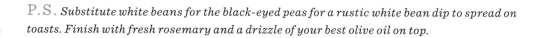

P.S. *Substitute white beans for the black-eyed peas for a rustic white bean dip to spread on toasts. Finish with fresh rosemary and a drizzle of your best olive oil on top.*

A BEAUTIFUL BOWL
OF
RICOTTA

serves 4 to 6

{all dolled up} Ricotta cheese is a sensational ingredient. It's simple in its origin {it starts with cow's or sheep's milk} that with a little extra love can stand as an expression of abundance and exuberance. Dress it up with a drizzle of your best honey or a superb, fruity extra-virgin olive oil and spices, and serve it as a first course with warm flatbread.

This dish is so simple, it's all about the quality of the ingredients. Get the freshest ricotta available, often made locally at Italian markets, which should taste of fresh milk with a touch of sweetness. Use your finest fruity finishing oil for the savory version, and raw, local honey or a specialty flavored honey such as acacia, lavender, or tupelo for the sweet.

{ SAVORY }

2 cups/480 ml fresh ricotta {locally made if available}

3 tbsp/45 ml your favorite extra-virgin olive oil

Pinch of red pepper flakes

Coarse sea salt

Coarsely ground black pepper

2 sprigs fresh thyme, flowering thyme, or basil

Crusty toasted bread or flatbread

Put the ricotta in a pretty, shallow bowl and use the back of a spoon to create dips and swirls.

Drizzle the olive oil on top and let it pool. Sprinkle with the red pepper flakes, sea salt, black pepper, and fresh herbs. Serve with crusty, toasted bread or flatbread.

{ SWEET }

2 cups/480 ml fresh ricotta {locally made if available}

2 tbsp water

1 to 2 tsp your favorite honey,
plus more for drizzling

1 large bunch concord or muscat grapes

Sprig of fresh thyme {flowering, if available}

Warm flatbread

Put the ricotta in a pretty, shallow bowl and use the back of a spoon to create dips and swirls.

Heat a small saucepan over low heat and add the water and 1 to 2 tsp honey, depending on the sweetness of the grapes. Add the grapes and thyme and toss to just glaze slightly and soften to the touch. Remove from the heat.

To serve, spoon the grapes over the ricotta along with a drizzle of the honey mixture.

MIDNIGHT MARINATED OLIVES

serves 6 to 8 for nibbling

{a jar full of flavor} I'm forever indebted to my friend Rori for teaching me that even a good olive can only get better when it is soaked in a good oil. I remembered this at midnight the night before friends were coming for dinner. So I threw together olives, bundles of herbs, and peels of citrus, which by the next day had already infused more flavor into both the olives and the oil than I could have ever hoped to do with any magic of my own. Now I always keep these in my fridge for impromptu entertaining. Spoon the olives into wooden bowls or serve them straight from the jar with a Virgin Mary of the Market {page 227}.

2 handfuls of picholine olives,
or your olive of choice
{cured, but not marinated}

2 cups/480 ml best-quality
extra-virgin olive oil

2 or 3 large strips orange or lemon zest

2 or 3 sprigs rosemary or oregano, or both

Combine all the ingredients in a pretty jar with a resealable lid. Set on the countertop overnight and up to a week, or in the fridge for up to a month. Bring to room temperature and spoon into a bowl for serving on a party tray.

P.S. *To make a dressing with the oil: Pour out 4 to 6 tbsp of oil. Whisk together with 1 tsp of Dijon mustard. Gradually drizzle in 2 tbsp of freshly squeezed lemon juice and whisk to combine. Season with salt and pepper.*

Marinating: This marinating technique works with mozzarella, too. Keep that version in the fridge.

ST. TROPEZ CRUDITÉS

serves 6 to 8

{an art} Anyone can put out raw veggies and store-bought dips on a pretty platter, but give your guests a good reason to come back dipping for more. In St. Tropez, where I spent two summers working as a private chef, the chicest beach restaurant served blanched vegetables, arranged artfully in a bowl made of cork. I served it this way with cocktails at least once a week, and as simple as it was, it always elicited a rousing interest from guests who couldn't quite figure out what was so different. The secret was to par-cook the carrots, snap peas, and string beans, which made them crisp and bright with a little more give to the tooth.

This makes a stunning intro to any main event, paired with Spicy Mayo or Herb Mayo.

---

2 handfuls sugar snap
or snow peas/mangetout,
green beans, or haricots verts

½ head cauliflower, broken into florets

Handful of baby carrots or 3 large carrots,
peeled and cut into batons

1 bunch French, breakfast,
or icicle radishes

Sea salt

Spicy Mayo {page 207} or Herb Mayo {page 207},
for dipping

Bring a large pot of water to a boil over medium-high heat. Meanwhile, have a bowl of salted ice water ready for an ice bath. Trim all your vegetables, leaving little bits of lovely tops or anything that gives them some personality and your guests something to hold onto while they dip. Salt the water generously and add the veggies {except for the radishes, which are best served raw}, one variety at a time, and cook until crisp-tender and bright in color. Remove with a slotted spoon and plunge them into the ice water to stop the cooking and keep the color. When the vegetables are cool to the touch, immediately remove them from the water and pat dry with paper towels/absorbent paper. If you're preparing the vegetables in advance, store each set of veggies wrapped in damp paper towels in the fridge until ready to serve. Remove from the cold about 30 minutes before serving for the best flavor {they'll all taste the same straight from the fridge}.

Arrange on a large tray or shallow bowl with sloping sides or stack and arrange each in different cups or rocks glasses. Serve with the mayo.

WILD MUSHROOM TOASTS

serves 4 to 6

{almost a meal} Twice a year, wild mushrooms pop up all over the forest floors after rains and melting of snow. Mixed together, as in this recipe {pictured on page 202}, they deliver an earthy bounty of flavor. You'll find the most exciting mushrooms at your local farmers' market, and if you're lucky enough to know foragers, treat them well. Many supermarkets now carry a variety of cultivated mushrooms as well. Morel, chanterelle, trumpet, oyster, and enoki mushrooms will turn heads, but even crimini mushrooms mixed in to stretch your dollar will do.

1 whole-wheat/wholemeal boule {rustic country bread} loaf, cut into ¼-in-/6-mm-thick slices

¼ cup/60 ml extra-virgin olive oil, plus more for brushing the bread

3 lb/1.4 kg wild mushrooms such as morels, chanterelles, trumpets, oysters, or enoki, cut into slices

Sea salt

Freshly ground black pepper

1 shallot, finely chopped

1 garlic clove

Sprig of thyme

¼ cup/60 ml half-and-half/half cream

2 tbsp water or chicken broth

1 tbsp cognac {optional}

2 tbsp unsalted butter

Small handful of fresh parsley leaves, coarsely chopped

Preheat the oven to 400°F/200°C/gas 6.

Brush the slices of bread with olive oil and lay on a baking sheet/tray. Bake until golden and just toasted but not completely dried out, 6 to 8 minutes. Set aside.

Heat your largest frying pan over medium-high heat. Add the ¼ cup/60 ml olive oil and the mushrooms and cook, stirring occasionally, until the mushrooms release all their liquid, about 10 minutes, seasoning gradually with salt and freshly ground pepper. Continue cooking until some of the liquid has evaporated. Add the shallot, garlic, and thyme and cook, stirring frequently, until fragrant, and the mushrooms are golden and crisp, about 4 minutes more.

Add the half-and-half/half cream, water, and a splash of cognac {if using}. Decrease the heat to medium-low and cook, stirring frequently, until the liquid thickens just slightly and coats the mushrooms evenly, a few minutes more. The mushrooms mixture should be saucy, like a gravy.

Remove from the heat. Pull out and discard the sprig of thyme and stir in the butter. Adjust the seasoning, adding more salt and pepper as needed. {Don't be surprised if it does; mushrooms soak up a lot of salt.}

Spoon over the toasted bread and sprinkle generously with chopped parsley.

EASIER-THAN-PIE OVEN FRIES

serves 4

{baked, not fried} There are only a few things that can convince me to turn on the fryer, such as Buttermilk Fried Chicken {page 140} and Fried Zucchini {page 191}. For everything else, the oven does a fine and dandy job. Fries are no exception. These are not French fries on a diet. On the contrary, they are all crunch and flavor, and practically guiltless!

2 large baking potatoes {about 1¾ lb/800 g}, cut into 4-by-½-in/10-cm-by-12-mm sticks

¼ cup/60 ml extra-virgin olive oil

1 tsp minced fresh rosemary

Sea salt

Freshly ground black pepper

Preheat the oven to 400°F/200°C/gas 6.

Toss the potatoes in the olive oil in a large bowl or plastic bag and spread onto a baking sheet/tray in a single layer. Bake on the top rack of the oven, turning a couple of times with a spatula, until golden and crispy, about 35 minutes. It's really important that you turn the fries partway through baking so that they crisp evenly.

Remove the fries from the oven, sprinkle with rosemary, and return to the oven to bake for 5 minutes more.

Season generously with salt and pepper and serve hot.

LITTLE DEVILED EGGS

serves 8 to 12

{*make them special*} No summer picnic is complete without deviled eggs, but they are pretty irresistible any time of year. When you're feeling like something special, make them with all the lovely pale blue or green eggs from heirloom breeds of hens, commonly found at farmers' markets, which yield rich sunset-orange yolks. For something truly memorable, try this with quail eggs, which turn deviled eggs into delicate bite-size wonders. One word of wisdom: bribe someone else to do the peeling.

1 dozen large organic eggs or 2 dozen quail eggs	Sea salt
1 tsp Dijon mustard	¼ tsp cayenne pepper or paprika, plus more for sprinkling
¼ cup/60 ml crème fraîche	Dill or chervil sprigs, for garnish
2 tbsp unsalted butter	
2 tsp pickle juice or freshly squeezed lemon juice	

Put the eggs in a pot with just enough cold water to cover. Bring them to a boil over medium-high heat. The minute they boil, remove them from the heat and cover. Set aside for 10 minutes for large eggs and about 8 minutes for quail eggs. Drain the eggs and roll them between your palm and the countertop to crack open the shell.

Peel the eggs under cold running water to remove the egg in one smooth piece. Halve lengthwise with a thin, sharp knife. Spoon the egg yolks into a medium bowl.

Mash the yolks together with a fork until they are smooth. Stir in the mustard, crème fraiche, butter, pickle juice, ¼ tsp salt, and cayenne.

Spoon or pipe {with a pastry bag} the yolk mixture back into the egg whites. Sprinkle with cayenne. Cover the eggs loosely or pack them into a sturdy container with plenty of space, and chill in the fridge until just before you're ready to serve them. Garnish with small sprigs of dill or chervil just before serving.

P.S: *The very freshest eggs are great for eating but hard to peel, so use eggs that are over a week old.*

{ SIPS }

The simplest way to spruce
up a table is something
refreshing in a pitcher.

sips

FRESHLY SQUEEZED LEMONADE

serves 4 to 6

1 cup/200 g sugar

5 cups/1.2 L cold water

8 large lemons, juiced {about 2 cups/480 ml juice}

2 cups/400 g ice

Bring the sugar and 1 cup/240 ml of the water to a simmer in a medium saucepan over low heat. Cook, stirring occasionally, until the sugar dissolves, about 4 minutes; you'll have about 1 cup/240 ml simple syrup.

Stir together the lemon juice, the remaining 4 cups/960 ml cold water, the simple syrup {to your taste; I usually start with about half of the simple syrup} and ice in a large pitcher. Stir and serve.

P.S. *You can add flavor to your lemonade by adding lavender, sage, or mint to your simple syrup after it cooks, and let it steep for about 25 minutes.*

ELDERFLOWER SPRITZERS

serves 1

Elderflower bushes grow all over András' family yard. My mother-in-law steeps her flowers into simple syrup that makes the most delicious cordial mixed with sparkling water. We served these at our wedding, and they are just as elegant with or without a little pour of gin.

2 capfuls {about 2 tbsp} elderflower syrup

1 tbsp freshly squeezed lemon juice

Club soda or seltzer water, chilled

Currants, lemon wedge, or strip of lemon zest

Gin

Stir together the elderflower syrup, lemon juice, and club soda in a chilled rocks glass. Stir in a capful or two of gin if you're feeling so inclined. Garnish with a sprig of fresh currants, lemon wedge, or curl of lemon zest.

SWEET PEACH-BASIL SUN TEA

serves 6 to 8

1 ripe peach, quartered, or the peel from 6 organic peaches

½ cup/100 g sugar

1 cup/ 240 ml water

Sprig of fresh basil

8 cups/2 L freshly brewed sun tea

Ice, for serving

Bring the peach, sugar, and water to a simmer in a medium saucepan over low heat. Cook until the sugar dissolves, about 4 minutes. Remove from the heat and add the basil. Set aside to steep until the syrup is fragrant with peach and basil.

Strain the peach and basil {you'll have about 1 cup/240 ml peach simple syrup} and use to sweeten sun tea. Serve over ice.

MINT-CHAMOMILE TEA

serves 4

2 cups/480 ml water, plus 2 cups/480 ml ice water

½ cup/100 g sugar

Handful of fresh mint leaves

Handful of fresh chamomile leaves and flowers, or 2 chamomile tea bags

2 cups/400 g ice

Bring the 2 cups water and the sugar to a simmer in a small saucepan over low heat. Cook until the sugar dissolves, about 4 minutes. Remove from the heat, add the mint and chamomile, and let steep for 10 minutes. Strain and discard the herbs {you'll have about 2 cups/480ml simple syrup}.

Add the 2 cups/480 ml ice water and the ice to the simple syrup. Serve in chilled glasses.

HIBISCUS-GINGER TEA

serves 6 to 8

1-in/2.5-cm piece fresh ginger, peeled and sliced

9 cups/2.3 L water

½ cup/100 g sugar

2 handfuls hibiscus flowers

Ice, for serving

Bring the ginger, 1 cup/240 ml of the water, and sugar to a simmer in a small saucepan over low heat. Cook until the sugar dissolves, about 4 minutes; Continue cooking to develop the ginger flavor, about 6 minutes more. Remove from the heat and let the ginger steep until the syrup is a touch spicy, about 1 hour {you'll have about 1 cup/240 ml simple syrup}.

Bring the 8 cups/2 L water just to a boil in a large saucepan over medium-high heat. Add the hibiscus and remove from the heat; let the hibiscus steep until the liquid comes to room temperature. Strain and discard hibiscus flowers. Serve over ice and sweeten to taste with the ginger syrup.

YERBA MATE—MINT SUN TEA

serves 8 to 10

¼ cup/16 g yerba mate leaves

1 bunch of fresh mint

2 gl/7.5 L filtered water

Ice, for serving

Combine mate leaves, mint, and water in a large jug. Steep in the sun for 1 day. Serve over ice.

VIETNAMESE
ICED COFFEE

serves 2

This is dessert and a drink in one. Cool and sweet, it is an afternoon pick-me-up not to be taken lightly.

6 tbsp/90 ml sweetened condensed milk

Ice

1½ cups/360 ml cold, freshly brewed coffee

1 cup/240 ml whole milk

Divide the sweetened condensed milk between two tall glasses. Fill each glass with ice, ¾ cup of the brewed coffee, and ½ cup/120 ml of the milk, and serve with a stirrer.

VENEZUELAN
CHOCOLATE SHAKE

serves 2

Who doesn't love milkshakes? Here's one you can love a little more often. This Venezuelan version is like a slimmer shake. Mostly ice and milk instead of ice cream, it's light on chocolate but very big on satisfaction.

2 cups/480 ml whole milk

2 tbsp cocoa powder

1 tbsp sugar

Small pinch of cinnamon

2 large handfuls ice

Blend all ingredients together in a blender until the ice is crushed completely and the drink is frothy. Serve in two tall, chilled glasses with fat straws.

VIRGIN MARY OF THE MARKET

makes 8

At the market from June to September, you can pick up everything you need to make this virgin bloody mary. The taste of the garden is so refreshing that you won't miss the vodka or bourbon. But feel free to slip a little in.

4 lb/1.8 kg vine-ripe tomatoes, cored and chopped

1 tbsp salt, plus more for seasoning

2 small cucumbers, peeled, seeded, and chopped

1 stalk celery with leaves, chopped

1 hot chile {such as jalapeño or serrano}, halved and seeded

2 tbsp freshly squeezed lemon juice

1 garlic clove, crushed

Freshly ground black pepper

Hot sauce {optional}

Ice, vodka or bourbon {optional}, young celery stalks with leaves, cornichon pickles, green olives, cherry tomatoes, or lemon and lime slices, for serving

Toss together the tomatoes and salt in a large bowl. Put the tomatoes in a fine-mesh strainer set over a large glass or plastic bowl. Let the tomatoes drain until all the juices have dripped out, about 1 hour. Press the liquid through or pass through a food mill if you have one, leaving the skins behind.

Puree the cucumbers, celery, chile, lemon juice, and garlic in a blender or food processor. Pass through a fine-mesh strainer into a large bowl to collect the juices, leaving the fiber and pulp behind.

Stir together the tomato liquid and the vegetable juices. Season with black pepper and more salt as needed, adding a dash of hot sauce if you like a little kick.

Serve over ice in tall chilled glasses. Stir in the alcohol, if you wish, and garnish with celery, cornichon, green olives, cherry tomatoes, or slices of lemon and lime, and swirl all the flavors together as you sip.

SCRATCH SANGRIA

serves 6

Nothing starts a party like a pitcher of sangria. Use a bottle of wine that's good enough to drink on its own. Choose something fruity and somewhat light and young, either red or white {but nothing oaky like chardonnay}. Sangria can swing the seasons easily and is excellent with chopped peaches or nectarines in the summer, apples in the fall, and bright, beautiful citrus all winter long.

1 lime, sliced

1 orange, sliced, or a handful of kumquats, halved

1 grapefruit or Meyer lemon, cut in pieces

¼ cup/30 g sugar

½ cup/120 ml brandy

¼ cup/60 ml Cointreau, Triple Sec, or Grand Marnier

One 750-ml bottle fruity red or white wine, chilled

Club soda, chilled {optional}

Stir together the fruit and sugar in a large pitcher. Add the brandy, Cointreau, and wine. Top off with a splash of chilled club soda {if using} for a fizzy finish.

P.S. *A good way to keep your sangria cold for a hot summer party is to slice and freeze your citrus for a few hours and up to overnight; they'll act like ice cubes and soften into the sangria as it sits.*

CHAPTER 10

INDULGENCES

Sweets to Love, Honor & Cherish

In books, you're not supposed to use a lot of exclamation points. I had to save all of mine up for this chapter. Both my hubby and I have insatiable sweet tooths. We were spoiled by mothers and grandmothers to whom daily dessert was not an unheard-of indulgence. I'm not talking about Ding Dongs and Oreos here, but real from-scratch desserts in little doses that ruined us from ever enjoying a lousy donut or pre-made pie.

Because of this, I am a lenient cook, but a devoted baker, preferring to spend my hours in the kitchen on the simplest dinners to leave time for measuring and turning raw ingredients into Sticky-Sweet Rhubarb Upside-Down Cake {page 255}, Bittersweet Chocolate Tart with Smoked Sea Salt {page 247}, or Chocolate Bread-&-Butter Pudding {page 235}.

Once you get started, it won't take long to find reasons for you to spoil each other too. These recipes are pure pleasure, not fussy or fancy, but requiring of the utmost commitment to loving whoever is on the other end. And it must be said that baking is not an entirely selfless act. Deep in the heart of the baker who pours her love into a Better-Than-Boxed Chocolate Cake {page 257} is an adoring little girl waiting to be smothered in the smiles and kisses that are sure to follow.

At their heart, these recipes are inspired by a grandmother whose simple peach or cherry cobblers made her table a touchstone for a marriage of over sixty-five years. They are guided by the soul and skill of a French pastry chef who is always ready to surprise and delight with texture and flavor. It is the best of both: homey heartland baked goods and big-city bake shops that together have yielded the most irresistible desserts.

These cakes, puddings, and pies find balance between the heart-warming flavors of farm-fresh fruits as in the Lazy Chef's Fruit Torte {page 244}, and the indulgent identities of ingredients like vanilla and bittersweet chocolate that make Black & White Cookies {page 262} that are hard to resist. Here sugar {or sometimes honey or agave nectar} plays a supporting role, never meant to overpower or outshine the main event, be it rich dark chocolate, velvety custard, or jammy stone fruits.

Here there is something for everyone {provided the everyone in question happens to love a good dessert}: crispy cookies marbled with slabs of chocolate {page 263}: warm, bursting cherries spooned over ice cream {page 239}; and biscuits with crumbly, golden edges and soft centers {page 241}.

Give yourself permission to indulge and enjoy life together, and always keep the cookie jar full!

COCOA

serves 2

{you can't resist} Real hot cocoa bubbling on the stove is the easiest way to seduce your beloved out of bed on a cold winter morning. Or better yet, pour it hot into mugs and crawl back in. There are months in our house when hot cocoa is an almost daily indulgence. It plays dessert, breakfast, or an afternoon treat so well that you'll soon find yourself stirring it together anytime you need something soothing and sweet. It's really worth it to keep a deep, Dutch-process cocoa around for this purpose. Keep in a sealed jar on the counter, at the ready.

2½ cups/ 600 ml whole milk

3 tbsp/15 g unsweetened
Dutch process cocoa powder

3 tbsp/20 g granulated sugar

Whipped cream/double cream
and chocolate shavings {optional}

Combine ½ cup/120 ml of the milk, the cocoa powder, and sugar in a medium saucepan with a heavy bottom and whisk thoroughly over low heat to make a thick chocolate paste. Whisk in the remaining milk until smooth and even with no lumps. Cook over medium heat, stirring constantly, until the mixture begins to bubble and thicken.

Smooth in the saucepan with an immersion blender if you have one, or beat vigorously with a whisk {but be careful since the mixture is hot} until smooth and frothy,

Pour into two sturdy mugs and top, if you wish, with whipped cream/double cream and chocolate shavings.

BROWN SUGAR PUDDING

serves 6

{southern comfort} My grandma, Virginia Copeland, always said "Learn to make what he loves." Top on my granddad's list was a brown sugar pudding that he first tasted at a boarding house where he stayed while working on the railroad after they first married. He loved it so much he brought back the recipe to his young bride. My Aunt Dorothy tells me that Grandma would make it for him just as often as he wanted for the rest of their lives. Though Granddad was forever tall and slim, he thrived on the way Grandma loved him through food. In this case, her love came in the form of tender cake dotted with plump raisins and smothered in brown sugar sauce. It's a perfect bed on which to drizzle fresh cream {as they would have} or melt vanilla ice cream.

Grandma and Granddad Copeland were mad about each other every day of their almost seventy-year marriage. If this was her secret, I wouldn't think of keeping it from anyone.

1½ cups/300 g packed brown sugar

2 cups/480 ml hot water

1 tbsp unsalted butter

1 cup/115 g all purpose flour

½ cup/100 g granulated sugar

1 tsp baking powder

¼ tsp iodized salt

½ cup/120 ml whole milk

½ cup/85 g raisins

1 tsp pure vanilla extract

Freshly grated nutmeg

Preheat the oven to 450°F/230°C/gas 8.

In a big, wide, cast-iron pan {about 10 in/25 cm} mix together the brown sugar and water until smooth. Add the butter. Bring to a boil over medium-high heat and cook until the sugar dissolves into a deep brown sauce.

Meanwhile, whisk together the flour, sugar, baking powder, salt, milk, raisins, and vanilla in a medium bowl to make a thick batter. Pour the batter into the boiling brown sugar sauce and stir just a little with a wooden spoon to encourage it to bubble to the top. Sprinkle freshly grated nutmeg over the top.

Bake the pudding until it is browned and just set with brown sugar sauce welled up in puddles between the cake, 15 to 20 minutes. Serve warm.

CHOCOLATE PUDDING

serves 4 to 6

{rich and pure} I adore chocolate pudding. I love it warm, I love it cold, I even love the pudding skin that forms on the top. This pudding is the taste of pure chocolate. Warm, it's rich and velvety, and thickens to a rich almost mousse texture in the fridge. If I didn't know better, I'd say it was almost the only chocolate dessert you'd ever need.

2 large eggs

3½ oz/85 g bittersweet
or semisweet/plain chocolate, chopped

1 tsp pure vanilla extract

2½ cups whole milk

⅓ cup sugar

¼ cup unsweetened cocoa powder

2 tbsp cornstarch/cornflour

1 hearty pinch fine sea or iodized salt

Whisk the eggs together in a sturdy, medium heatproof bowl and set the bowl near the stove. In another bowl, add the chopped chocolate and vanilla. Set a fine mesh strainer over the top and keep it nearby.

Combine ½ cup/120ml of the milk, the sugar, cocoa powder, cornstarch/cornflour, and salt in a medium saucepan with a heavy bottom and whisk thoroughly to make a thick chocolate paste. Whisk in the remaining milk until smooth and even with no lumps. Cook over medium heat, stirring constantly until the mixture begins to bubble and looks like a good hot chocolate. Keep cooking and stirring over a medium-low flame as the sauce boils and thickens to coat the back of a spoon with a thick layer, about 4 to 6 minutes.

Remove from the heat. While stirring the eggs with a whisk, use a ½ cup/120 ml measure to pour a little of the hot liquid into the eggs very slowly. Continue whisking to allow the eggs to adjust to the heat without scrambling. Add the egg mixture to the pan with the milk mixture and cook over low heat, stirring constantly until it is hot to the touch and a spoon or spatula leaves a thick trail as you pull it through the pudding. Immediately pull the pudding from the heat and quickly pour through the strainer into the bowl with the vanilla and chocolate. Use a rubber spatula to push the pudding through the strainer until only any lumps remain behind. Whisk the chocolate into the pudding until it is completely melted.

Divide the pudding among four to six small dishes and serve warm, cool, or chilled from the fridge.

MASTER PUDDING: Pudding is not a hard dessert to master, but like all custard desserts it can take a little practice to cook the eggs without curdling them. Read the recipe through once first and get everything set up before you begin. Straining your pudding at the end is an extra step of security to ensure the silkiest pudding, one you may decide to skip once you become a pudding pro.

CHOCOLATE BREAD-&-BUTTER PUDDING

serves 4 to 6

{almost naughty} In the earliest days of culinary school, before they let us loose with expensive ingredients and our own wild ideas about how to mix and match flavors, we often listened to the chefs talk about flavor, texture, or the history of certain foods. On those hungry evenings, there was always a good fresh French bread, butter, and dark chocolate in the classroom pantry, which we munched on layered together like sandwiches. This is a shamelessly decadent version, improved by custard and the magic that happens when all the components come together in a warm oven. Eat this warm or at room temperature, when the chocolate chunks are still warm enough to melt away the biggest worries of your week.

6 oz/170 g bittersweet chocolate, coarsely chopped

4 tbsp/44 g unsalted butter {at room temperature}, plus more for brushing

7 oz/200 g pugliese or rustic white bread {about ½ loaf}, cut in ¼-in-/6-mm-thick slices

3 large eggs, plus 3 egg yolks

¼ cup/50 g packed brown sugar

¼ tsp ground cinnamon, plus more for sprinkling

Pinch of fine sea salt

2¾ cups/ 660 ml half-and-half/half cream

1 tsp pure vanilla extract

1 tbsp turbinado or coarse sugar

Preheat the oven to 350°F/180°C/gas 4.

Sprinkle ¾ cup/90 g of the chocolate all over the bottom of a 7-by-11-in/17-by-28-cm baking dish.

Spread the butter on one side of the bread slices. Place the buttered bread on top of the chocolate, overlapping at the edges in a single layer like shingles.

Whisk together the eggs, yolks, sugar, cinnamon, and salt in a medium bowl. Stir in the half-and-half/half cream and vanilla and whisk to combine well. Pour the custard over the bread, and press any floating bread slices down into the custard to ensure the custard will soak all of the bread. Sprinkle the remaining chocolate pieces over the top, tucking them into the custard slightly to fill in the gaps where the bread meets. Set aside for 20 minutes to soak. Sprinkle the turbinado sugar over the top and dust very lightly with cinnamon.

Place the pan inside a roasting pan filled with 1 in/2.5 cm or so of warm water {the water should come about halfway up the sides of the baking dish}. Bake until the custard is just set but a touch wobbly in the center and the pudding puffs slightly, about 55 minutes.

Let the pudding cool for about 15 minutes. Serve warm.

GREEK YOGURT
WITH
FRESH FIGS

serves 4

{make caramel} One summer when I was working as a private chef in the south of France, there was a fig tree along the walkway between my bedroom and the kitchen. I waited all summer for the fruit to turn from green to deep purple, with the best intentions of making them into some-thing sweet for the family. But they seemed to ripen only one per day, and it was me against the birds to get them at their best, so I savored them one by one, straight from the tree.

Fresh figs, when you can get your hands on them, are so delicious eaten raw. But whenever I have more than a handful of ripe ones at one time, this is what I make, a subtle improvement {if that's possible} on nature's best.

⅓ cup/65 g packed brown sugar

2 tbsp water

3 tbsp cold unsalted butter

2 cups/480 ml Greek or strained yogurt

8 fresh figs, halved

Combine the brown sugar and the water in a small saucepan over medium-low heat. Cook until the sugar dissolves completely and begins to melt into a thick sauce, about 8 minutes. Decrease the heat and whisk in the cold butter until the mixture reaches the consistency of melted caramels. Remove from the heat and spoon the warm cara-mel over swirls of Greek yogurt and fresh figs.

WARM CHERRIES
WITH
PISTACHIO ICE CREAM

serves 4

{in season} All it takes is ten minutes to delight. Well, there is the matter of pitting the cherries, but for the short season they come on the scene, this is worth it. You won't complain when you taste them spooned warm over your favorite ice cream as a sweet summer sundae.

2 cups/340 g fresh
sweet red cherries, pitted

⅓ cup/40 g sugar
1 pt/480 ml pistachio ice cream

Toss the cherries and sugar together in a medium saucepan. Cook over medium heat until the cherries burst, about 6 minutes. Remove the cherries with a slotted spoon to a medium bowl and set aside. Continue to cook the juices until they are the consistency of syrup, about 6 to 8 minutes. Cool slightly {so the ice cream doesn't melt in an instant} and stir the cherries back in.

To serve, scoop the ice cream into small bowls or juice glasses and spoon the cherry sauce over the top.

PISTACHIO HUNTING: Good pistachio ice cream isn't easy to find, but gelato and artisan ice cream companies that are springing up all over the country are expanding your options by leaps and bounds. Go for the good stuff if you can find it, made with all natural ingredients and no added artificial colorings or flavors. And this sauce goes splendidly with classic, dependable vanilla ice cream as well.

SUMMER BLUES BROWN BETTIES

serves 4

{baked berries} I can remember every spoonful of my first brown betty. It was at the home of my dear friend Frances, who never ceases to amaze at what delights she turns out of her tiny kitchen. Her brown betty was all bursting blueberries and buttered bread crumbs with a dollop of ice cream—warm, sweet and so simple yet such a revelation. It was everything lovable about a luscious fruit cobbler or crisp made easier—all finesse and no fuss {the secret of most accomplished entertainers!}

Even if you've never turned on your oven, there's no excuse not to serve a fresh summer dessert when it is this easy, and this good. Go ahead, give your summer blues their moment.

TOPPING

4 thick slices stale sourdough, French, or hearty white bread, crusts removed, and cubed

¼ cup/50 g packed light brown sugar

¼ cup/50 g granulated sugar

1½ tsp ground cinnamon

¼ tsp ground ginger

FILLING

1 pt/punnet fresh blueberries

1 pt/punnet fresh blackberries

⅓ cup/65 g granulated sugar

1 tsp freshly squeezed lemon juice

4 tbsp/55 g cold unsalted butter, cut into pieces

Premium vanilla ice cream

Preheat the oven to 375°F/190°C/gas 5. Butter four shallow individual baking dishes or one 9-in-/23-cm-square or round shallow baking dish {such as a casuela}.

MAKE THE TOPPING: Pulse the bread cubes in a food processor or spice grinder to make coarse crumbs. {You should have 1½ cups/85 g crumbs.} Combine the bread crumbs with the brown and granulated sugars, the cinnamon, and ginger in a medium bowl.

MAKE THE FILLING: Toss the berries with the granulated sugar and lemon juice in a separate bowl. Sprinkle the bottom of each casserole with just enough of the crumb mixture {about one-third total} to lightly coat the bottoms. Divide the berries among the dishes and top with the remaining crumbs. Lay the nubs of butter over the top. Bake until the crumbs are golden brown and the fruit is bursting, about 20 minutes.

Transfer to a wire rack to cool, about 15 minutes. Serve warm with vanilla ice cream.

BERRIES & CREAM BISCUITS

serves 6

{summer's best} I grew up with spongy store-bought shortcakes smothered in fresh strawberries and freshly whipped cream. To tell you the truth, they were pretty delicious, since real berries and fresh cream can make most things taste good. One day I had this all-American treat at the hands of a British baker whose shortcakes were a cross between a buttery French Breton and an American cream biscuit—golden, crumbly, and sweet with so much more texture to soak up the saucy berries. Ever since, I've been rolling, pressing, and baking my way toward my memory of that perfect shortcake. This is it, all grown up with sliced almonds and berries tossed in Grand Marnier. Shortcakes are cheap to make, so this is the perfect time to spring for fresh, high-quality cream and local berries from your farmers' market. You'll be so glad you did.

SHORTCAKES

1¾ cups/200 g all-purpose/plain flour, plus more for dusting

1 tbsp baking powder

½ tsp fine sea salt

6 tbsp/85 g very cold unsalted butter, cut in pieces

⅔ cup/165 ml cold heavy/double cream or half-and-half/half cream

2 large eggs, beaten

1 to 2 tbsps sliced/flaked skin-on almonds

1 to 2 tsp turbinado or coarse sugar

TOPPING

3 cups strawberries, hulled and quartered

1 pt/punnet blackberries, huckleberries, or mulberries

3 tbsp sugar

1 tbsp freshly squeezed lemon juice or Grand Marnier

1½ cups/360 ml cold whipping/double cream

1 to 2 tbsp sugar

MAKE THE SHORTCAKES: Line a baking sheet/tray with parchment/baking paper and set aside.

Whisk together the flour, baking powder, and salt in a large bowl. Rub in the 6 tbsp/85 g cold butter with your hands until the flour is coated in the butter and some pieces clump together. Lightly stir in the cream and half of the beaten egg with a fork until the mixture just comes together into a rough, shaggy, but not sticky, dough.

Turn the dough out onto a lightly floured countertop and fold over once or twice. Don't overwork it; the layers of cool butter and flour are what give this biscuit its distinctive rise and texture. Pat the dough into a 6-by-4-in/15-by-10-cm rectangle that is about 1½ in/4 cm tall.

Using a pastry cutter or a sharp knife, cut the dough into six 2-in-/5-cm-square biscuits. Transfer the shortcakes to the prepared baking sheet, evenly brush the top of each

CONTINUED

shortcake with the remaining beaten egg, and sprinkle with sliced almonds/flaked almonds and turbinado sugar. Transfer to the freezer to chill for 30 minutes.

Meanwhile, preheat the oven to 375°F/190°C/gas 5.

MAKE THE TOPPING: Toss the berries and the sugar together in a medium bowl; add the lemon juice to help draw the juices out of the fruit. Cover and set aside while you bake the shortcakes.

Bake the shortcakes until they are an even golden brown and just cooked through, 25 to 30 minutes. When finished, remove from the oven and transfer to a wire rack to cool completely.

Meanwhile, whip the cream with 1 to 2 tbsp sugar, depending on how sweet you like it, until it just holds soft peaks. You want your cream to be light and luscious, and dollop easily off the side of a spoon.

To serve, split shortcakes or pry into halves. Layer with whipped cream and berries, and spoon berry drippings all over the top. Be generous.

THE FLAKIEST SHORTCAKES AND SCONES: The tender flaky texture of a good shortcake, biscuit, or scone depends entirely on cold butter and a dough that's been barely worked. Freezing the shortcakes before baking them is a must—it helps them hold their shape and grow tall and stately in the oven, so they're perfect for presentation.

LAZY CHEF'S FRUIT TORTE

serves 8 to 10

{easy breezy} A cake that can highlight the fruits of almost every season is a baker's best friend, especially one that comes together as quickly as this one. Ripe with the flavors of seasonal fruit, this is as good with peaches, plums, and blackberries in the summer as it is with pears and cranberries for Thanksgiving. I find this torte to be especially seductive as the seasons turn with a bit of the last of the blueberries and first of peaches and figs, for example. This torte needs only a dusting of confectioners' sugar or lightly whipped cream to warrant its praise, so put your feet up and grab a good book while it bakes!

¾ cup/170 g unsalted butter {plus more for the pan}, at room temperature

1½ cups/300 g sugar

3 large eggs, at room temperature

1 tsp pure vanilla extract

1½ cups/175 g all-purpose/plain flour, plus more for dusting

1½ tsp baking powder

Pinch of fine sea salt

TOPPING

1 tbsp sugar

1 tsp ground cinnamon

1 ripe pear, nectarine, peach or plum, pitted, peeled, and sliced

Handful of berries, pitted cherries, cranberries, fresh currants, or quartered figs

Confectioners'/icing sugar

Sweetened whipped cream/double cream

Preheat the oven to 375°F/190°C/gas 5. Butter and lightly flour a 9-in/23-cm springform pan.

Beat together the butter and sugar in a large bowl with an electric mixer until light and fluffy. Add the eggs, one at a time, beating well after each addition, until fully combined. Stir in the vanilla.

Whisk together the flour, baking powder, and salt in a small bowl. Add to the butter mixture and stir to make a thick batter.

MAKE THE TOPPING: Stir together the sugar and cinnamon. Transfer the batter into the prepared pan. Top the batter with the fruit and sprinkle with the cinnamon-sugar.

Bake until the torte springs back in the middle, is evenly domed, and the top is caramelized and golden brown, about 1 hour and 10 minutes.

Transfer to a wire rack to cool until easy to handle. Remove the pan sides and let the torte cool further until just warm to the touch. Sprinkle generously with confectioners'/icing sugar. Slice and serve with sweetened whipped cream/double cream.

A FRUIT FOR ALL SEASONS
Try these four fruit combinations, one for each season.

FALL: *Pear and Blackberry*
WINTER: *Pear and Cranberry*
SUMMER: *Peach, Fig, and Blueberry*
SPRING: *Strawberries*

BITTERSWEET CHOCOLATE TART
· · · · WITH · · · ·
SMOKED SEA SALT

serves 12

{amaze with ease} For my parents' fortieth anniversary, my siblings and I threw them a party to celebrate. We filled the house with fresh artisan cheese, handmade crackers and cookies, and one flawless bittersweet chocolate tart, to satisfy their mutual affection for chocolate. I should have made twelve of them—it was gone before we offered the toast, and I'm still getting requests to share my recipe.

Despite its handsome finish, this couldn't be easier. The crust gets its tenderness from sugar and melted butter, pressed in instead of rolled for ease. It is completely simple, and sinfully elegant. The flavor comes from the chocolate and the cream, so splurge on the highest quality of both you can find. Your loved ones are worth it.

CRUST	FILLING
½ cup/115 g unsalted butter, melted	½ cup/120 ml heavy cream
3 tbsp sugar	½ cup/120 ml whole milk
½ tsp pure vanilla extract	2 tbsp sugar
Pinch of fine sea salt	Pinch of fine sea salt
1 cup/115 g all-purpose/plain flour	7 oz/200 g high-quality bittersweet chocolate, chopped {1 heaping cup}
	1 large egg, beaten
	Smoked sea salt {optional}
	Crème fraîche {optional}

Preheat the oven to 350°F/180°C/gas 4.

MAKE THE CRUST: Whisk together the melted butter, sugar, vanilla, and salt. Add the flour and stir until it feels like damp sand. Press the dough evenly along the bottom and up the sides of an 8-in/20-cm square or 9-in/ 23-cm round tart pan/flan tin with a removable bottom {which makes it much easier to remove the tart in one piece. If you don't have a tart pan/flan tin, you can make this tart in a springform pan; press the dough evenly across the bottom and only about 1¼ to 1½ in/3 to 4 cm up the side of the pan}. Use wax/greaseproof paper or buttered fingers to even out and press the dough tightly into the corners. Prick the crust all over with a fork and chill in the fridge until ready to bake, about 30 minutes.

CONTINUED

Set the pan on a baking sheet/tray and bake until the crust is golden brown, about 25 minutes.

MAKE THE FILLING: While the crust bakes, bring the cream, milk, sugar, and salt to a simmer in a medium saucepan over low heat. Remove from the heat and add the chocolate. Let it sit for about 2 minutes, without stirring. Starting in the middle of the pan, whisk together until the chocolate is evenly melted and the mixture is smooth and a shiny dark brown.

Whisk the beaten egg into the chocolate filling and pour the filling directly into the hot crust. Decrease the oven to 300° F/150°C./gas 2 and return the tart to the oven. Bake until the filling is set, but still a little wiggly in the center, about 15 minutes {temperatures vary from oven to oven, so the visual clue is more important than time}. Set your timer for

13 minutes. If it looks mostly set at that point, test it by opening the oven door a crack and carefully jiggle the tart pan/flan tin with the edge of your oven mitt. Only the center third should wobble. If it wobbles all the way to the edge, close the door quickly and continue baking about 2 minutes more.

Remove the tart and cool completely on a rack at room temperature. Just before the tart cools and sets completely, sprinkle a few large flakes of smoked salt on the surface, or leave plain.

Remove the tart from the pan sides and carefully transfer to a platter before serving. Let it cool just until it slices easily. It melts in your mouth when served slightly warm, with a dollop of crème fraiche, if you wish, for extra decadence. Or cool completely, and serve by itself.

P.S. *The deep, smoky flavor of smoked sea salt is a fine complement to the rich chocolate, but this tart is just as elegant with big flakes of white sea salt, or if you're a chocolate purist, no salt at all.*

MY GIRL'S BROWNIES

makes 9 to 12 brownies

{make him proud} He'll never get over his mom's brownies, until he's had yours. These will become a favorite of everyone who likes dark, fudgy brownies that stay soft from the center to the outer edges, even when fully baked {no more fighting over the middle pieces!}. These are the ultimate pantry brownie, drawing their richness from butter and cocoa powder instead of chopped chocolate, which means you can whip up a batch fresh and cheap whenever the craving hits.

10 tbsp/140 g unsalted butter, plus more for the pan

1 cup/200 g sugar

1 tsp pure vanilla extract

2 large eggs, chilled

½ cup/50 g cocoa powder

½ cup/60 g all-purpose/plain flour

1 generous pinch {about ⅛ tsp} of fine sea salt

½ cup/55 g toasted walnuts {optional}

Preheat the oven to 325°F/165°C/gas 3. Lightly butter an 8-in-/20-cm-square baking pan/tin. Line the pan with parchment/baking paper: cut two strips 8 in/20 cm wide and long enough that they hang about 2 in/5 cm over each side of the pan to create flaps. Tuck the paper into the edges of the pan and butter the parchment.

Cream the butter and sugar together with an electric mixer until light and fluffy, about 2 minutes. Add the vanilla and the eggs and mix to combine. Add the cocoa, flour, and

salt and stir to bring together, stopping to scrape the bowl as needed. Lightly stir in toasted walnuts, if you wish, with a spatula.

Transfer the batter to the prepared pan and bake until the top cracks and a toothpick inserted into the center comes out moist but not gooey, 30 to 35 minutes.

Transfer to a wire rack to cool. Cut into 9 to 12 bars, and serve warm or cool completely.

P.S. *These are the perfect brownie for a sundae, and soften into rich folds of vanilla ice cream like a dream.*

CARROT CAKE BARS
···· WITH ····
CREAM CHEESE FROSTING

serves 12

{my favorite} For as long as I can remember, I've been crazy for carrot cake. Any carrot cake will do, with or without walnuts, coconut, or pineapple, as long as it's slathered in cream cheese frosting. But there's no carrot cake in the world like my mom's: so tender it truly melts in your mouth. Each year for my birthday, no matter what theme cake creation I'd asked for on the outside {aqua-blue pool for a pool party, a yellow-studded pineapple for a luau party}, whenever she'd slice it open, there was my favorite orange cake.

When I finally made it myself, it was still perfect. But since I'm always looking for ways to make things just a touch healthier, I tried it again with white whole-wheat flour, and agave nectar in the icing to cut back on some of the sugar. I fell in love all over again, and I hope you will, too.

BARS

4 large eggs

1⅓ cups/315 ml grapeseed or canola oil

10 oz/300 ml pure carrot puree or jarred carrot baby food

2 cups/225 g sugar

2 cups/255 g white whole-wheat/wholemeal flour or all-purpose/plain flour

2 tsp baking soda/bicarbonate of soda

1 tsp ground cinnamon

FROSTING

½ cup/115 g unsalted butter {at room temperature}, cubed

8 oz/225 g cream cheese or Neufchâtel cheese, at room temperature

¾ cup/70 g confectioners'/icing sugar

2 tsp agave nectar or honey

1 tsp pure vanilla extract

MAKE THE BARS: Preheat the oven to 350°F/180°C/gas 4. Lightly butter a 9-by-13-in/23-by-33-cm pan. Line the pan with a wide piece of parchment/baking paper cut so that it tucks neatly along two opposite sides and hangs over the edges by about 1 in/2.5 cm on the other opposite sides to create flaps.

Beat the eggs in a bowl with an electric mixer on medium-high speed until thick and pale, about 4 minutes. Add the oil and carrot puree. Add the sugar, flour, baking soda/bicarbonate of soda, and cinnamon and stir together until evenly combined. Pour into the prepared pan and

bake until the cake spring back lightly when touched, about 40 minutes. Transfer to a wire rack to cool completely.

MEANWHILE, MAKE THE FROSTING: Check to make sure that the butter and cream cheese are soft but still cool. Beat them together in a bowl with an electric mixer until smooth and fluffy with no lumps. Sift in the confectioners'/icing sugar and add the agave nectar and vanilla extract. Beat until light and fluffy.

Spread the frosting evenly over the top of the cooled bars. Cut into 12 bars. Serve at room temperature.

OLIVE OIL CAKE
WITH
TANGERINE MARMALADE

serves 8

{tastes like the sun} There is an elegance to an olive oil cake, especially one layered in shingles of shiny, candied citrus that make it an instant centerpiece. But what are good looks to a dessert without the flavor and texture to back it up? This cake wins in all categories. It borrows a little trick from savvy Italian nonnas, who have long known olive oil as their heart healthy secret to a moist cake. Made with your best mild fruity finishing oil {one whose flavor you like all on its own}, this becomes a special-occasion cake that's far simpler to make than it looks.

While your cake cools, make your own luxurious homemade marmalade out of sweet citrus. We fell in love with fresh squeezed tangerine juice on our honeymoon in Mexico. I love tangerines for their beautiful balance of sweetness and tang and the way their tender skins soften with sugar and add a glistening finish to this tender cake. You can use whatever citrus you love, or a mix of all of your favorites.

OLIVE OIL CAKE

4 large eggs

¾ cup/150 g sugar

⅔ cup/165 ml your favorite extra-virgin olive oil

⅓ cup/75 ml melted unsalted butter

Finely grated zest and freshly squeezed juice of 1 tangerine, orange, or lemon

1½ cups/175 g all-purpose/plain flour

1 tbsp baking powder

¾ tsp fine sea salt or iodized salt

TANGERINE MARMALADE

4 large tangerines, Minneolas, lemons, Meyer lemons, or Temple oranges {about 1¾ lb/800 g}, or a mix

1 cup/200 g sugar

Crème fraîche or whipped cream/double cream, for serving

MAKE THE CAKE: Preheat the oven to 325°F/165°C/gas 3. Lightly butter a 9-in/23-cm springform pan with a removable bottom.

Combine the eggs and sugar in a large bowl and beat with an electric mixer on high speed until the eggs are thick and pale yellow, about 3 minutes. Drizzle in the olive oil and melted butter and continue to beat. Fold in the citrus zest and juice.

CONTINUED

Whisk together the flour, baking powder, and salt in a separate bowl. Add the dry ingredients gradually to the egg mixture and stir until evenly combined, scraping down the sides of the bowl with a rubber spatula to make sure there are no dry bits at the bottom.

Pour the batter into the prepared pan. Bake until the top is lightly brown and a skewer inserted into the center comes out clean, 40 to 45 minutes, rotating once during baking to make sure it cooks evenly. Cool the cake on a wire rack for about 10 minutes. When cool enough to handle, remove the pan sides and cool the cake completely on the rack.

MEANWHILE, MAKE THE MARMALADE: Scrub and dry the tangerines and trim off their tops and bottoms. Slice two of them as thinly as possible while still keeping their shape, about ⅛ to ¼ in/3 to 6 mm thick, discarding the seeds as they appear. Place the tangerine slices in a small pot with a heavy bottom. Juice the remaining two tangerines {you should have a scant 1 cup/240 ml of juice} and pour the juice over the sliced fruit. Set aside for 20 minutes.

Cook over medium-high heat until the liquid comes to a boil. Decrease the heat and simmer until the tangerine peel is soft, about 20 minutes. {Don't stir, which will destroy the pretty round shape of the citrus.} Add the sugar and continue cooking until the sugar is dissolved. Cook until thickened and the juice has gelled slightly and is syrupy, about 20 minutes. Remove from the heat and let it cool to room temperature.

Arrange the candied citrus slices over the top of the cake, overlapping to make beautiful jeweled tiles of fruit. Drizzle some of the citrus syrup over the slices and allow it to drip down the sides of the cake. Slice and serve with crème fraîche or whipped cream/double cream.

P.S. *If you love the flavor of this citrus marmalade, make a batch or two using chopped citrus and keep it in jars in the fridge to serve with toast and biscuits.*

STICKY-SWEET
RHUBARB UPSIDE-DOWN CAKE

serves 6

{our secret} Packaged miniature marshmallows go against all the principles of fresh, local, seasonal food. But you'll have to forgive yourself just this once. They are the secret ingredient in this irresistible summer sweet, made with the crisp, tart rhubarb that makes a fleeting appearance at the market in early spring.

I learned to make this cake from my mother, who learned it from hers. Mom would send one of us into the backyard to snap off fat stalks of rhubarb that grew up over our heads. I remember the ruby color, the snap as she sliced them into chunks, rhythmically rocking her well-used Chicago Cutlery against the cutting board. The smell of the house as the cake cooks can still take me back to the sounds of my dad, licking his lips with his standard "oh honey, honey," as he drizzled fresh cream over his steamy portion.

Years later, when I was learning French pastry at the three-star restaurant Café Boulud in New York City, I made this for the staff and sheepishly plated up a portion for the pastry chef, Remi, whom I both feared and adored. He raved. His praise for this humble dessert reminded me how often good things come in simple packages. Now I make this for everyone, and of course András, with the rhubarb from our own garden. It never fails to surprise and seduce.

CONTINUED

5 tbsp/70 g unsalted butter {plus more for the pan}, at room temperature

1¼ cups/140 g cake/soft-wheat flour

1¼ tsp baking powder

1¾ cups/350 g sugar

¼ tsp fine sea salt

½ cup/120 ml whole milk

1 large egg, beaten

1 tsp pure vanilla extract

4 large stalks rhubarb, cut in ½-in/12-mm pieces {about 4 cups/2 kg}

Handful of miniature marshmallows

High-quality vanilla ice cream, for serving

Heavy/double cream {optional}, for serving

Preheat the oven to 350°F/180°C/gas 4. Butter a 9-in-/23-cm-square baking pan.

Whisk together the flour, baking powder, ¾ cup/150 g of the sugar, and salt in a medium bowl. Mix in the 5 tbsp/70g soft butter with a fork or your fingers. Whisk together the milk, egg, and vanilla in a small bowl. Add the milk mixture to the flour mixture, using a fork to bring all together into a loose batter.

Toss together the rhubarb, the remaining 1 cup/200 g sugar, and marshmallows in a medium bowl; spoon in an even layer in the prepared baking pan. Spoon the batter over the top in an even layer. The batter will drip down between

the rhubarb allowing some of the rhubarb to show {don't worry if some of the marshmallows and rhubarb show, they will melt into a caramelized crust as the cake cooks}.

Bake in the center of the oven until the rhubarb is bubbly, the top is puffed and caramelized {slightly golden-crisp in spots}, and the cake springs back lightly when touched, about 40 minutes.

If you can resist the intoxicating smell, let the cake cool a few minutes on a rack. Then spoon out into small bowls, flipping the cake so the rhubarb side faces up, and serve with a scoop of vanilla ice cream. If you're feeling really decadent or have a bit of Southern in you, drizzle fresh cool cream over the top.

BETTER-THAN-BOXED CHOCOLATE CAKE

makes one 9-in/23-cm layer cake; serves 8

{not just for birthdays} This cake is completely delicious, and not the least formal, which I've learned, from the staunchly loyal, old-fashioned cake lovers in my family, is a very good thing. It is filled with the love of my mother whose chocolate cake was never, ever remiss at a birthday or milestone even if it meant staying up past midnight while the rest of us slept. Her chocolate cake has flown miles and ridden over mountains in the backseat of a car to make it to our most special meals or occasions just in time, and it even made it on the menu at our wedding. And it's kept my dad never far from her side for over forty years.

For the ones you love, you won't mind putting in the extra effort to make them a cake from scratch, especially when it's almost as easy as cake from a box. This one is based on ingredients from your pantry and comes together all in one bowl. And when you taste its luscious textures, you may just swear off your old mix for good. The rich, silky, buttery chocolate icing is what really takes this over the top and makes it just the thing to make your chocolate cake legendary.

CAKE

3 cups/385 g all-purpose/plain flour

2⅔ cups/530 g granulated sugar

1 cup/100 g cocoa powder, plus more for dusting

1½ tsp baking soda/bicarbonate of soda

¾ tsp baking powder

½ tsp fine sea salt

1¾ cups/420 ml warm water

1 cup/240 ml vegetable or grapeseed oil

4 tbsp/55 g melted butter, plus more for the pans

5 large eggs

1 tsp pure vanilla extract

CHOCOLATE FROSTING

1½ cups/340 g unsalted butter, at room temperature

3 tbsp/45 ml agave nectar or honey

½ cup/50 g confectioners'/icing sugar

1¼ cup/120 g cocoa powder

¼ cup/60 ml warm water

¼ cup/60 ml cool heavy/double cream

CONTINUED

MAKE THE CAKE: Preheat the oven to 350°F/180°C/gas 4. Lightly butter two 9-in/23-cm round cake pan/tins. Line with parchment/baking paper. Butter the parchment. Dust the inside of both pans with cocoa powder and knock against the side of the counter to settle a thin dusting of cocoa inside the pans; discard any extra cocoa.

Whisk together the flour, sugar, cocoa, baking soda/bicarbonate of soda, baking powder, and salt together in the bowl of a stand mixer.

Add 1 cup/240 ml of the warm water, the oil, and melted butter and mix on medium speed until combined. Stop the mixer to scrape down the sides of the bowl and make sure all the ingredients are fully incorporated. Add the eggs, one at a time, mixing well between additions to incorporate and aerate the batter, which gives the cake a more even crumb. Add the remaining ¾ cup/180 ml warm water and vanilla and beat until smooth and aerated, about 2 minutes. The batter will look loose and watery, about the consistency of heavy cream or hot fudge.

Divide evenly between the prepared pans and tap lightly on the counter to smooth the top. Bake until the cakes are evenly domed and spring back lightly when touched, about 40 minutes. Test the cakes with a toothpick inserted into the centers; if it comes out clean your cakes are done.

Remove the cakes from the oven and let them cool on a wire rack until they are just warm to the touch, about 15 minutes. The cakes will pull away from the sides of the pans slightly as they cool. Flip the pans to unmold the cakes onto a rack to cool completely, 1 hour.

MAKE THE FROSTING: Before you begin, check to make sure the butter is room temperature, just soft enough to press easily with your finger. Beat together the butter, agave, confectioners'/icing sugar, cocoa powder, and warm water with a stand mixer until light and creamy and evenly combined, about 2 minutes. Stop to scrape down the sides of the bowl and make sure all the butter is fully combined. Add the cool cream and beat on medium high until fluffy and creamy.

When the cakes are completely cooled, slice off the dome from one of the layers with a serrated knife so that you can stack the layers easily. Lay the trimmed cake layer on a cake stand or serving platter, trimmed-side up. Tear four sheets of parchment/baking paper or wax/greaseproof paper into long strips and tuck under the edges of the cake around all the sides {this will help to keep your serving platter clean as you frost}. Scoop about one-third of the frosting onto the top of the cake. Using an offset spatula or the back of a spoon, spread the frosting evenly over the top of the cake and around the sides. Cover with the second cake layer, domed-side up, and press down slightly to flatten. Look down at the cake and slide the top cake layer until it lines up perfectly with the bottom layer. Add another one-third of the frosting to the top and spread evenly over the top. Spread the remaining one-third of the icing around the sides of the cake to create a smooth, even layer.

Make careless swirls of icing all over the top of the cake using the back of a large spoon. Serve immediately or store in a cool place until ready to serve.

If you plan to make ahead and refrigerate, note that the icing will set up in the fridge and will sweat slightly when it comes out. Remove from the fridge about 1 hour before serving to restore the frosting to its luscious, creamy state.

P.S. *If you want a deep, dark chocolate flavor, use Dutch-process cocoa. For an old-fashioned-quality cake, use natural cocoa.*

{ THE COOKIE JAR }

Before I was married, I always gave my dearest brides-to-be the same gift at their shower—a vintage cookie jar filled with a girlish apron, something delicate, and a stack of my favorite cookie recipes with a note that said "keep the cookie jar full"—a nod to the flirtatious fun I wished for their marriage. Now that I am married, I realize what good advice that was! Here's what keeps our cookie jar full.

DEEP-DARK-SECRET CHOCOLATE COOKIES

makes 3 dozen cookies/biscuits

{pure chocolate} This is the kind of cookie for which you'd reveal your deepest, darkest secret. The cookie's secret is four kinds of chocolate and a brownie-meets-truffle texture so be careful not to overbake them. This recipe makes a big batch, so keep extra dough in the fridge for easy last-minute baking and an unparalleled chocolate fix. Cracked, roasted cacao beans are worth hunting down in a specialty food store or online. You can skip them, but you'll miss their deep, dark chocolate crunch. See Sources {page 293}.

7 oz/200 g bittersweet chocolate, chopped

½ cup/115 g unsalted butter, cut in pieces

3 large eggs

½ tsp pure vanilla extract

¾ cups/150 g sugar

1 cup/115 g flour

2 tbsp Dutch-process or natural cocoa powder

1 tsp baking powder

¾ tsp fine sea salt

3 oz/85 g milk chocolate, coarsely chopped

¼ cup/30 g cacao nibs

Melt the bittersweet chocolate and butter together in a glass bowl set over a pot of simmering water. Stir occasionally until melted and smooth. Set aside to cool.

In a separate medium bowl, whisk together eggs, vanilla, and sugar until combined.

In another medium bowl, sift together the flour, cocoa, baking powder, and salt.

Gradually whisk the egg mixture into the melted chocolate. Sift the dry ingredients into the chocolate mixture in batches, folding in until completely blended. When the dough is completely cool, stir in the milk chocolate chunks and cacao nibs.

Like any cookie/biscuit or dough, chilling the dough here results in a more even shape when you bake. Refrigerate for 25 minutes before scooping. {If you really can't wait, they will bake up in slightly irregular shapes, but they'll still taste delicious, so go ahead with the next step.}

Preheat the oven to 350°F/180°C/gas 4. Line a baking sheet/tray with parchment/baking paper.

Scoop portions of dough with a tiny cookie/biscuit or ice-cream scoop and roll into small 1-in/2.5-cm balls. Place on the prepared baking sheet/tray 1 in/2.5 cm apart. Bake until just set but still soft to the touch, with shiny tops, about 8 minutes. Let the cookies cool slightly on the baking sheet.

Serve while the milk chocolate is still melty and warm. The cookies keep in an airtight container for up to 2 days, or in the freezer for 2 weeks.

P.S. *Make these into incredible ice cream sandwiches with your favorite ice cream!*

BLACK & WHITE COOKIES

makes 16 cookies/biscuits

{chocolate and vanilla} Chocolate, Vanilla, Chocolate, Vanilla? God bless the baker who invented the cookie to end that debate forever. Part cookie, part cake, a good black-and-white can steal your heart. You'll find any number of versions aross the Northeast, where they found their fame. The best version I've ever had came from a small family-run bake shop in Boston. This one is inspired by their light, cakey version, with a thick schmear of fluffy frosting full of real vanilla and rich cocoa.

COOKIE

1 cup/225 g unsalted butter, at room temperature

1¾ cups/200 g granulated sugar

1 large egg

1 cup/240 ml buttermilk

1 teaspoon pure vanilla extract

4 cups/510 g all-purpose/plain flour

1 tsp baking powder

1 tsp baking soda/bicarbonate of soda

Pinch of fine salt

ICING

14 tbsp/200 g unsalted butter, at room temperature

1 lb/455 g confectioners'/icing sugar {about 3¾ cups}

2 tbsp agave nectar or honey

1 vanilla bean/pod, pulp scraped, or ½ tsp vanilla bean/pod paste

½ cup/50 g cocoa powder

2 tbsp lukewarm water

Preheat oven to 350°F/180°C/gas 4. Line 2 baking sheet/trays with parchment/baking paper or silicone baking mats.

MAKE THE COOKIES/BISCUITS: Beat the butter and sugar together with a stand mixer fitted with the paddle attachment until light and fluffy, about 2 minutes. Add the egg and beat on low to incorporate.

Combine the buttermilk and vanilla in a small pitcher or bowl. Whisk together the flour, baking powder, baking soda/bicarbonate of soda, and salt in another bowl. Add one-third of the dry ingredients to the batter on low speed. Add half of the wet ingredients, followed by another one-third of the dry, and finally the rest of the wet. Stir on low speed to create a smooth, even batter. Stop and scrape down the bowl and then beat on medium-high until completely smooth and silky, about 1 minute. Batter will be thinner than a typical cookie/biscuit dough, more like a cake batter.

Using a cookie/biscuit or small ice cream scoop {about 2-tablespoon size}, scoop portions of dough onto the prepared tray in smooth, egg-sized mounds. Leave about 2 in/5 cm

between each cookie/biscuit since the batter will spread slightly. Bake until they are puffed in the center and spring back lightly when touched, about 12 to 15 minutes. Remove from the oven and let cool a few minutes. Transfer cookies/biscuits to a wire rack to cool completely.

MEANWHILE, MAKE THE ICING: Beat together the butter, confectioners'/icing sugar, and agave to make a smooth, fluffy icing. Remove two-thirds of the icing {about 1½ cups/360 ml} and stir in the vanilla bean/pod pulp. Add cocoa powder to the remaining icing and beat to combine thoroughly, adding about 2 tablespoons lukewarm water to bring it together.

When the cookies/biscuits are completely cool, spread the vanilla icing over half of each cookie/biscuit, using about 1 scant tablespoon per cookie/biscuit. Finish with the chocolate icing. These are best eaten the day they are baked, but you can store them for 1 day in an airtight container.

THOUSAND-LAYER
CHOCOLATE CHIP COOKIES

makes 20 cookies/biscuits

{an artist's way} Imagine the countertop of your favorite bakery piled high with stacks of crunchy cookies marbled with sheets of chocolate. Now imagine that in your very own kitchen. These are worth the effort. The layered chocolate provides unparalleled texture, flavor, and a bakery-style finish that will make you very proud to call these your chocolate chip cookies.

1 cup/225 g unsalted butter,
at room temperature

¾ cup/150 g packed dark brown sugar

¾ cup/150 g granulated sugar

4 egg yolks, at room temperature,
plus 1 large egg, lightly beaten, for brushing

1 tsp pure vanilla extract

2¼ cups/280 g all-purpose/plain flour,
plus more for dusting

¾ tsp baking soda/bicarbonate of soda

¾ tsp fine sea salt or table salt

9 oz/255 g high-quality bittersweet chocolate

¼ tsp fleur de sel {optional}

Preheat the oven to 375°F/190°C/gas 5. Line two baking sheets/trays with parchment/baking paper.

Cream the butter and both sugars together with an electric mixer on medium-high speed until light and fluffy, about 3 minutes. Beat in the egg yolks, two at a time, followed by vanilla.

Whisk together the flour, baking soda/bicarbonate of soda, and salt. Stir the dry ingredients into the butter mixture on low speed until just mixed. Stop and scrape down the bowl to make sure all the butter is evenly incorporated and then give the dough a final mix.

Divide the dough into three portions. Put each dough portion on large piece of plastic wrap/cling film, and pat into a 4-by-6-in/10-by-15-cm rectangle. Wrap and refrigerate on a flat shelf in the fridge until well chilled, about 30 minutes. {This helps to set the butter and make the dough easier to work with. Chilling cookie dough also helps cookies keep their shape when they bake, the secret of most fine bakeries!}

Meanwhile, coarsely chop the chocolate into thin shards using a serrated knife. Set aside.

When the dough is chilled, lay one portion on a lightly floured countertop. Sprinkle with half of the chocolate and top with another piece of dough. Repeat with remaining

chocolate and dough until you have a slab of dough with two layers of chocolate. Dust lightly and evenly with flour and roll gently with a rolling pin into a large 9-by 6-in/23-by-15-cm rectangle that's about 1½ in/ 4 cm thick.

Using a 2-in/5-cm round cookie or biscuit cutter or a thin-rimmed glass, cut out ten rounds of dough. Gather the scraps together, pat lightly, and cut out the remaining cookies.

Divide half of the cookies/biscuits between the two prepared baking sheet/trays, leaving about 3 in/7.5 cm between the cookies since they will spread. Brush the tops of each cookie with the beaten egg, and with a light hand, sprinkle with a few grains of fleur de sel, or leave plain.

Bake until the cookies are set, 12 to 15 minutes, switching the sheets halfway through top to bottom if you're baking two sheets at a time. Let cookies cool slightly, about 3 minutes, then transfer the cookies with a thin spatula to a wire rack to cool completely {or, just slide the parchment directly onto the cooling rack}. Let the baking sheets cool completely before using to bake the remaining dough {lining with more parchment, if needed}. Bake as directed, switching the sheets top to bottom halfway through baking, and cool.

Store in an airtight container for up to 4 days.

CHAPTER 11

GATHERINGS

Your wedding meal is the meal of all meals, the greatest of gatherings. There may never be another day when you are completely surrounded with the people you love, feeding and feasting side by side in honor of the two of you.

Ours was the meal of our lifetime, with our ninety-seven nearest and dearest all gathered at one long table in the shade of a poplar grove. The meal itself was outstanding, every detail and dish an expression of our gratitude for our families and a tribute to the memories we had made together in the years before we became husband and wife {of course, there were figs!}. But what we remember even more than the food itself was the music made of voices we know and love, laughing and sharing stories all around us. It was the clinking of forks and glasses as friends and family devoured the meal we'd so carefully planned for them that gave us a fullness that seemed to last and last for days.

There's a place for that in your everyday life. Though your wedding may be the greatest gathering of all, don't let it be the last! In asking your friends and family to be a part of your life and your table from this day forth, you're asking them for their support, to believe in your decision, and to help you walk through life together. You're also asking them to share in some of your new favorite foods, like Dutch Babies with Poached Rhubarb {page 58} served up as a His & Hers Brunch {page 273}.

Far less work or money goes into {and needs to go into} a gathering of friends at your home than you put into your wedding, but the sentiment should be the same. The meal you serve can be as simple as Pizzeria Facile {page 274} or you can use it as an excuse to crack the case of wine you got as a gift and show off your grill pan to make flatbread for A Platter of Plenty {page 280}. Even new friends will quickly become family when they're invited next to you at the stove to spoon up French Onion Soup {page 134} for a cozy Snow Day {page 273}. That is the spirit of gathering.

If you've been using this book for the two of you at home, you're already ready to entertain. These casual feasts build on the recipes you've already made and mastered during the week, sometimes doubled and tripled for a crowd, plus any extra details you need to round it all out and make it a party. Before long, yours will be the table or picnic blanket your friends love to return to.

And in the sweetness of friendship let there be laughter, and sharing of pleasures.
—Kahlil Gibran

THE HOSTS WITH THE MOST

Consult entertaining tomes of the 1950s and 1960s, and you'll find dozens of rules for entertaining, including stern advice like this: "See that every bit of silver on your table is as bright as vigorous polishing can make it. Be strict about this."

While these are admirable standards, rules for entertaining leave little room for spontaneity, which is in the spirit of every good host. Make room for friends, new and old, planned and unexpected, by ditching your ideas about being the perfect host and adopting gracious but no-nonsense philosophies instead. You and your guests will have a lot more fun, and they'll know that you're the couple to call for a good time.

BE THOUGHTFUL: When you invite friends, choose a set-up that will show them {and as important, you} a good time. If there's a newbie in your crowd, include a couple of great storytellers who can keep the conversation going if you have to step away to stir the soup. Mix and match old friends and new, couples and singles, with a little thought to ensuring that no one is left the odd ball at the table.

ENLIST THE TROOPS: As the hosts, you have the privilege of delegating—encourage everyone to participate in a way that makes them feel included, and you feel relieved.

MAKE YOUR GUESTS FEEL SPECIAL: If you've asked your friend the baker to bring her famous potato rolls, make her feel like a star. Put them front and center and make a point of praising them.

BE FLEXIBLE: When you open your home and your hearts to others, there will be surprises {early arrivals, no shows, and spills}. Be gracious. You may find yourselves in the other shoes someday and will appreciate the hosts who let it all slide off their backs.

MAKE ANY OCCASION A SPECIAL OCCASION: Every day is an occasion. Bring out your best bottle of wine for an unexpected guest, or set aside your plans and whip up something sweet when your dearest friend calls to say she's skipping the gym to stop by for a chat. And when your best friends call to say they got engaged, clear the counter and pull out the pizza dough. There's probably no one they'd rather celebrate with.

SPARE THE EXPENSE BUT NOT THE PLEASURE: The fastest way to make your table green and glam is to use what you have. Take a look around the house with fresh eyes and see what you can turn into a spread without spending a dime. Check your entertaining pantry, fridge, and freezer for stowaways like leftover aioli and frozen bread. Then make a list of what's missing {crackers, a bit of good sausage, sparkling water, and a bottle of wine}. Narrow it down to the essentials and pick out only the things that make the most impact {skip the crackers, spring for the sausage}. Snip from your windowsill garden to make an instant herb bouquet and turn on the tunes.

SPRING FEAST

serves 6 to 8

{serve proudly} Your first gathering cooking for the family could be daunting, especially if your mother-in-law {or your own mother} is a regular Martha Stewart. You need something that doesn't require constant attention, big messes, or last-minute cleaning. Let your oven do the work by serving a low-and-slow-roasted leg of lamb. Serve it with a heaping bowl of luscious polenta and pretty-as-a-holiday-picture green beans. For dessert, pull out the chocolate tart you made the night before and start the storytelling. It's time to find out what's really behind that photo of your honey you spied in their high school yearbook.

MENU

Effortless Leg of Lamb {this page}

Melted Polenta, doubled {from Grilled Lamb Chops with Melted Polenta, page 175}

Green Beans with Tomatoes & Bread Crumbs, doubled {page 199}

Bittersweet Chocolate Tart with Smoked Sea Salt {page 247}

SIP

Ripe, old-world Châteauneuf-du-Pape

EFFORTLESS LEG OF LAMB

serves 6

6-lb/2.7-g bone-in leg of lamb

Sea salt

Olive oil for rubbing

16 garlic cloves

4 or 5 sprigs rosemary

Trim all but a thin layer of fat from the lamb {you can ask your butcher to do this for you} and trim any loose or excess bits. Season all over with the salt, using a more generous hand on the thicker middle section. Cover with plastic wrap/cling film or aluminum foil and set the meat aside to absorb the seasoning while it comes completely to room temperature, about 1 hour.

Preheat the oven to 300°F/150°C/gas 2.

Rub the lamb all over with olive oil. Make 16 small slits that are ½ in/12 mm wide and ½ in/12 mm deep around the lamb using a thin, sharp knife. Stuff a clove of garlic inside each slit. Lay the lamb on a shallow roasting rack or rimmed baking sheet/tray with at least 1 in/2.5 cm sides {to collect the drippings}, and add the rosemary.

Roast until the lamb is falling-off-the-bone tender and just a touch rosy inside, about 3 hours. If you have an internal thermometer, now is the time to use it. Your lamb should be about 118°F/48°C for juicy blush pink. Let the lamb rest 20 minutes before slicing and serving.

SNOW DAY

serves 6

{a fireside feast} Snow Day, Snow Day! The streets are closed and that means only one thing: Put those onions and potatoes in your pantry to good use. Call up your friends and inspire them to put on their heaviest boots and hike on over for a bowl of French Onion Soup and Potatoes Rösti. Bring out Scrabble and set up a cozy circle around your coffee table. This meal doesn't require fancy table settings, just extra sets of wooly socks, big spoons for slurping soup, and deep pots of chocolate pudding.

MENU

French Onion Soup {page 134}

Potatoes Rösti, doubled {page 186}

Chocolate Pudding {page 234}

SIP

A nutty, caramely American brown ale

. . . .

GOOD OLD-FASHIONED GAMES
TO GET THE PARTY STARTED

Scrabble
Bingo
Dominoes
Charades

. . . .

HIS & HERS BRUNCH

serves 4 to 6

{for valentine's} Marriage is a year-round opportunity to show love, so I'm not sure how so much pressure got put on Valentine's Day. Skip the syrupy sweet talk and invite over a couple of buds and their beloveds. Make it really easy on yourself by whipping up two loaves of quick bread the night before. Bake off the Dutch babies {one recipe per couple} or the baked eggs to order when guests arrive {depending if they like their breakfast sweet or savory}. Serve a little champers or mimosas, and fresh brewed coffee.

MENU

Dutch Babies Poached with
Rhubarb {page 58} or
Little Beauty Baked Eggs {page 78}

Golden Zucchini Bread {page 75}

Fruit Salad

SIP

Mimosa or Virgin Mary of the Market {page 227}

PIZZERIA FACILE

serves 6 to 8

{mingle} Homemade pizza for a crowd gets real easy real fast if you've made it a point to befriend your local pizza guy. Drop in to see him on your way home from work to buy about 4 lb/1.8 kg of his fresh dough, already resting at ideal temp. Next, skip the sauce and instead spend a little time prepping the gleanings from your garden or latest trip to the market in groupings that complement each other, and bake the pizzas per the Gardener's Pizza that has become your old stand-by.

This is the party for breaking the ice and bringing old and new friends together, since the party centers around the kitchen countertop and a hot oven. Fire up the oven or the grill and let it preheat while you pour wine. Next, send in the troops and let them loose on the toppings bar. Rotate the pizzas in and out of the oven, depending on how much or little cooking the toppings need, and line them up on wooden boards on the counter for your guests to slice and help themselves as they come fresh out of the oven.

For dessert, skin and slice up the juiciest market muskmelon or cantaloupe and arrange it on a platter with a bowl of sour cream or Greek yogurt sprinkled generously with dark brown sugar.

MENU

Gardener's Pizza, with a shortcut {page 158}

Window-Box Green Salad for Two {page 86, quadruple recipe}

Muskmelon with Sour Cream & Brown Sugar

SIP

Sweet Peach-Basil Sun Tea {page 224}, Champagne

A snappy, crisp sauvignon blanc

CONTINUED

PIZZA: GRILL IT! During the heat of the summer, take pizza night outside to the grill/barbecue. Heat an outdoor grill/barbecue on medium until the grill grates are hot and coals are deep red. Lightly oil the prepared dough and the grill grates. Season the dough with salt and lay it across the grill/barbecue. Cook until golden and crisp on one side, about 6 minutes. Flip and repeat, cooking until it has puffed and evenly cooked. Add toppings and anything that needs to melt, like cheese, in the last 3 minutes of cooking. Close the grill/barbecue grate to melt the cheese. Use a large sturdy spatula to transfer the pizza to a wooden board. Top with herbs, salt, pepper, and a drizzle of your best olive oil.

PIZZA TOPPINGS BAR

Here are three winning combinations to top sauceless pizza {each is enough to top 1 lb/450 g of pizza dough}.

{ GARLIC & GREENS }

2 handfuls spinach, kale, mustard greens, or Swiss chard {or a mix}

2 tbsp extra-virgin olive oil, plus more for drizzling

6 garlic cloves, smashed

Sea salt

Freshly ground black pepper

Red pepper flakes

½ cup/120 ml fresh whole-milk ricotta cheese

Parmigiano-Reggiano cheese, shaved in large shards

Wash the greens and remove any woody stems or ribs. Chop Swiss chard stems {if using} into 1-in/2.5-cm pieces. Cut the remaining leaves into 1-in/2.5-cm strips.

Heat the olive oil in a medium frying pan over medium-low heat. Add the garlic and cook until fragrant, about 2 minutes. Add the Swiss chard stems and cook to soften, 2 minutes more. If using a mix of greens, add heartier ones like kale or mustard greens first, letting them wilt before adding the more tender greens like spinach or chard. Cook, tossing with tongs to coat in oil until the greens are wilted and tender, about 12 minutes total. Season with salt, black pepper, and red pepper flakes toward the end. Set aside.

Follow the directions in Gardener's Pizza {page 158}. Bake until puffed and crisp. Spoon cooked greens and garlic over the baked pizza crust. Remove from the oven to a cutting board or pizza peel. Top with the ricotta and Parmigiano-Reggiano. Drizzle with additional oil, and season with salt and pepper. Slice and serve.

{ BELLE FLEURS }

1 small zucchini/courgette, plus 6 zucchini/courgette blossoms

2 garlic cloves, thinly sliced

Extra-virgin olive oil, for drizzling

2 ears corn, kernels shaved off in slabs

½ cup/120 ml fresh whole-milk ricotta cheese

Sea salt

Freshly ground black pepper

Using a vegetable peeler or a sharp knife, slice the zucchini/courgette into thin strips and arrange them on the dough. Sprinkle with garlic and drizzle with olive oil.

Follow the directions in Gardener's Pizza {page 158}. Bake until puffed and crisp and almost cooked through. Add the corn, zucchini/courgette blossoms, and ricotta to the hot pizza and bake just 1 to 2 minutes more to warm through. Remove from the oven to a cutting board or pizza peel. Drizzle generously with your best olive oil, sea salt, and freshly ground black pepper. Slice and serve.

{ MARGHERITA FRESCA }

3 medium heirloom tomatoes or 2 handfuls baby heirlooms {about 1½ lb/ 680 g}

8 oz/225 g buffalo mozzarella, sliced

1 small handful fresh basil leaves

Extra-virgin olive oil

Sea salt

Freshly ground black pepper

Follow the directions in Gardener's Pizza {page 158}. Bake the pizza until slightly browned, 4 to 6 minutes. Arrange the tomatoes, mozzarella, and basil leaves on the pizza overlapping slightly. Season with the olive oil, salt, and pepper and bake until the mozzarella melts but holds its shape and the tomatoes are just warm but not too juicy, another 4 minutes. Remove from the oven to a cutting board or pizza peel. Slice and serve.

CRACK-YOUR-OWN CRAB FEST

serves 4

{get messy} When crabs are in season, put everything on hold, lay down a big sheet of butcher paper, and invite the neighbors. Fresh crab is so tender and sweet you'll want to pounce on them the minute they hit the table. The buttery meat needs little but lemon to be enjoyed. What on earth could you add to improve it?

The first order of business is picking the best batch of crabs {see Under the Sea, below}. Once you've put so much thought into the quality of the crab itself, you're off the hook for accoutrements and decor. Fry a few dozen sticks of fresh zucchini to whet appetites. Then, boil baby potatoes in a pot next to your crab and toss them in oil and fresh chives. Rush your hot potatoes and steamy crab to the table with crab crackers or a clean wooden mallet and then take your sweet time cracking claws and sucking out all the tender meat. For dessert, serve the most lazy, luscious fruit torte {made the night before} and wash it down with big batch of lemonade.

MENU

Fried Zucchini {page 191} with
Spicy Mayo {page 207}

Fresh Hard-Shell Crabs

Boiled Baby Potatoes
with Garden Chives {page 184}

Lazy Chef's Fruit Torte {page 244}

SIP

Fresh-Squeezed Lemonade {page 223} or
a mild, refreshing German-style Helles lager

CONTINUED

UNDER THE SEA: Dungeness Crab {from the Northwest} are sustainably raised and caught, and wild-caught Jonah {also called Atlantic Dungeness} or U.S. Blue crab {from the Eastern Seaboard}, are both good alternatives. Dungeness, which are in season from November to late May, yield much more meat to shell than Jonah, which can be found year-round, and Blue crab, which you're most likely to find in spring and summer. Plan your party around whatever crab is local and in season for you, which is often the easiest to find too. Cook all live crab the day you bring them home.

HOW TO COOK AND CLEAN HARD-SHELL CRABS

serves 4

4 live Dungeness or 16 small live Blue crabs {about 8 lb/3.6 kg}

Sea salt

2 large lemons, halved

Rinse the crab in cold water. Fill a 10-qt/9.5-L pot with about 6 qt/5.7 L of water; bring to a boil over high heat. Salt it like salt water. Put the crab in the pot and cover the pot to bring it back to a boil quickly. Cook the crabs until the shells turn dark red and the flesh is slightly opaque, 6 to 10 minutes for small crabs {Blue} and 12 to 15 minutes for larger ones {Dungeness}. You can test this by pulling away a leg from one of the crabs and checking the meat that comes with it. Remove the cooked crabs from the pot with tongs, transfer to a strainer, and rinse with cold water. Snip the rubber bands from the claws with scissors.

Place a crab belly-side up and pull off its belly flap {apron}. Remove the top shell and take out the feathery gills on the two sides, the intestines, and the yellowish crab butter. Rinse the crab in bowls of water to wash off any remaining gills. Twist off the claws and legs and use crab crackers or a mallet to crack the shell; pull out the meat {careful, a crab's legs are heavily armored with sharp spikes}. Snap the crab in half {or use a sharp knife for larger crabs} and pick out the meat with your fingers or a fork, or if you're in good company, your teeth. There are lots of little pieces of shell to work around, but it will be worth it for every bite of sweet meat. Serve with lemons for squeezing over the meat and cleaning hands.

A PLATTER OF PLENTY

serves 6 to 8

{starring ricotta} This is the party that you will throw over and over again. It won't always look the same, nor should it. It stars a simple bowl of dressed-up ricotta with warm flatbread. From there, take any number of your favorite dishes from the earlier chapters to fill out your spread. You can start with the menu below. This sultry combination of fatty charcuterie and crisp veggies calls upon your well-stocked kitchen. Though it could take a few hours or more of preparation if you are starting from scratch, this menu rewards the clever cook who has been storing away goodies all week {extra beets roasted Wednesday night, pizza dough from Friday night} so that by Saturday nearly all the work is done. What's not on hand can be bought or prepped ahead so that there are no dirty dishes in the way when friends arrive. Just before they walk through the door, toss together your salad, drizzle your ricotta, and lay your flatbread on your well-loved grill pan.

MENU

A Beautiful Bowl of Ricotta {page 213}

Grilled Flatbread

Sliced charcuterie, such as salami, mortadella, or saucisson sec

Roasted Beets with Pistachios {page 195}

Arugula, Grapefruit & Fennel Salad {page 88}

Midnight Marinated Olives {page 214}

Fresh & Pretty Peas with Radishes {page 200}

SIP

A food-loving grenache, mourvèdre, tempranillo, or sangiovese wine

MAKE FRESH FLATBREAD: Preheat a grill/barbecue or grill pan to medium-high, or the oven with a pizza stone to 450°F/230°C/gas 8. Divide 1 lb/450 g of prepared pizza dough into four pieces. Stretch or roll the dough to rounds or rectangles. Brush generously with olive oil, season with salt and pepper, and sprinkle with chopped fresh rosemary or oregano. Set aside to rise 10 minutes. Cook the flatbreads on the hot grill or in the oven on a pizza stone {or a flat baking sheet/tray} until set and lightly charred, about 6 minutes. If you're cooking on the grill/barbecue, flip them carefully and cook on the other side. Drizzle the tops with olive oil and season with coarse finishing salt. Transfer the flatbreads to a large cutting board and cut or tear into pieces. Serve warm.

GLAMMED-UP SOUTHERN SUPPER

serves 8

{bring your manners} Fried chicken, glamorous? Oh yes, and it's never looked so good. Put it on the prettiest platter you have and serve up the whole menu with Southern style.

Champagne and fried chicken are a match made in heaven. Citrusy, acidic Champagne flirts wildly with the crispy, unctuous skin of fresh fried chicken. Make your biscuits, black-eyed pea dip, and deviled eggs {this is the time to go for quail eggs if you can find them} in advance so you can concentrate on the fryer the day of your party. Bake a cake full of all that good-old-fashioned Southern lovin' and set it on a cake stand like a proud grand dame.

MENU

Buttermilk Fried Chicken {page 140}

Cheddar-Cornmeal Biscuits {page 70}

Little Deviled Eggs {page 221}

Black-Eyed Pea & Manchego Dip {page 212}

Sliced Tomatoes with Salt & Pepper

Better-Than-Boxed Chocolate Cake {page 257}

SIP

Sweet Peach-Basil Sun Tea {page 224}, Champagne

STEAK NIGHT, FOR THE GUYS

serves 4

{give him steak} Gals, he honed his steak skills back on date night—return the treat. But this time, go the extra mile with a move that shows him just how much you love him—invite the guys. Set him up with his well-seasoned frying pan, a couple of steaks, and a growler of his favorite beer {the good stuff}. Put out a plate of your home-baked brownies before you slip out the door to meet the girls for a night on the town. Once the other guys taste your lovin' in action, he'll never get a bad rap for staying in with you again.

MENU

Iron Skillet Steak {page 176, doubled}

Easier-Than-Pie Oven Fries {page 219} with Spicy Mayo {page 207}

My Girl's Brownies {page 249}

SIP

Growlers of artisan brew

BREWER'S FEAST: Beer lovers rejoice; there is much to learn about and enjoy in the world of brewing. The ingenuity of craft brewers has reinvented centuries-old beer styles, creating more to enjoy than ever before. From local to domestic to imported Belgian beauties, beer comes in a myriad of characters. Here are a few basics to help find a brew you both love.

Embrace diversity. There are more than 125 different styles of beer, each with its own unique characteristics and flavors. When you taste different types, make a note of what you like and seek out other brands and brewers in the same styles.

Know the basic types. Most beer can be divided into two categories—ales and lagers—based on the type of yeast used during fermentation. In general, ale yeast ferments at warm temperatures and creates fruitier flavors. Lagers ferment at cooler temperatures and produce drier, subtler flavors.

Let style and region be your guide. If you loved the German beer you had last weekend but want to try something new, look for another German brewer. If you prefer to drink locally, check out the local breweries and give their selection a taste.

Look for quality ingredients. Just like in food, the quality of the ingredients that go into a beer equals the quality that you taste in your glass. Look for breweries that pride themselves on using quality ingredients.

CHAPTER 12

ESCAPES

Campfire Cooking, Pretty Picnics & Portable Parties

Sometime between your honeymoon and your next big trip, you may get a little antsy for adventure. Every so often, you just might need to run away together.

After our wedding, we postponed our honeymoon and took a mini-moon instead, made out of a long drive along Virginia's Blue Ridge Parkway with stops at roadside farm stands and little cabins along the way. After all of the excitement and rush of the wedding itself, the best thing we could imagine was to just be together, anywhere, alone. We've been taking mini-moons ever since.

A mini escape just for the two of you is fun to dream up, but sometimes gets passed over with busy schedules and limited budgets. It doesn't have to cost a thing or even take much planning. Your next adventure could be to the state park, nearest campground, or anywhere you can rent a canoe. Pack a fresh baguette, a bottle of wine, and make your next meal a picnic.

PACK A PICNIC

Picnics anywhere, even just outside your back door, can make you feel like honeymooners again. It only takes a minute to unwind as soon as you get outside. Suddenly it's okay to have snacks for dinner and eat with your hands, sitting Indian-style. It hardly takes special skills or instructions to pack a picnic. Anything that can be kept in portable containers can be picnic food {sliced sausages, cheese, olives, sliced fruit, egg salad, fruit salad}.

But never was there a better picnic food than the sandwich. The very best sandwiches start with good bread. A baguette is a splendid choice that can turn into spectacular sandwiches in three easy steps.

STEP 1 Find yourself a reliable bakery that bakes up fresh baguettes daily.

STEP 2 Spread both cut sides generously with butter or mayo, which seals the bread and keeps it from getting soggy.

STEP 3 Fill it with one of the following combinations:

- **BLT:** Crispy bacon + salted tomato + spicy mayo + lettuce
- **JAMBON-BEURRE:** Ham + unsalted butter
- **CAPRESE:** Beefsteak tomatoes + fresh mozzarella + basil + salt + pepper

P.S. *Salt and drain tomatoes on paper towels/ absorbent papers before adding to sandwiches.*

{ IN THE BAG }

Picnics aren't just for lunches and afternoons. In our first two years of marriage, we were always inviting friends for over for feasts that spilled over our petite kitchen counter and pair of bar stools. We got in the habit of tucking everything into a big canvas bag with a blanket and heading down to the park or the strip of city beach just practically in our front yard. It felt like a little respite from routine for all of us, and after a while, our picnic bag was always packed and ready for an impromptu escape.

Keep your picnic basket {or any sturdy bag} packed with:

- A thermos big enough to hold wine, sangria, or lemonade to serve four
- Reusable plates and utensils
- A portable knife
- A small wooden cutting board for cutting or serving cheese, sausage, melon
- Enameled metal bread box or aluminum lunchbox, sturdy enough to protect sandwiches from getting squished
- Napkins or hand wipes

SET UP CAMP

Sometimes you're having so much fun together in the great outdoors, you don't want to head back to civilization any time soon. Pitch a tent and stay overnight—there is lots of fun and feasting to be had at a campsite.

The first time András and I went camping, I swooned when I saw how quickly he set up camp {he clearly had done this a lot more than I}. Determined to show him I was the outdoors gal he'd always dreamed of, I pulled out my 6-in/15-cm cast-iron frying pan and made us veggie paella. It was a touch over the top for camping grub {sometimes a good sausage cooked on a stick over the fire is just the thing}, but it was delicious. And we could hardly wait to wake up and put the pan to good use again in the morning for griddle cakes.

{ CAMPING GEAR FOR GOURMANDS }

- Quick-boil stove
- Coffee percolator
- Keep-dry salt and pepper
- 6-in/15-cm cast-iron skillet
- Portable grill
- A serious knife
- Portable olive oil {in paper cartons, not glass}
- Pie iron or Campfire Cooker sandwich press
- Enamel or bamboo plates
- Folding eating utensils

There are all kinds of outdoor gear to acquire if you plan to do lots of camping, everything from portable grills/barbecues that disassemble into tiny tubes to pie irons for making all kinds of elaborate campfire courses. But when you've packing light, all you really need is a good Boy Scout knife, a percolator {if you drink coffee}, a quick-boil stove, and a 6-in/15-cm cast-iron skillet and a small metal spatula. Here's how to get from breakfast to bedtime with little else:

PACK {IN A COOLER WITH AN ICE PACK}:

- 1-gl/3.8-L jug of clean water
- Ground coffee
- 1 pt/480 ml milk
- ½ cup/115 g of butter
- 1 mini jug pure maple syrup
- 1 package sausage patties or bacon
- Half-dozen eggs
- Several slices of your favorite cheese
- Kaiser or dinner rolls
- Homemade salsa
- Handful of fresh spinach
- A package of corn tortillas
- Keep-dry salt + pepper shaker
- Beer

PREP {AT HOME BEFORE YOU HEAD OUT}:

- 1 batch griddle-cake dry mix {see Breakfast—Griddle Cakes, following}
- 1 onion, sliced

CONTINUED

COOK {AT THE CAMPSITE}:

BREAKFAST—GRIDDLE CAKES: At home, mix together ¾ cup/90 g white whole-wheat/wholemeal flour, ¼ cup/ 35 g cornmeal or semolina flour, 2 tsp baking powder, ½ tsp salt in a sturdy plastic or stainless-steel container big enough to stir your batter in the next day. At the campsite, add 1 egg and 1 cup/240 ml of the milk you brought for coffee. Melt 2 tbsp of butter in the cast-iron frying pan, and pour into the batter. Seal the container tightly and shake it around to mix well, or stir with a fork. Add an extra pat of butter to the pan. Pour about 3 tbsp of pancake batter {you can eyeball this} into the skillet and cook until bubbly. Flip with a spatula to cook through. Repeat with remaining batter, adding a little more butter if you like extra crispy edges. When you're all done, wipe the skillet with paper towels/absorbent paper so it's ready for lunch.

LUNCH—SAUSAGE {OR BACON}, EGG + CHEESE ON A ROLL: Drop two pats of butter in the cast-iron frying pan. When hot and bubbly, add sausage patties {skip the butter if you're using bacon} and cook on both sides until cooked through. Move them to a plate. Crack 2 eggs into the pan. Stir them around with a spatula to scramble. Tuck the edges of the egg up into a little square and top with a slice of cheese. Transfer to soft dinner or Kaiser rolls, stack with sausage or bacon, and dig in.

DINNER—QUESADILLAS: At home, slice 1 Vidalia onion and pack it in a self-sealing plastic bag. At the campsite, add the last two pats butter or a little oil to the frying pan followed by the onion. Cook until the onion is soft, about 8 minutes. Scoop it out onto a plate. Add a tortilla and crisp over medium heat. Layer the tortilla with your cooked onions, cheese, and a handful of torn spinach. Top with another tortilla. When the cheese melts, flip the quesadilla to crisp the other side. Cut in wedges with your pocket knife and serve hot with salsa and cold beer.

Don't forget to pack plenty of fresh fruit, GORP {page 21}, and water for all the hiking and climbing you do in between.

There is nothing in the world like sitting around a live fire under the stars, soaking in the smells and sounds of the forest around you. A dinner cooked on that fire and the s'mores that follow are an experience to remember for a long, long time. If you camp at a site that allows a fire, make sure to build it a safe distance from your tent. Once you have a

{ CAMPING TRICKS ONLY BOY SCOUTS KNOW}

- Set up your tent near a very cold spring. If you don't have an ice chest or are staying a few days, sealed packaged meats like hot dogs can be tucked between two rocks deep under the ice-cold water and kept overnight.

- Always set up your tent at least 2 hours before sundown.

- Light your fire at least 6 to 7 steps from your tent.

- Never, ever keep food in the tent overnight, unless you really like critters.

- If you run out of food, s'mores make a very tasty breakfast.

good fire with rosy red coals, just about anything can cook wrapped in a packet of foil and tucked into the embers. Start with a main ingredient and add fat and flavor. Close up the foil tightly, since it's the steam and the heat of the coals that actually cook the food, and let the fire do the work.

FIVE WINNING FOIL PACK COMBOS

- Corn-on-the-cob + butter + cilantro/fresh coriander + lime
- Sweet potatoes + sage + salt + butter
- Shrimp/prawns + smashed garlic + cherry tomatoes + black pepper
- Salmon + scallions/spring onions + ginger + sesame oil
- Bananas + butter + brown sugar + cinnamon

Start with a generous square of foil and pile the ingredients in the center. Season with salt and pepper and a drizzle of oil and fold up all four corners. Crimp to make a tight seal {you can make them up to this point at home, stick them in a cooler and bring them out when your fire is toasty}. Tuck into hot but not flaming coals, using tongs or long twigs to place them in hottest portion. Cook until the meat is cooked through or the veggies are tender {use your tongs to pry open your hot foil to check} and serve straight from the foil on bamboo or enamel plates.

When you're ready to step it up a notch or are circling the tents with the whole gang, divvy up the packing and prep lists and get creative.

SOURCES

ABOUT FOOD & SUSTAINABILITY

The very best source for produce is always your local farmers' market. Here's where to find the market and CSA nearest to your zip code:

www.localharvest.org

For more help navigating the world of local food:

www.locavores.com

Issues on sustainability change frequently. To stay informed, get to know the resources on these two sites:

Sustainable Table
www.sustainabletable.org

Monterey Bay Aquarium Seafood Watch
www.montereybayaquarium.org/cr/seafoodwatch.aspx

INGREDIENTS

CHARCUTERIE, BACON & SPECIALTY MEATS

Burgers' Smokehouse
800-345-5185
www.smokehouse.com

Nueske's
800-392-2266
www.nueskes.com

Salumeria Rosi
212-877-4800
www.salumeriarosi.com

CHEESE, CHARCUTERIE, OILS, OLIVES & SPECIALTY FOODS

Artisanal Cheese
877-797-1200
www.artisanalcheese.com

Di Bruno Bros.
888 322 4337
www.dibruno.com

Formaggio Kitchen
888-212-3224
www.formaggiokitchen.com

Gourmet Sleuth
408-354-8281
www.gourmetsleuth.com

Murray's Cheese
888-692-4339
www.murrayscheese.com

Saxelby Cheesemongers
212-228-8204
www.saxelbycheese.com

Vermont Butter and Cheese Creamery
800-884-6287
www.vermontcreamery.com

Whole Foods markets
www.wholefoodsmarket.com

CHOCOLATE

Callebaut Chocolate
www.callebaut.com

Chocolatesource.com
800-214-4926
www.chocolatesource.com

Scharffen Berger
www.scharffenberger.com

Valrhona Chocolate
www.valrhona-chocolate.com

GRAINS & FLOURS

Anson Mills
803-467-4122
www.ansonmills.com

Arrowhead Mills
866-595-8917
www.arrowheadmills.com

Bob's Red Mill
800-349-2173
www.bobsredmill.com

King Arthur Flour Baker's Catalogue
800-827-6836
www.kingarthurflour.com

INTERNATIONAL INGREDIENTS

Amazon
www.amazon.com

SALTS

The Meadow
888-388-4633
www.atthemeadow.com

SPICES & VANILLA

Kalustyan's
800-352-3451
www.kalustyans.com

Penzey's Spices
800-741-7787
www.penzeys.com

The Spice House
847-328-3711
www.thespicehouse.com

KITCHEN & BAKING TOOLS

Crate & Barrel
800-967-6696
www.crateandbarrel.com

JB Prince
800-473-0577
www.jbprince.com

KitchenAid Appliances
800-541-6390
www.kitchenaid.com

New York Cake and Baking Distributor
877-692-2538
www.nycake.com

Pfeil & Holing
800-247-7955
www.cakedeco.com

Sur La Table
800-243-0852
www.surlatable.com

Williams-Sonoma
877-812-6355
www.williams-sonoma.com

SEEDS

The Cook's Garden
800-457-9703
www.cooksgarden.com

Johnny's Selected Seeds
877-564-6697
www.johnnyseeds.com

Seed Savers Exchange
563-382-5990
www.seedsavers.org

CAMPING GEAR

Gander Mountain
888-542-6337
www.gandermountain.com

REI
800-426-4840
www.rei.com

INDEX

LEARN TO MAKE HIS FAVORITE THINGS

—Virginia Edwards Copeland